LŌAL KASHMIR

Praise for *Lōal Kashmir*

'Caught amidst a landscape of violence and guns in Kashmir, how do the young navigate their romantic urges, dreams and relations? Subtle, uplifting and yet heartbreaking, these are the lesser-heard stories of personal desires, longing and the spirit of love jostling for space in a region torn by war and suspicions.'

—Anuradha Bhasin

'A tender compendium of love stories that traverse polarities of beauty and tragedy.'

—Farah Bashir

'In the midst of a plethora of books on Kashmir about the last three-and-a-half decades of its recent history, comes *Lōal Kashmir* by Mehak Jamal as a breath of fresh air. Her simple yet compelling prose draws attention to the razor's edge on which Kashmiris have to walk, negotiating between the diktats of the security forces and the militants. It is a chronological collection of vignettes of ordinary lives lived through extraordinary times. "Lōal", a Kashmiri word meaning love and longing, is the leitmotif in Kashmiri poetry from the sixteenth century onwards. Thus, it is an appropriate prefix to the story of Kashmir for the past thirty-five years. Lōal is what allows Kashmiris to get through hartals, curfews and bomb blasts. It is a heart-warming book because it tells you that life can and does go on.'

—Neerja Mattoo

‘In collecting testimonies of Kashmiris in love, Mehak Jamal has created something remarkable: a heartbreaking and subversive account of life in a state where normalcy remains elusive. You’ll find yourself rooting for the people in these pages to find each other.’

—Rahul Bhatia

‘Fragile and persistent, like tendrils making their way around—sometimes through—what must feel like a wall of stone, these simple stories of love and longing allow us an unexpected engagement with the young in Kashmir, with a generation that has come of age in a conflict that began in the early 1990s, and seems never to end ... As phones are throttled by endless communication shutdowns, it is the paper planes that must carry hopeful messages of love onto curfewed streets ... The stories that Mehak Jamal brings together help to reconstruct a history through their memories, and a fierce insistence on loving turns into another weapon in what is no less than a battlefield.’

—Sanjay Kak

‘In *Lōal Kashmir*, Mehak Jamal masterfully captures the essence of a region where beauty and conflict intertwine. With a keen eye for detail and profound empathy, she brings to life Kashmir’s untold stories, revealing the warmth, resilience and humanity so often overshadowed by headlines. This is a debut at its finest—honest, insightful and deeply moving.’

—Sonia Faleiro

LŌAL KASHMIR

LOVE AND LONGING IN A TORN LAND

MEHAK JAMAL

FOURTH ESTATE · *New Delhi*

First published in India by Fourth Estate 2025
An imprint of HarperCollins *Publishers*
4th Floor, Tower A, Building No. 10, Phase II, DLF Cyber City,
Gurugram, Haryana – 122002
www.harpercollins.co.in

2 4 6 8 10 9 7 5 3 1

P-ISBN: 978-93-6569-063-7
E-ISBN: 978-93-6569-848-0

Typeset in 11.5/16.2 Scala Pro at
HarperCollins *Publishers* India

Printed and bound at
Replika Press Pvt. Ltd.

MIX
Paper | Supporting responsible forestry
FSC™ C016779

This book is produced from independently certified FSC® paper to ensure responsible forest management.

For my grandmother Wijaya,
who made sure we read the latest books

The world is full of paper.
Write to me.

—*Agha Shahid Ali*

Come friend, let's go fetch water
The world is lost to sleep and dreams—
Still I wait for what he'll say
Come back, my flower-decked lover!

—*Habba Khatun*
Translated by Neerja Mattoo

The detailed notes pertaining to this book are available on the *HarperCollins Publishers* India website. Scan this QR code to access the same.

CONTENTS

INTRODUCTION

Lōal is the kashmiri word for love and affection.

To pronounce it, it is—lōal like whole. Lōal like soul.

This book contains sixteen such stories of lōal. Not all of them are romantic tales, though most are. Beyond romantic, familial and platonic love, these stories span decades, religious identities, age groups, sexual orientations and gender identities in Kashmir. Each one of these narratives belongs to a real person (or persons) who has graciously shared her/his life story with me with trust, generosity and warmth.

Who am I? And why am I telling these stories? I was born in Srinagar to a Kashmiri Muslim father and a Maharashtrian Hindu mother; my lineage is unusual to say the least. I grew up in Kashmir, struggling with language, religion and belonging. I always felt that I belonged to Kashmir, but I wasn't sure if Kashmir belonged to me.

As I traversed my teens between the late 2000s and the early 2010s, I went through several summers of unrest. Till that point in my life, I had witnessed multiple hartāls, imposed post encounters, grenade blasts and killings; I had seen exams and birthday parties being cancelled or postponed on account of them. The heavy paramilitary presence around us—that could come as a shock to someone from outside—had become a part of the scenery. That I lived in a place of conflict had always been a reality for me. It was a way of life. But beginning in 2008, the conflict started to take a whole new meaning. From the Amarnath Land Row in 2008 to the Machil Fake Encounter in 2010, each summer, like clockwork, I was plunged into curfews and hartāls that seemed never-ending. I wasn't allowed to go outside, but I saw the death toll in the newspaper rising each day.

When I was in the eleventh grade, I missed months of school due to the hartāls. With nothing to do, I spent hours by myself, whiling away each day at home, missing my sister who was by then away at college. I read books and watched TV, but all I craved for was to put on my school uniform and be with my friends—the only others who understood what I, as a teenager, was going through; who understood the dichotomies and responsibilities that came with being a Kashmiri, while yearning to live a regular life.

In those warm, sleepy afternoons when there was nothing of consequence to be done, I always wondered if anyone in the world knew about what was happening inside all of us who were cooped up in our homes in Kashmir. The news spoke about the political situation, the facts and figures were all documented. But did anyone know that I—along with countless others—had to go to school on Sundays, the only day free of hartāls? Did anyone know that I couldn't spend my birthdays with my friends for consecutive years? Did they know that we skipped an entire book of eleventh grade physics because we didn't have enough time to finish the syllabus? The internet listed the number of days of shutdown each year, but not one article talked about the number of childhood dreams that evaporated each passing summer.

As the world outside grew more hostile, my plight seemed negligible in comparison. Besides, what I was experiencing wasn't new to me, and certainly not to Kashmir.

Kashmir has gone through various periods of unrest over the last several decades and the past century. These waves of conflict have been documented and cemented in history. What I found dwindling in many of these narratives were the lived experiences of people going through those troubled times. In protecting the history of a people, we often forget to preserve their memories as well.

The idea for this book was born after the abrogation of Articles 370 and 35A in August 2019. As the abrogation happened, Jammu, Kashmir and Ladakh were kept under a complete communication lockdown. The Kashmir Valley had witnessed many such blockades, but the extent of this one was unprecedented. Phone and internet services were disconnected by the authorities and continued to be dead for several months. Civilians faced concertina wires blocking roads wherever they went, unable to make even a simple commute.

In all that stifling silence, I kept hearing stories of how Kashmiris reached out to each other in dire times and how they found ingenious ways to keep in touch. I was immediately transported back to the time when I was confined in my house in my teens. That seemed like a simpler era compared to this.

In the stories I heard, those that piqued my interest were the ones of lovers seeking out each other in the midst of the communication and physical clampdown. My heart went out to them, and I started to wonder how they had coped with volatile times. What had gone through their minds when they were away from one another? What were the first words they uttered when the phone lines worked again? Were there as many heartbreaks as there were reaffirmations of love? How did all the uncertainty of what was happening on the outside affect them on the inside? Did they come out more resilient or fainter in their hearts? And just like that it clicked—what better way to preserve the memories of the Kashmiri people than through the lens of love?

The whole point of blocking communication during 2019 was to *deny* that something was happening on ground in Kashmir. To make something *undeniable* in history, we must share our lives, our stories, our laughter, our sadness—everything that we have been through.

Thus, *Lōal Kashmir* was born. To make the trials of Kashmir as undeniable as the air we breathe. To bear witness to them.

I set out to collect stories of love, longing and loss in Kashmir during the various periods of unrest that the Valley had faced. I wished to understand how living in a place of conflict had shaped these lovers' lives for better or for worse. As I searched for true narratives, I found that Kashmir had a storehouse of them that needed to be told and retold, lest they fall through the cracks and get lost forever. When I put out a call for *Lōal Kashmir,* I was overwhelmed with the response I got. In almost every conversation I had, one line was constant: 'No one *ever* asks us about this.' Since the Kashmir conflict dominates all talk around the Valley, the participants were eager to say—*this is not all we are.* They wanted the world at large to remember how bravely they had fought, but equally how fiercely they had loved.

Interviewing and listening to all the contributors in this book gave me strength and purpose. In a conservative place like Kashmir, where speaking aloud about love can be a huge taboo, I found courageous voices willing to bare their souls to me—a complete stranger. There was a sense of urgency in their voices.

As I got closer to completing my book, there were dozens of stories that didn't make it to the final collection. There were also some contributors who chose to retract their stories. Though they had a range of reasons for the decision, the majority had the same looming fear—that someone could come after them for what they had said. The silencing of those who tell the truth in Kashmir is a familiar story. Yet, such silencing brings with it a slow erasure of the history of a people. Such erasures may seem slight at first, but with time, who is to tell what all we may end up losing? When I set out to collect the stories in this book, my initial goal was to preserve memory, but my later hope became to preserve some of the history of this land as well.

I am thankful to all the people who shared their lives with me. I would like to pay homage to a few of them who didn't make it to the book ...

To the man who walked 3 kilometres back and forth, between his home and the bank his girlfriend's sister worked at, just to dispatch letters to his beloved. Each time he walked back through a highly volatile area, reading his beloved's letter reduced his fears; in fact, he barely realized when he reached home.

To the two best friends, the guy from Kashmir, the girl from Uttar Pradesh, who got into a heated argument before the phone lines got cut, and immediately regretted a quarrel that would be denied a resolution. Months later, when they spoke for the first time, she had shaved her head; he offered to shave his to give her company. Years later, they fell in love.

To the man who took a wāzèwān majmè from his sister's wedding to his beloved's house just to catch a glimpse of her once.

To the two boys who faked a wedding invitation card so that one of them could see his girlfriend under the guise of inviting her to a non-existent wedding.

To the teenage lovers whose code words for 'I love you' were 'three words'. Whenever they spoke on the phone and someone passed by, they ended their calls by saying, 'Three words.'

To the photojournalist who walked and hitchhiked 27 kilometres from Boniyar to main Baramulla to the school his girlfriend taught at, never showing his press card for easy travel, having been beaten up by the army for that in the past. The times he took his camera along, he learnt to hide his memory card when they checked.

To the two engaged doctors who scheduled their night shifts such that they could meet and talk freely. When he passed her home, he would often leave chocolates on her car bonnet, much to the shock of her parents.

To the girl pursuing an MBBS in Bangladesh who found solace in her Palestinian friend when she couldn't reach anyone back home. This boy, who was used to not being able to speak to his family for months at a time, gave her comfort and support. Both children of conflict formed an intense bond.

I'd like to pay homage to so many others. But that would span another book entirely. If it wasn't for each and every one of these narrators, you would not be holding this book today. In all my conversations, I was astounded to find how similar experiences could be in times of absolute alienation. To anyone who has gone through this, I want the book to be a reminder that you are not alone in what you're feeling, especially when you are from Kashmir.

Equally, I want this book to be a statement on the power of love. In a place where people are afraid to speak their minds—for fear of eavesdropping; for fear that conversations will be misconstrued—I found brave-hearts wishing to talk about the most universal emotion in the world: lōal.

Having always questioned if I belonged to Kashmir—or more significantly, if Kashmir belonged to me—writing this book has brought me closer to this place and its people. I want *Lōal Kashmir* to be a beacon of hope for anyone who has questioned their sense of belonging in the world they inhabit.

Kashmir belongs to lovers, and I am one of them.

This is my love letter to Kashmir.

A BRIEF HISTORY OF KASHMIR

From time immemorial, the seat of power has changed hands in Kashmir. In the sixteenth century, the last indigenous Kashmiri king, Yusuf Shah Chak, was exiled by Mughal Emperor Akbar, who later annexed the region. Mughal rule lasted until the eighteenth century, after which the Afghans took over. The subsequent Sikh rule imposed heavy taxes on the poor. Following the first Anglo–Sikh war in 1846, the Sikhs were defeated by the East India Company, which went on to acquire Kashmir as part of the Treaty of Amritsar, but later sold it to the Dogra rulers of neighbouring Jammu for 75,00,000 Nanakshahee rupees. The Dogra rulers levied even more taxes, causing further suffering for indigenous Kashmiris.[1]

In the twentieth century, across the Indian subcontinent, there was a call for freedom from foreign rule. By 1931, in Kashmir, political rallies against both native and colonial oppression brought Sheikh Abdullah, the son of a shawl trader, into prominence. Abdullah aligned himself with the social-revolutionary nationalism of Jawaharlal Nehru and the Indian

National Congress, rather than the Muslim League.[2] He promised liberation from Dogra rule and pledged land reform, which became the backbone of his Naya Kashmir manifesto.

In 1947, with the end of British colonial rule, the independent states of India and Pakistan emerged post-Partition. Princely states were asked to join either India or Pakistan, considering the wishes of their people. Maharaja Hari Singh, the Hindu Dogra ruler of Jammu and Kashmir—with a Muslim-majority Kashmir—delayed his decision. Muhammad Ali Jinnah attempted to woo the Maharaja into joining Pakistan, a move that did not sit well with Abdullah.

In October 1947, armed tribesmen from Pakistan's North-West Frontier Province entered Kashmir to join an ongoing internal revolt in Poonch against the Maharaja's high taxes. The tribesmen went on a violent rampage. The Maharaja requested help from India to quash the invasion. In return for receiving assistance, the Maharaja signed the Instrument of Accession to India—with the provision for a plebiscite in the future to determine the will of the Kashmiri people—thus acceding Jammu and Kashmir to India.[3] Indian military forces were airlifted to Srinagar to push back Pakistani militia. Pakistan sent in regular forces and the fight later escalated into the first Indo–Pak War of 1947–48.

In 1948, a United Nations resolution called for an immediate ceasefire and a plebiscite in Kashmir. The ceasefire, brokered by the UN, ended the first Indo–Pak War, with both nations agreeing to a plebiscite and troop withdrawal behind the ceasefire line. This left two-thirds of Kashmir under Indian control, with the rest referred to as Pakistan-occupied Kashmir by India.

In 1950, the Indian Constitution came into effect, incorporating Article 370, which granted autonomous status to Jammu and

Kashmir, limiting Indian jurisdiction to defence, foreign affairs and communication. Since its inception, Article 370 has been diluted through various constitutional orders.

The second Indo–Pak War in 1965 was followed by the 1972 Simla Agreement, which redefined the ceasefire line as the line of control (LoC) and called for bilateral talks between India and Pakistan to resolve the Kashmir dispute.[4]

In Kashmir, there's a common belief that the people have never been given a fair chance to choose their representatives. Since the first elections in 1951, ruling parties were often those backed by New Delhi. Sections of the Kashmiri leadership consistently boycotted elections, demanding the promised plebiscite. In 1987, the Muslim United Front (MUF), a coalition of local political parties, contested state assembly elections against the National Conference and Congress. They saw elections as a route to a plebiscite that had not yet been implemented.[5] The popular MUF lost the elections to the Congress–Conference Alliance amidst allegations of poll rigging. The unpopular reinstated government of Farooq Abdullah (Sheikh Abdullah's son) was met with the ire of Kashmiri people, thus igniting armed resistance in Kashmir in 1989.[6] Many young men crossed into Pakistan, received guerrilla warfare training, and returned to fight Indian rule. Militancy surged in the 1990s, with various outfits emerging; this was met by the Indian state's intensified militarization in the region.

In 1989–1990, as calls by Kashmiri Muslims for self-determination gathered pace, many Kashmiri Pandits viewed the call as anti-national.[7] Panic and fear was set off in the Pandit community following some high-profile killings of Kashmiri Pandit and Muslim officials by militants. The rumours and uncertainty were accompanied by the absence of safety guarantees by the state government.[8] After many Pandits lost their lives to militants and unidentified gunmen, the Kashmiri Pandits started leaving the Valley in large numbers, to Jammu, Delhi and other parts of India. Post this displacement, a majority of the Kashmiri Pandit families have not been able to return to their homes.

The Kargil War in 1999 between India and Pakistan took place in the Kargil district of Jammu and Kashmir. With the dawn of a new millennium, there was a shift from armed struggle to mass, non-violent protests in the Valley. While India and Pakistan restored diplomatic talks and tried implementing confidence-building measures, this did not result in the demilitarization of Kashmir, nor did there seem to be any agreement on future demilitarization.

From 2008 onwards, Kashmir experienced almost annual summer protests. The region saw widespread, sustained non-violent civilian uprisings against Indian rule, with significant unrest in 2008, 2009 and 2010, leading to prolonged military curfews and the deaths of numerous Kashmiris. In 2016, the death of Hizbul Mujahideen commander Burhan Wani in an encounter triggered months of protests and lockdowns, with a frequent shutdown of phone and internet services to control information dissemination.

In August 2019, the Indian government abrogated Articles 370 and 35A under the 'Jammu and Kashmir Reorganisation Act, 2019'. They also bifurcated the state into two union territories: Jammu and Kashmir, and Ladakh.[9] While the act was being passed in the Indian Parliament, the erstwhile state confronted a severe communication blockade. The phone and internet lines remained closed for months to come. Promises of restoring statehood were made, but as of 2024, Jammu and Kashmir remains a union territory. Local assembly elections were held in 2024, marking a decade since the last ones.

Kashmir's history post-1947 has been marked by protests, an armed struggle, heavy militarization and human rights violations. The Armed Forces (Special Powers) Act (AFSPA), which grants special powers to the Indian armed forces to maintain public order in 'disturbed areas', is applicable to the whole of Jammu and Kashmir.

The Kashmir region remains to this day one of the highest militarized zones in the world.

Names and details in the following chapters have been changed at the discretion of the contributors: 'Matador', 'Kashmiri in Gaza', 'Paper Maps', 'Visa', 'Roohani', 'Doraemon', 'Blue Salwar Kameez', 'Forty-four Days', 'Lilly', 'Newspaper'.

ŌTRÜ

day before yesterday

1

LOVE LETTER

JAVED HAD STARTED SEEING a girl in the ninth grade. It started off innocently as these things often do. Her house was close to their school, so he would walk her home each day. Meaning, he'd stay on one side of the road and she on the other side with her giggling friends. This was all the time they had with each other.

The association grew—exchanging looks, exchanging food, exchanging letters. She would bring him home-cooked food as he usually only carried biscuits to school. It was first love.

In 1992, Javed turned seventeen. He was in the eleventh grade. He and his girlfriend had been dating a few years. But now they were in separate schools, so the letter-writing had increased. Urdu was the language of choice, the language of love.

Javed lived in a village in Anantnag, often called Islamabad locally. One morning, after getting a new letter from his beloved, he was all set to show it to his friend who lived in a neighbouring village. It was a beautiful letter, with Urdu poetry that his girlfriend had penned specially for him. As half the fun of young love was showing off to your pals, Javed wanted to begin his regular post-mortem of the letter with his friend. Or he wished to make him jealous ... who is to say? But the actual reason Javed wanted to leave home that day was because he had heard early in the morning at the kāndur's—the baker's—that a crackdown was going to happen in his village.

Crackdowns were carried out by army troops in Kashmir to look for militants. All the men of an area would be called out with their identity cards. After a preliminary check, they would be paraded in front of a mukhbir—an informant of the army. One by one, the men would be brought in front of a row of jeeps, one of which the mukhbir would be sitting in. If he recognized any man with affiliations to the taḥrīk—the armed movement—he pressed the car horn. The person's face would be covered and he would be sent to the interrogation centre. Some men made it back home after getting interrogated, beaten up or tortured. Most never returned.

Just a year before, Javed had been made to strip down completely during one such crackdown. That memory still haunted him, and he wanted to stay as far away as possible this time around.

So, he got ready, put his beloved's letter in the front pocket of his shirt for good luck and left the house. But he was too late. It was 8 a.m., and the army had already arrived. They started their routine—knocking on doors and yelling commands for the men to vacate houses. Soon Javed was standing in line with the rest of the men of the village. The crackdown had begun.

One by one, the men were checked by the army, their possessions examined, their identity cards scrutinized. If they passed this round, they would be sent off for the identification parade with the mukhbir, which would mean standing in the sun for hours at end. Javed desperately wanted to get out of here, but he was stuck for good. As he waited for his turn, he watched his father being sent off for round two.

Finally, Javed's turn arrived. The soldier patted him down from head to toe. He felt his front pocket. Javed gulped. He didn't want to part with his letter. The soldier got the folded piece of paper out and opened it.

All written in Urdu.

He looked at Javed suspiciously and asked him, 'What is this?'

Javed couldn't think of what to say apart from the truth. He stammered, 'Love letter.'

The soldier raised his eyebrows in surprise. He went and discussed the situation with the other soldiers. They kept looking back at Javed and then at the letter inquisitively.

Javed was a bundle of nerves. 'They don't believe me. They probably think it's some militant code,' he panicked.

Javed wondered if he could ask for help from the elders around him; maybe one of them could back him up that the letter indeed was penned for a lover. But telling them about his love life seemed like a fate far worse. If his father got a whiff of this afterwards, Javed would probably never get to see his girlfriend again. So, he simply waited. Finally, the soldier returned and gave Javed's letter back to him. Javed was about to join his father, when the soldier asked him to stay back. The soldiers finished with the rest of the men. All of them were sent off for identification by the mukhbir. All except Javed.

The four soldiers approached him. Javed trembled. 'This is how I go ... over a damned love letter,' he thought.

But instead of hurting Javed, all four soldiers sat down in a circle on the grass. They gestured, asking him to join them.

He sat down tentatively. They took off their helmets and kept their guns aside. Under those heavy helmets, they were young men. Twenty-two or twenty-three maybe?

Javed couldn't think about their age when his life was on the line.

'What is this new game?' Javed wondered as the soldiers got comfortable. Then one of them spoke. *'Ab suna apna love letter.'*

Recite your love letter now.

Javed stared in shock. Surely he was dreaming. Surely they were pulling his leg. This was a ploy to humiliate him. But no. The soldiers were genuinely interested in him and his missive. It wasn't each day during these searches and crackdowns that they came across declarations of love. Quite the opposite, actually. It seemed that they wanted a break from the crackdown as much as Javed did. Javed—because he found them traumatizing; the soldiers—because they were exhausted. Javed was taken aback by the turn of events. He also knew that complying was his only way out. He didn't want to test fate by refusing the soldiers' request. So, he took out his girlfriend's love letter—his prized possession—and started reading it. Slow and succinct.

Line by line.

Javed saw the soldiers around him open up. They laughed and giggled like love-struck teenagers as he continued. Maybe the letter spoke of their own longings. Maybe they had someone they wanted to get letters from, too.

They didn't understand the Urdu properly, so after reading each line of the poem, Javed would translate it in great detail. That way, he also bought himself more time. The longer he was here, the longer he wasn't over there with the rest of the men.

Javed wasn't used to seeing the softer side of the army. He had always seen the soldiers as formidable creatures, as beings he was supposed to be afraid of. 'Don't get on the wrong side of soldiers' had been drilled into him at home. But here they were—soldiers—happily following his adolescent romance as though it held within it a Bollywood film monologue.

And did Javed put on a show for them! He painted a grand picture, gesticulating wildly and enunciating words with a flourish. They were eating out of the palm of his hand. So much so, they decided to arrange tea for themselves and him. A little chai and charcha.

NOW, AT THAT TIME, being a doctor was a really reputable professional choice. There was only one doctor in the whole village, and his vocation also saved him from crackdowns. One of the soldiers walked up to his house and knocked on the door. When the doctor unlatched it tentatively, the soldier asked him to organize tea for all of them, including Javed.

The women didn't want to serve tea to the soldiers, so the doctor appeared minutes later with a tray. Javed was mortified. He couldn't wrap his head around the idea that he was being served by this man he looked up to. As the doctor started pouring out the tea, Javed sprang to his feet in protest. He offered his own services. The soldiers, who were treating him like their buddy, told him to sit down.

The doctor looked back and forth, confused. He didn't know whether to proceed or stop. He was also shocked to witness the camaraderie between Javed and the soldiers. But then, he had learnt not to ask any questions.

Javed, who never would've thought of arguing with an army man, felt compelled to speak up before things got more awkward or heated. He gathered the courage to tell the soldiers that he held the doctor in high regard and couldn't bear to be served by him. It would be disrespectful and go against his values.

The soldiers listened with reluctance and grudgingly saw his point of view. 'No worries, love doctor,' they said. 'We'll leave this doctor be.' The soldiers laughed at their joke. Javed and the doctor did not. Javed prised the kettle out of the doctor's hand and told him that he would gather the empty cups himself. The doctor gave Javed one last disapproving look and moved away. Javed poured the Lipton chai—what sweet tea is referred to as in Kashmir—into the cups and served the soldiers and himself.

At seventeen, when Javed didn't think much of himself, being given more respect than the most respected man in the village was overwhelming. He wasn't sure he liked it. He prayed that no one would hear about what had transpired this afternoon, and that the doctor kept his mouth shut.

The tea was slurped. The biscuits were eaten. Javed stuffed his letter back into his pocket, almost wishing there was more to it. This was not the post-mortem he had planned for, but it was what had presented itself. In the process, he had seen the soldiers transform—a fact that felt surreal to him.

Now the soldiers started putting their helmets back on. Once again they were turning into the formidable creatures that he knew so well. Just moments ago, they had appeared human to Javed. That moment was passing.

The soldiers probably wouldn't speak of the events of the preceding hours to anyone. Javed wouldn't speak of them either. A silent understanding had been reached between the two.

The crackdown was coming to a close. The men were trudging back home slowly, and Javed wasn't part of the queue.

Javed bid adieu to the soldiers. They slapped him on the back like he was their pal and started making their way back to their team. Javed scrambled to collect the cups and got away from there before the onlookers could deduce anything more.

As he walked back home, his mind was racing. He was sure his father had reached. Javed was in for some drama for sure. He needed a backstory and fast. The storyteller he had become that day—it came to the fore again. A plan came to him faster than he had anticipated.

Javed reached home to find his mother hysterical. When she had asked his father about Javed, he had told her that he hadn't seen him during the crackdown at all. On hearing this, his mother had almost collapsed. Surely her son hadn't been picked up?

Before she could have a complete nervous breakdown, Javed arrived.

'Where were you?' she yelled.

Javed obviously couldn't tell her that he had been saved because of a love letter. However, he had found the perfect alibi.

During crackdowns, the army would often take a man from the village—someone who knew the houses well—for talạshī—a quick and efficient search. Javed told his panic-stricken parents that he had been picked for talạshī this time around. Though initially sceptical, they came around to believing his story.

Javed was off the hook. He was force-fed nun-chai and tsoṭ—salty tea and bread. He had already had too much tea, but he couldn't tell his mother this.

The day passed. Javed couldn't make it to his friend's village anymore. He would have to show him the letter the next day in school.

After this unusual crackdown, though Javed didn't feel like a changed person—nor did he see the army in a kinder light—one thing did change. From that day onwards, Javed always carried a love letter in his pocket.

Just in case.

2

MATADOR

For Sagar, the conflict began one fine day in 1989. He was all of ten years of age. Shabir Shah had just got arrested. Shah, who would become the founder of the Jammu and Kashmir Democratic Freedom Party in 1998, had been an advocate for the self-determination of the Kashmiri people for many years.

The day of the arrest, Sagar, his elder brother and their father had gone to Maharaja Bazaar in Srinagar to exchange a crate of cold drinks. Back then, one had to take the wooden crate full of empty glass bottles to the dealer to get a new one of full bottles in return. It was 6.30 p.m. and the last slivers of light were still hanging in the air. Sagar and his brother waited in their sky blue Maruti Omni van as their father scurried across the street, legs buckling slightly under the weight of the clattering bottles.

As the brothers waited for their sweet fizzy delights, suddenly they heard a commotion outside. A stone flew through the air and hit the back window of the car. The kids ducked down. Sagar craned his neck a bit to see men pelting stones outside; his eyes searched for his father. His brother protectively pushed his head down. Sagar heard the car door open, the urgent sound of keys clattering and the engine revving to life. With the kids' heads still low, their father drove them out of the chaos. The men pelting stones had been protesting against Shah's arrest. As they drove away, Sagar's heart sank. No cold drinks for him this time.

That day was the first time Sagar realized his family lived in a place of conflict.

SAGAR'S FATHER WAS A well-known maths and geometry teacher at Tyndale-Biscoe School in Srinagar. He was fondly called 'Masterji' both within and outside the school. Both his sons studied in this all-boys' school that shared a boundary wall with its all-girls' sister school, Mallinson.

Schools in Kashmir had three-month-long winter vacations, and Sagar's family would pile into the blue Omni van and drive down to Jammu each year to see the grandparents. After spending several lazy weeks there, they would head out to Chandigarh or Delhi. Jammu would be chilly in the winters, but not as cold as Kashmir, so Sagar welcomed the change in temperature.

In January 1990, they made the same annual journey to Jammu. But this time around, Sagar noticed visible lines of stress on his parents' faces when they left their house in Indira Nagar, Srinagar. Sagar's youngest aunt was getting married in Jammu the following month. The family was going to attend the wedding, enjoy the festivities and come back towards the end of February before schools reopened in March. The plan was in keeping with the holidays they had enjoyed in the past, so Sagar couldn't tell why his parents' faces seemed drawn.

Sagar's grandparents lived in Bhagwati Nagar near the Tawi river in Jammu. As wedding preparations gathered steam, Sagar was quick to pick up bits of the adults' conversations exchanged in hushed whispers. He heard of fellow Kashmiri Pandits leaving the Kashmir Valley in hoards. By end January, his parents were contemplating whether it was wise go back to the Valley or stay put in Jammu. In the midst of all the wedding chaos, Sagar wasn't able to understand his parents' full predicament nor was he privy to the finer details of all that was happening in Kashmir. Sagar's brother, who was only a couple of years older, seemed equally clueless.

Eventually, the things Sagar had overheard became a reality. He started seeing lines of trucks carrying people enter Bhagwati Nagar. The first refugee camps for the exiled Kashmiri Pandits emerged around the area. They weren't even set up by the government at first. Sagar heard that it was a wealthy businessman who had donated his money to build them. Each family in the camp was to receive one kilo of sugar, two kilos of wheat flour, one bed sheet, one bucket, one mug and some other essentials to survive.

In this sombre atmosphere, Sagar's aunt got married. The adults tried to look happy, but their faces gave away their despair. They felt guilty for celebrating at this time when their brethren were getting displaced from their homes.

Sagar's family extended their stay a little longer, waiting for the hālāth to settle down in the Valley. February turned to March. Sagar started getting antsy, for by now schools back home would have begun, and he was scared his friends would forget him. The family had started considering going back by the first week of April, when an incident in Kashmir shook them to the core.

At the beginning of April, two connected kidnappings of Dr Mushir-ul-Haq, the vice chancellor of Kashmir University (in conjunction with his personal secretary Abdul Gani Zargar), and Mr H.L. Khera, general manager of the HMT watch factory, took place.[10] The abductors were members of the Jammu and Kashmir Students Liberation Front (JKSLF) and demanded the release of three arrested militants in exchange for the kidnapped men. The governor of the state at that point, Jagmohan, refused to meet their demands, and the three men were found dead a few days later, the two colleagues in one location, and Mr Khera in another.

Khera uncle, as Sagar called him, was their next-door neighbour in Indira Nagar. He knew the entire family. The incident hit too close to home. Sagar's extended family gathered for an intervention and told his father firmly, 'You are not going back.'

By this time, the schools in Jammu had started additional classes for the displaced Kashmiri Pandit students. Sagar was admitted into St. Peter's. His classes would start at 2 p.m., as part of the second shift, after regular school ended. The teachers were working double time. For Sagar, until now, none of the unfolding events had felt real. But when he put on his new uniform and went to an unfamiliar school, a firm thought took root in his head—'I'll never see home again.'

Summer vacations arrived, and Masterji went back to Kashmir along with a few other Kashmiri Pandit colleagues—essentially to check on their homes and understand the situation. He returned a few weeks later and with some hesitation announced that they would be moving back to Kashmir. 'The conditions are permissible, and it is our home after all.' Sagar's mother was scared and relieved at the same time.

Sagar had turned eleven during his Jammu stay but remained too young to be part of the decision-making process. The elders pronounced and the children followed. Within a month, when they piled all their belongings back into the blue van to finally go back to Srinagar after a prolonged hiatus, Sagar experienced bittersweet emotions. He was happy that he would be home again but sad that a lot of people he knew wouldn't be there anymore. He had overheard the fact that Khera uncle's entire family had vacated their house next door.

Sagar's house compound in Indira Nagar had a hotel—named Hotel Sandhya—that Masterji owned in partnership with his neighbour. If one were to map out the compound, this would be the layout—the hotel up front, followed by the partner's house, and then Masterji's house right at the back. Khera uncle had been renting the partner's residence.

Sagar could always see the Kheras' house from his bedroom window and felt comforted by the warm yellow glow of the lights there. Now those windows would be dark and cold. Little did Sagar know that wasn't the only unfamiliar sight about to greet him.

A little after Masterji had inspected their Indira Nagar house, but before Sagar's family could return from Jammu, Masterji's partner rented out Hotel Sandhya to the Indian army without consulting him. Back then, hotels in Kashmir were running empty—tourists weren't visiting—and the paramilitary slowly started moving into such abandoned properties and setting up army bunkers.

When Sagar's family returned to Srinagar and saw bunkers all around their home, it came as a big shock to them. There were no boundary walls between the three houses, so the bunkers basically spilled right into Sagar's home compound.

They knew how this appeared to the world. All of a sudden, not only was Masterji a Kashmiri Pandit in a place where there were few Pandits left, but he also had to contend with the presence of the army on his premises. Rumours started swirling. 'Did you hear ... Masterji has gotten the CRPF to stay at his hotel for the family's security!' From being a cordial neighbour, Masterji became part of the problem.

When Sagar's father tried to get the army out, they coaxed him: 'Sir, your whole house is exposed, your walls are low, you need some protection with our bunkers.'

But Masterji remained adamant. 'Fine, I will build a wall around my house. But I don't need your bunker on my premises.'

Masterji knew that the army wouldn't leave easily, so he built a boundary wall between the hotel and their house. That was the only way to separate his family from the army shelter. Sagar overheard his father muttering as he watched the wall being raised, '*Our* protection my foot, it's for their protection.'

SAGAR AND HIS BROTHER re-joined Tyndale-Biscoe School with their father. Sagar was in the sixth grade now. From the moment he stepped in, Sagar could tell that things were very different. Not one of the Kashmiri Pandit students was around. He was the only one in his class. Sagar started sensing an invisible gaze on him at all times, as if everyone was wondering why he was still here. At one level, the perception felt oddly funny ... but he didn't feel like laughing.

While Sagar wasn't afraid of being back—admittedly, he didn't understand the gravity of the situation, at least for the first year—he often found himself at loose ends. Curfews and hartāls were a norm, and Sagar went to school irregularly and only when his father did. This meant that the awkwardness of being the only Pandit during roll call wasn't a regular occurrence either.

Sagar started noticing small things, which in themselves felt enormous. His mother had rejoined the State Bank of India branch she used to work at before they'd left. The office was in the Akhada building in Maisuma, the area famous for kani-jang—stone pelting. Sagar used to watch perplexed as she'd wipe off her bindi and take out her dejhoor—the ear ornaments worn by married Kashmiri Pandit women—before she left the house each day. He slowly realized that she was removing identifying markers before leaving home. As she mostly travelled by public transport, she was being extra careful about not bringing attention to herself. She was safe in the bank, but her commute was what worried her.

Sagar's mother followed a specific protocol at home as well. She made sure that her husband and two sons were home by 5 p.m. each day. The roads in the evenings would be deserted, save for the stray dogs howling. She would bolt the gates and lock the front door. If there was a knock at the gate at night, she would never let Sagar, his brother or her husband open it. Her view was simple—be it a militant or the army, they would hesitate before shooting a woman. With a man, they wouldn't even think twice. While a shootout hadn't taken place in their neighbourhood, her survival instinct was sharp and deeply ingrained.

A few months after returning, Sagar's parents took the executive decision of taking him out of Biscoe and putting him in Kendriya Vidyalaya (KV) in the Badamibagh Army Cantonment, relatively closer to where they lived. As Sagar was still quite young, they felt that sending him to a school closer to home would be safer. His brother was passing out of school soon, so he remained in Biscoe right till he graduated.

Till they could form new relations and friendships in the neighbourhood, it was just Sagar and his brother hanging out together. By 1992, his brother had passed his twelfth-grade exams and was sent to Bangalore to study engineering. As a result, he didn't end up spending as much time in the conflict zone as Sagar did. Sagar studied in KV for three years, and in the tenth grade, when he was deemed old enough to commute on his own, was admitted back into Biscoe for good.

Sagar was a teenager now. All the kids he had studied with earlier still remembered him, but he didn't make friends right away. It took time for him to slowly develop his own small circle of buddies with Bilal and Adil—the 'trio' was what they called themselves. By the middle of tenth grade, they were thick as thieves.

Sagar had started seeing noticeable changes in Biscoe by then. If someone in a student's family was a militant, or had connections with a militant organization, everyone knew. It was everyone's business. That said, the invisible gaze that Sagar had felt when he had just returned wasn't there anymore—not in the school at least, and not on him. Here, everyone knew him as '*Masterji ka beta*', the teacher's son—and while there was nowhere to hide, Sagar felt no pressing reason to conceal his identity.

Outside school was a different story. Sagar had picked up on social cues and grew aware of how to interact with people beyond the comfort of home and school. What to do, what not to do; what to say and how to say it—there was a protocol. And Sagar had learnt that all protocol revolved around: a) Being a Kashmiri; and b) Being a Kashmiri Pandit.

Something he learnt pretty quickly was never to reveal his full identity. If someone asked him his name, he always replied, 'Sagar.' He never added the Razdan in the end. Sagar was a Muslim name, too, so no one batted an eyelid. It wasn't like Sanjay or Sunil, which were clear giveaways. As long as he said 'Sagar', he was fine. But if he happened to let slip 'Sagar Razdan', expressions changed. (Though sometimes even if he didn't divulge his full name, his Pandit features gave him away.)

Once he had his small circle of friends he trusted, the trio, Sagar finally started living a normal teenage life—or as normal as normal could be in a conflict zone. In this, the trio led comparable lives, going through the same rigmarole. There was no distinction between him, Bilal and Adil.

SINCE THE RAZDANS' RETURN, Sagar's house had been a safe haven for many Kashmiri Pandits. Often the guests included fellow teachers, colleagues, neighbours, acquaintances and distant relatives. Sometimes the guests had no relationship at all with the family. Yet, each found security in the company of the Razdans, sometimes living in their home for up to six or seven months.

A lot of Kashmiri Pandits had got displaced from downtown Srinagar and the neighbouring villages and had come to Indira Nagar. As several Pandit inhabitants of Indira Nagar had left Srinagar, these displaced people would rent those accommodations. Now even Khera uncle's house was being inhabited by another family.

The Kashmiri Pandits who were from downtown Srinagar had been living there for generations. Their houses got ransacked after the families left—not so much by the neighbours, but by youngsters from other areas who caught a whiff of empty homes with decades' worth of possessions. Authorities didn't look into this matter. At that time, the priority was to curb militancy, and no one was bothered about thefts. Once the paramilitary forces gained hold over Kashmir, they ransacked the houses as well. It was a free-for-all, no questions asked. As the army started moving into and building bunkers in abandoned Pandit houses, the few remaining memories that held those homes together also evaporated.

Indira Nagar was unlike downtown Srinagar. It was built by people who came from all over Kashmir, bought land there and constructed their homes. In other words, it comprised of first-generation families, along with the Razdans. Everyone knew everyone. Even without the army bunker that had moved into the hotel next door, Sagar's home would have been safe from ransacking if the Razdans were away. The Razdans trusted everyone who lived around them, and Sagar was sure the neighbourhood trusted his family.

As more people moved into the abandoned houses next door, Sagar was constantly meeting new people and building new relations. There were kids his age that he hung out with, though his deepest friendships were still with his friends from school.

IN THE DAYS TO come, Sagar kept hearing the elders say, 'We don't have anything to worry about.'

They'd continue, 'We are not the targets out here. The army is against the militants. All you need to tell the army if they stop you is that you are a Pandit.'

What they implied was that he could emphasize he was Hindu and not Muslim. Sagar understood the subtext well.

He felt reassured that if he ever got stopped by the army, 'he was okay'. His identity was going to bail him out. Where once he tried to pass off as a Muslim, he now decided to leverage his Hindu identity.

One day, when Sagar was returning home from Biscoe in one of the many Matador buses that lined Srinagar's streets, his vehicle was stopped by the army for checking. The bus had just reached Burn Hall, another boys' school in Sonwar. There was a Border Security Force (BSF)—as against a Central Reserve Police Force (CRPF)—check-post next to the school. BSF, CRPF—all these abbreviations were a blur in Sagar's mind. He didn't make any distinctions when it came to the army. They were all the same. And as he would learn soon enough, so was he to them.

Everyone in the bus was asked to step down and stand in a single file for checking. Sagar knew the drill. Take your ID card out, keep both hands above your head with the ID flashing in one hand throughout. This time around, Sagar just kept his hands above his head but didn't take his ID out. After all, his elders had told him that his name would be enough. The Sikh army guy was moving down the line, frowning at the ID cards and comparing them to the scared faces they belonged to.

Finally, Sagar's turn came. The army guy looked at Sagar's empty hand and then down at him. 'ID?', he asked curtly. Sagar confidently replied, 'Sir, my name is Sagar Razdan.' He emphasized his surname and gave the army guy a 'we're cool right?' look. The army guy smirked, and the next thing Sagar remembered was that the side of his face grew hot and red from a hard slap. As Sagar regained his composure to look at the army guy's angry face, the man spat out a few expletives. 'What the hell are you still doing here? Your people have left. What do you think of yourself?'

Sagar understood the tone immediately. This man wasn't curious or empathetic. He was raging. He raged at Sagar's audacity to still show his face around here.

This incident changed Sagar's views forever about what the conflict signified. He understood that out here, they were all Kashmiris first, and then Hindu or Muslim. It didn't matter what community or religion they belonged to; for the army, they were all 'the others'. They were all part of the problem. This was the status quo.

From that day, Sagar learnt that his identity was not his defence; that it could well pose an issue for someone who didn't trust him or didn't know him at all. He had to remain cautious and only divulge his first name. He continued to avoid unknown people and only explored the city in the company of his friends.

Sagar loathed being a minority in his own hometown, but he gathered that it was not everyone's intention to scare, threaten or harm. Even so, the small things got to him. A simple joke could turn offensive.

Dāl-e-battè—loosely translated as lentil Pandit—was a belittling term used to describe Kashmiri Pandits. It sounded like Dāl-e-batè, which meant lentils and rice, but the connotation was that since Pandits included dal or lentils in their day-to-day meals—unlike the mutton consumed by the Muslims—they were weak in comparison. It was an everyday expression, which didn't bother Sagar when there were other Pandit kids in his class. Back then, there was no way to tell if the term was directed at him or them.

However, in the later years, when he was the only Pandit kid in class, Sagar knew the term was directed at him. It wasn't meant to make him feel weak or inadequate, nor did the person referring to him as Dāl-e-battè know of his strengths and weaknesses. They were kids, after all, the same age as him. They weren't thinking about what the term actually conveyed. But it did lead to Sagar feeling more like a minority than ever.

Fuelled by this feeling, Sagar stopped watching cricket matches altogether. Under normal circumstances, if there happened to be an India–Pakistan match, he'd have supported India. Not because he felt an affinity to the team, but because this was his default response and had always been. There was nothing political about it. Now, if India did win a match, there was no way to celebrate in Kashmir. He couldn't burst crackers or yell from the windows. If Pakistan won, he knew he had it coming the next day. He would be picked on in school and those around him would gloat. So, Sagar adopted a mask—he appeared nonchalant—when there were cricket matches. He just shrugged his shoulders and said, 'I didn't even watch the match. I don't care about cricket. Who won?' This became Sagar's permanent stance till finally he stopped caring about cricket altogether.

The most important lesson Sagar learnt during adolescence was to survive. Surviving a conflict was not easy, but he managed by keeping his interactions to the minimum and his business to himself. But with his hormones playing up, Sagar couldn't always be canny. Hot-headed, he often did stupid things and got into fights that were hard to wiggle out of. Sagar's Pandit identity didn't bode well in such situations. As soon as he got into a tussle and the opponent found out that Sagar was a Pandit, he'd hear, 'Either your dad is working with the police or is with the army as an informer. Because where the hell did you find the guts to start this fight?'

BY 1994, A NEW army battalion had shifted into Hotel Sandhya. Again, the commander came to meet Sagar's father to deliver his protection spiel. 'We are happy to give you protection along with a gypsy car and a guard.' To which, an amused Masterji's reply was, 'How long will you do that? Right now your battalion is here, tomorrow when you leave, then what happens? If I do this today, I'll be putting a mark on myself. I can't go to Biscoe, my wife can't go to work, my son can't go to school. So, thank you, but no thank you.'

It wasn't as if Sagar's father never got calls from the other side. Sagar often picked up phone calls on their landline, and a gruff male voice would say, 'Tell Masterji to come to this place at this time with this much money.' Masterji would get regular intimidating letters from Hizbul Mujahideen and the Jammu Kashmir Liberation Front (JKLF) demanding Rs 50,000 or Rs 1,00,000 in return for 'protection'—the elusive protection that everyone seemed to be offering. The subtext across those calls and letters was—give us the money and we won't kill you. These were huge amounts of money back then and impossible to pay. 'All because we have the CRPF bunkers nearby,' Masterji sighed.

It was a norm for militant organizations to have the names and numbers of anyone whose hotels, cinema halls, properties or premises had been taken over by the army. Often, after the evening nẹmāz, the loudspeaker at the Syed Sahib shrine in Sonwar would read out a list of names. The people milling outside the shops, buying hot nadụr' mọnji and hạlụwè would all stand still to listen, afraid that they'd recognize one of their own. The list would carry the names of all those who had rented out their places to the army—Muslims and Pandits, both. They'd get summoned to covert locations to meet with the militants. Sagar's father's name was often on the list, even though he wasn't the one who had rented out the hotel. But who cared about technicalities?

Soon after the evening prayers, news would reach Sagar's house, and Masterji would start calling colleagues frantically, figuring out what to do, how to get out of it. They would, in turn, contact someone they knew, and in a few weeks or months it would be sorted out. Even so, the cycle repeated itself every few months, like clockwork.

A lot of Masterji's colleagues would tease him when he called about the letters and the lists. 'As if your students will cause you any harm. Go, see what they want. Set them right.' Biscoe boys were excellent at trekking. Legend was that they could go up and down the Shankaracharya hill in thirty minutes. Some of these young boys had crossed over to Pakistan, making the arduous journey across the mountains. These boys, who received arms training and had become militants, were often Masterji's ex-students.

Masterji never went to the places specified in the letters or the announcements. One man on the list had gone to the address and had been shot dead. He was a Muslim whose property had been taken over by the army without his consent, just because it was empty. This was the 1990s. The army didn't ask politely, 'Sir, your house is empty, may we move in?' They just did ... and one found out later. While in Masterji's case, the hotel partner had given away the keys willingly, in most instances they were forcefully taken. It took a couple of years for these property owners to fill out applications to get rent from the army. Whether they got the money remains uncertain.

Over the years, Masterji stopped driving his Maruti Omni van around Srinagar. That car model was mainly used by Indian intelligence agencies and had been banned for common use by the militant organizations. Plus, as Sagar had seen on TV, it was always used to kidnap people in Bollywood movies.

So, the Omni remained in the garage for the majority of the year and only came out in the winters when the family made their annual trip to Jammu. Sagar's father would write 'FOR JAMMU' in big, bold, black letters on a piece of paper and stick it to the windshield, so that anyone who saw the conspicuous van knew it was going out of the Valley, and not roaming around anywhere local. On their return, the sign would say 'FOR SRINAGAR'. The car would then be swiftly unloaded and locked in the garage again, seeing the light of day only over the next round of winter vacations.

BY THE ELEVENTH GRADE, Sagar started getting himself a reputation. He was seventeen now. The trio—Bilal, Adil and Sagar—was learning martial arts and working out regularly. There was an active rivalry between Biscoe and S.P. College students—they were perpetually at loggerheads—and they'd often get into fights. So, Sagar and his friends started carrying knives in their backpacks, just in case.

Once, there was a (now infamous) fight in Lal Chowk, where the two schools decided who got to dominate the area. Sagar and his friends were coming back from their tuition classes in a Matador bus when they were told that there was a problem in Lal Chowk. Some guy from S.P. was pursuing the sister of a guy from Biscoe; he had tried flirting with her.

This is how all the fights started back then. Over girls. The girls who themselves were oblivious to it all or didn't care. Nevertheless, big battles were fought over their honour. The rhetoric was, 'Unless you want to marry her, stop looking at her.' This was young blood, and the hunger to fight egged all the boys on. They just needed a reason, however random.

Sagar's bus with half a dozen boys from Biscoe entered the Matador yard at Lal Chowk. They could see the other Matador full of S.P. guys waiting. Someone started running across the yard and closed both the gates.

As Sagar looked around his Matador, it dawned on him that he finally belonged. What had seemed impossible to him just a few years ago now felt close—that, here, he was a part of something, even if that 'something' was a gang war. His adrenaline started pumping.

As soon as the gates closed, the boys spilled out of their respective Matadors. Sagar and his friends pounced on the S.P. guys like a swarm of angry bees. The young men fought each other for what seemed like hours for a reason that was mundane at best. There could have been a stabbing—they certainly had the weapons for it—but luckily both sides escaped without grievous injury. Biscoe won the battle and secured 'dominance' over Lal Chowk.

Post that fight, Sagar's ego soared ... and how. He started getting into random tussles. People who once knew him as 'Masterji's son' now knew him by his name. The son of a renowned teacher becoming something of a delinquent was not looked upon kindly. The news would reach the school sooner or later. But before the news could, the fights did.

Sagar was in the twelfth grade when some guys from S.P. College infiltrated Biscoe. They had a beef with Sagar and his friends. Sagar, Bilal and Adil, upon hearing that the S.P. boys were on the school premises, coolly walked out of their class mid-lecture. The S.P. boys had cornered a Biscoe student in the bathroom and would only let him go if the trio showed up. As soon as they did, a fight broke out in the loo. The cornered student ran away, not wanting to be part of this.

Sagar chased the S.P. boys into the main field, which was circled by the school building. If you happened to be in the field, the whole school got a clear view. So did Masterji. Sagar didn't think about this as he caught hold of an S.P. guy's shirt collar. He started relentlessly slapping the boy he had cornered in the middle of the field. Suddenly, he felt someone staring at him and looked up to see the shocked face of his father, chalk still in hand.

'What has he become!' Masterji roared at home. 'In front of the whole school, that too.' Sagar's mother, distraught that her son was a gunda now, stayed mum.

Post that incident, Masterji would make surprise visits to Sagar's classroom to check if he was there. Stubborn as Sagar was, he was barely in class. The school was divided into two groups of people—those who would rat Sagar out to his father, and those who would make sure Sagar was in class when Masterji was on one of his 'Sagar checking rounds'.

Once, Sagar was chilling at a chaiwala's tapri in Hari Singh High Street. Suddenly the watchman from school emerged through the crowds, completely out of breath. Between huffing and puffing, he said, *'Mōl čhuy tshānḍān, mōl čhuy tshānḍān!'* He was informing Sagar that his father was looking for him. Sagar ran back to school to find a livid Masterji waiting outside the classroom door. 'I had gone out to get a pen,' Sagar lied. 'Where's the pen?' Masterji asked. Unable to furnish an answer, Sagar stared at his feet. Masterji told him, 'This is not the first time. I've come here often, and you're never in class! The teacher doesn't even know that you are supposed to be in this class. She's never seen you.' All the students pressed their ears to the door to hear Sagar getting told off.

Sagar's parents were clearly worried about him—worried that he'd eventually mix with the wrong crowds and get shot somewhere. They'd taken a gamble and come back to Kashmir when everyone in their family had advised them against it. They firmly believed it would be safe for their children. But here was their reckless child, walking into the fire himself. What were they to do?

SAGAR DIDN'T KNOW OF Aalmeen's existence till Bilal fell in love.

Bilal had spotted a girl from Mallinson who was in the eleventh grade, and in his words, he was 'in love'. It was as simple as that back then—you saw a girl and you were in love. The plan was to secure enrolment in the same tuition centre she was in—the famous Excel, with Shah sir for chemistry and Ashraf sir for physics. Bilal was adamant that Adil and Sagar enrol too, to test their chemistry with the girls.

Sagar wasn't interested. He was already going to tuition classes for both the subjects closer to home. Convincing his parents that he wished to go to Excel in distant Jawahar Nagar was a task he wasn't keen to take on.

'She has really cute friends, too. Maybe if we're lucky, by the end of the month, we will all have girlfriends!' Bilal pleaded with Sagar and Adil. 'At least come once and have a look.'

Sagar and Adil relented—after all, they wished to see who these cute girls were. Bilal was over the moon. On the designated day, Sagar bunked his tuition classes and went with his friends. Bilal planned to catch a glimpse of his beloved at Excel.

Sagar had always been amazed that girls tended to travel in packs of five or six at all times; he remained astounded by the fact at the Jawahar Nagar bus stop, too. On one side of the road stood the trio. On the other side, all the girls. Sagar looked around and noticed that other boys stood next to the trio, too, supposedly for the same reason, to watch the girls at the bus stop. Slightly disgusted with what he was becoming, Sagar was about to call the entire escapade off.

That's when Bilal hissed under his breath. 'There she is in ... in pink.' Sagar and Adil's heads swivelled fast enough to give them whiplash. Sagar saw the girl who had become the object of his friend's affection. But not for very long—for Sagar couldn't take his eyes off the girl she was talking to.

Dressed in a blue phẹran, jeans and sneakers was a tall girl. When she smiled, she looked exactly like Sonali Bendre, who was Sagar's present crush. Her head was covered with a muffler to keep the cold out, but a few stray strands of hair kept breaking free. She tucked them behind her ear every few seconds; they seemed to revolt against the inconvenience and wiggle out again. She looked around, and her eyes briefly caught Sagar's across the road. She looked away quickly, colour rising to her cheeks. A Matador came to a halt at the bus stop, and she got in.

And just like that, Sagar whispered the dreaded words he had rolled his eyes at just the day before: 'I think I'm in love.'

Her name was Aalmeen.

Aalmeen was a Muslim, and Sagar was a Pandit. Both Bilal and Adil were concerned about this from the beginning and tried to dissuade him. 'Don't do it, Sagar, you're going to get hurt. Either physically or mentally.' Not once did they suggest, 'Don't date a girl from our community.' Rather, what they were saying was, 'If you date a Muslim girl, you won't be happy. People will make sure you are miserable.'

Sagar understood their fears, and he knew that history was not on his side. But he also knew that he would do just about anything to talk to Aalmeen, even if it was once. Bilal and Adil could gauge this as well when they talked to their smitten friend. 'We are with you, whatever happens,' they finally said.

Soon, Sagar knew everything about her. Aalmeen Bhat was a year younger than Sagar, in the eleventh grade. She studied in Mallinson, right next door to Biscoe, and wanted to become a doctor. The next step was to make himself known to her.

Sagar somehow managed to persuade his parents that he needed to shift to Excel. It took a week of convincing, but at last, he managed to enrol himself there. This was the only way he could see Aalmeen every day.

They were in different tuition batches, but at least Sagar got to see his beloved leave when his classes began. After almost a month of this, Aalmeen also started noticing Sagar—the fact that he was always around and he didn't look at any other girl but her. She realized that he was interested.

Sagar started receiving the occasional smile from her, even a stray look every now and then. Sometimes the two took the same Matador, sitting far away from each other, but very aware of the other person's presence. This dance went on for a few months.

Adil's cousin sister was in the same batch as Aalmeen. The trio begged her for the girls' phone numbers—something, anything that they could get their hands on. Adil had also started fancying a girl from Aalmeen's batch, so he had a similar petition to make and his was the most desperate.

At that time, finding a girl's landline number was a huge deal. In the past, whenever the trio got their hands on a number, they'd called the house randomly. If the girl answered, they'd remember, 'She picks up the phone herself!' They would then keep bothering her. It was inane behaviour. Adil's cousin—keenly aware of the antics of these teenage boys—obviously didn't want to give any girl's number to them. She was a tough cookie. 'There's something called trust, hello?'

But she took pity on Sagar, the most lovelorn of the lot. Seeing his forlorn face, she presented her straightforward plan. 'I will point you out to Aalmeen tomorrow, tell her your name and say that you want her number. If she says yes, I will give you her number. If she says no, then no it is. No further questions. Are you okay with that?'

This wasn't an easy decision for Sagar. He obviously didn't want Aalmeen to say no, but he knew that this was his only chance to move beyond the coy looks that they were currently exchanging on the Matadors. He said yes to the plan. The next day, Sagar watched with bated breath as Adil's cousin went over to speak to Aalmeen. As they giggled about something, he hoped they weren't laughing at him.

After what seemed like ages, the cousin gestured towards Sagar. Aalmeen looked at him as he pretended to read something interesting in his chemistry textbook, which was upside down. Too late to turn it now. After a few moments, a torn piece of paper from a notebook landed on his book. He looked up to see Adil's cousin smiling. 'Well, that was easy,' she giggled.

Sagar thanked her profusely. 'I'll get you a big chocolate tomorrow.' As soon as she left, he studied the piece of paper and the landline number written in blue ink.

Adil's cousin had been firm about one thing. 'Till she doesn't ask you to call, don't call. Don't even dare. Anyone can pick up the landline, and you don't want her getting into trouble.' This was the general rule of thumb—never call a girl's house without prior intimation. Sagar remembered her instructions and waited for a signal from Aalmeen. He had memorized her phone number by now. Often he'd dial the number at night without the last digit, just to feel the thrill of it.

Sagar and Aalmeen never spoke to each other in the Matadors. Sometimes if they were lucky, Sagar would even sit next to her, making sure there was enough space between them, no part of his attire touching hers. In the small, crowded Matador with people pushing and yelling *tal sā, tal sā*—move on already!—giving her that much space was a massive feat. That was the extent of their interaction. Sagar couldn't bring himself to open his mouth and form words yet. Aalmeen was probably afraid of what the onlookers would think of her talking to a guy in the open.

A few months passed without them making the transition to phone calls. Then one autumn evening, as Aalmeen was getting off the bus, she muttered under her breath, '10 p.m. tonight.' There was little anyone could do for the rest of the bus ride to wipe the silly smile off Sagar's face.

As winter rolled in, Aalmeen and Sagar were speaking for long, long hours, burning the phone lines.

They were finally dating.

All their friends knew about them, of course, and at home, Aalmeen's elder sister, Bareen, was in on the secret. They had formulated an intricate system for calling.

If Sagar had to call Aalmeen's home, they would fix the date and time three days in advance. He would give three rings and cut the call. She would call him back. Or she would give Sagar two rings, and he would know that no one was at her home and that he could call. They divided the phone calls so the parents wouldn't get suspicious about the phone bills.

The plan wasn't foolproof. Sometimes Aalmeen's parents would answer the phone before the three rings ended. On such occasions, Sagar hung up. But this was a girl's house, and Aalmeen had an elder sister. Their parents weren't stupid. They knew blank calls meant that boys were calling. Eventually, so Aalmeen's folks didn't give her the third degree, if anyone answered besides Aalmeen, Sagar wouldn't cut the call. On the phone, Sagar's voice sounded deep, which made him seem much older than he was, almost like a grown man. If Aalmeen's mother or father answered, he'd immediately ask, *'Ghulam Mohammad sạb chuy yetẹth?'* They would say that it was a wrong number—no Ghulam Mohammad lived here—and he'd hang up. After some time, he'd get a call from Aalmeen, and they'd laugh over the episode.

Sagar was always more romantic on the phone than in Aalmeen's presence. It had nothing to do with her, she was lovely. But he felt more at ease when no one was watching. Outside the tuition class or in the Matador, Sagar always felt on edge. He kept glancing at the people around him and felt that they were darting looks at Aalmeen or him. 'Are they staring because I'm with a girl, or are they staring because they know I'm a Pandit and she's a Muslim?' His thoughts would spiral. On the phone, thankfully, he was at peace and could focus on the lovey-dovey side of things.

Sagar was too shy to touch Aalmeen or even to hold her hand or give her a hug. Not even if they caught an auto rickshaw—on the rare occasion they had money to splurge—did they sit close together. Sagar was too reticent, and Aalmeen didn't initiate.

The maximum time they'd get together in private was in a PCO near the tuition class. If you had good relations with the PCO owner, he'd let you talk alone in the booth for a few minutes. Sagar and Aalmeen did this a lot before jumping on to the Matador to go back home.

Over time, they found other places to meet. There was a gift shop called Dreams in Lal Chowk that they used to frequent. They made friends with the owner, a sweet fellow who was sympathetic to their romantic cause. He would let them wander in the aisles far longer than anyone else, so they could have the dating experience. He would mind his business for the length of their rendezvous, and sometimes he'd get them chips and Coke, which they would eat right there in the shop.

Every day, after Aalmeen's morning tuition class and before school, Sagar would wait inside Dreams. Aalmeen's Matador would stop on the other side of the street. Through the stacks of Happy Birthday cards, Sagar would watch her cross the road. She would duck into the shop, the tiny bell on the door signalling her arrival; its jingle sounded as joy-filled as Sagar himself.

Sagar wasn't afraid of anyone in his family seeing them together. There were barely any relatives left behind anyway. But for Aalmeen, it was a different story. Her whole extended family was in Kashmir, many had businesses and shops around the area. Speaking to any guy would get her into trouble—but a Pandit boy? She didn't even want to know what the end of that sentence portended.

So, to stay out of the public gaze, Dreams became their safe haven. The only place where they weren't under the scrutiny of anyone. They never went to a restaurant or even had an ice cream outside. Sagar didn't try to push his luck or convince Aalmeen to experiment outdoors—especially since she had made her stance clear.

Sagar and Aalmeen usually walked to school together from Dreams, separating just a few metres before the school gates. She would walk into Mallinson and Sagar into Biscoe.

Hartāls and curfew were a dampener on their relationship—for, when the city came to a halt, everyone was at home, parents, relatives, the works. There was no school to attend or tuition class to visit, and therefore, no ready excuse to leave the house. Sagar definitely couldn't call Aalmeen without her prior permission. So, the two didn't speak to each other for extended periods of time when there were hartāls.

Sometimes hartāls would go on for days and weeks. Close to losing his mind, Sagar would attempt making up reasons for stepping outside, but was never able to get past his fretting mother. Once the curfew was lifted, Sagar wasn't always sure if Aalmeen would be allowed to step out on the first day. He'd wait at Dreams anyway, hoping and praying she'd get off a Matador. Some days, his prayers would get answered; most days they would not.

Over time, in a land of routine unrest, Sagar and Aalmeen devised systems to meet. If there were blasts or if there was firing, they'd demarcate safe spaces. If there was conflict somewhere around Lal Chowk, then they would meet in Jehangir Chowk in the Matador yard. If trouble erupted outside the perimeter of Lal Chowk, then they would meet indoors in Dreams. The general idea was to wait for each other for at least thirty minutes before giving up and moving on. Sometimes, if roads were cordoned off, Sagar would somehow reach Aalmeen's last stop on her Matador route and wait for her there.

These weren't well-planned strategies. They worked, but rarely. After all, crises were unpredictable, and inconspicuous spots were few and far between.

By the end of 1996, both Sagar and Aalmeen had completed their exams. Sagar was done with the twelfth grade and was waiting for his results. In the interim, he was attending tuition classes for his entrance exams. Aalmeen had started attending tuition classes for the twelfth grade and would have to go to Zaina Kadal in the mornings to Jalu sir for physics.

The Matador guys had started recognizing Sagar and Aalmeen, as they were regulars. So, the lovers came up with another meeting system.

Sagar would wait at the Matador stand in the morning. As soon as Aalmeen walked in and clambered on to a bus, he would get in behind her. The bus conductor who knew them would close the doors. The driver would then zoom out of the bus stand with an almost empty bus. For the most part, it would just be the two lovers in the whole Matador. But sometimes, there were one or two more passengers who looked most perplexed on finding themselves in a near-empty bus—a rarity in Kashmir.

Sagar paid for all the empty seats in the Matador. Back then, it was a hefty amount of Rs 50. All of this, so that they could enjoy some private quiet time. Both the driver and conductor were fine with it. There was no hanky-panky going on. Sagar and Aalmeen yearned for these moments where they could speak without distraction or the fear of anyone following or eavesdropping. Sagar would bring his own recorded cassettes to the bus. A lot of Jagjit Singh ghazals played during those cold winter mornings.

When Aalmeen would get down at Zaina Kadal for her tuition class, Sagar waited in the Matador with the driver and conductor. They'd get him tea and snacks from the chai tapri outside, and the three of them would hang out till Aalmeen came back. They had a good thing going.

Sagar would ride back in the bus with Aalmeen, walk with her till school, and drop her off. He was pretty clueless about what he wanted to study in college, and would barely make it to the entrance tuition class he was enrolled in. This right here, being with Aalmeen each day, was Sagar's priority.

ZAINA KADAL WAS IN Srinagar's downtown area. Downtown was not easy to navigate if you weren't from there. The houses were clustered together, and the impact and volatility of militancy was much higher and more visible. Sagar's friend's cousin used to be a militant and had been picked up by the army in the downtown area. He had been tortured for several years before getting released and was now a shadow of the man he used to be.

Such stories were a dime a dozen at the time. Sagar had heard all the gruesome ones. And, of course, he had heard about Krishna Flour Mill (KFM). In the early to late 1990s, if anyone needed to be 'interrogated' by the militants, he was taken to KFM. It was an abandoned flour mill in the downtown area that had a huge compound. The army was known to steer clear of it.

Whether this was fact or fiction was hard to tell—as is true of so many things in Kashmir.

As folklore went, if you got a visit from a militant, and if he wanted something from you, he would say, 'Are you going to tell me right now, or should I take you to Krishna Flour Mill?' You would, of course, spill the beans immediately. All this wasn't something one read about. One heard it from close friends or friends' cousins who hung out with militants.

'No one returns from there normal,' kids would whisper in class. Intense fear overwhelmed the body at the mere mention of the mill. It was infamous the way that Papa II, the army interrogation centre, was. No one returned 'normal' from there either.

Aalmeen had a cousin sister—also in the twelfth grade—who lived in Hyderpora. A boy from their batch, Shameem, was interested in her. Shameem's father was a famous judge in the sub-district court. Somehow Sagar always had a feeling that he was, in fact, besotted with Aalmeen and not her cousin. But he didn't dwell on the matter very much. That is, until one day Sagar got a call from Shameem.

'Sagar, there's a problem,' Shameem started. When Sagar asked what the problem was, Shameem told him that someone in the Zaina Kadal tuition class was interested in Aalmeen. Apparently, they had been following her and had connections with militants. 'We have to do something,' Shameem said.

Sagar was more annoyed about Shameem's deep investment in Aalmeen's safety than he was about the boys following her.

'Why are you so worried?' he asked Shameen. 'She hasn't said anything to me about this. And it isn't like she's your girlfriend. Unless ... are you interested?'

Shameem quickly defused the situation. 'I'm telling you because your reputation precedes you. I've heard about the fights you've gotten into. I know that you have a short fuse. I just wanted to give you a heads-up, that's all.'

Sagar was unconvinced. He couldn't understand why Shameem was going out of his way to call him. Whether Shameem informed him or Aalmeen did—it would lead to the same fuse getting blown. Shameem's reasoning made no sense. There was something off-putting about this call ... as though Shameem had an ulterior motive.

Shameen was right about one thing though—that Sagar was hot-headed. The young, fiery blood in Sagar raged.

Shameem continued, 'They've called us to meet them in Zaina Kadal tomorrow morning at 9.'

Now Sagar was even more suspicious. 'Who is "they" and why are you invited as well? And why the hell are they calling you in the first place? They have your number and not mine? That's strange.'

Shameem claimed he had no idea. He was just the messenger.

Sagar let it go and reached out to Bilal and Adil immediately. If he was going the next day, he needed his entourage with him.

Bilal asked him to postpone the meeting. 'It's Eid tomorrow, Sagar. At least push it to the day after tomorrow?'

Adil didn't have a landline phone to call, and it was already too late in the evening to go to his house.

Sagar asked Shameem to delay the meeting by a day. Shameem replied saying that it wasn't possible since the people who had summoned them had affiliations with militants. 'Better not to test their patience I would suggest.'

Already riled, Sagar at once decided to go without his friends. 'It's just you and me then,' he told Shameem and cut the call.

He didn't have a phone conversation scheduled with Aalmeen that night, so he would have to go without telling her. He didn't want to ruin her Eid anyway.

The next morning at 9 a.m. sharp, Sagar reached the spot in Zaina Kadal where he had been summoned. He looked along the empty road stretching before him, and he didn't see Shameem anywhere. A niggling feeling started bothering Sagar. Had he been set up? Only Bilal knew about this meeting, that too not a whole lot. If something were to happen to Sagar, Bilal wouldn't even know where to look. Putting on his bravest face, Sagar waited it out.

After ten minutes, Sagar saw a man wearing a nun-chai coloured Khan suit and a dark brown waistcoat walking towards him. He was clean-shaven with hair cut like Amitabh Bachchan's. He appeared to be in his early thirties. He was flanked by two guys on either side who looked only a year or two older than Sagar. They were both wearing phẹrans, which immediately struck Sagar as odd. The weather was still quite warm for phẹrans.

Sagar felt that there was something unusual about this guy approaching him. He had an enigmatic personality—as if he owned the street he was walking on. As the three figures approached Sagar, he felt it in his bones—'I'm not supposed to be here.' All the years of never going anywhere alone and staying away from strangers, and here Sagar was, walking willingly into a rat trap.

The man reached Sagar and asked, 'What's your name?' Blankly Sagar answered, 'Sagar Razdan.' As soon as he said Razdan, he bit his tongue. The man looked visibly surprised. In the span of that second, Sagar regretted every decision that had led him to this moment, right down to his parents having brought him back to Kashmir. 'I'm screwed,' he thought.

The man asked for his ID card. Sagar mutely handed it over. The man scanned it with curiosity, making a low humming sound after reading the information that seemed to interest him. 'Name ... father's name ... hmm ... school ... hmm ...' He then put the ID card in his suit's breast pocket, put his arm around Sagar's shoulder like they were buddies, and muttered, *'Pakh.'* He was telling Sagar, 'Let's go.'

They were at Zaina Kadal's last Matador stop. Sagar knew it from his many commutes to drop and pick up Aalmeen. Would he ever see her again?

If they took the steps and walked down, they would be right at Aalmeen's tuition centre, though she wouldn't be there. She was at home, celebrating Eid, adjuring the elders for Eidi. Sagar tried to comfort himself with her imagined presence.

But they didn't go towards the tuition centre. The man led Sagar down another route. Sagar gulped, for he knew where that road went. To KFM.

As they walked, the man chatted with Sagar as if they were talking about the weather. He asked Sagar why he was there. Sagar divulged everything—about someone bothering his girlfriend and about the news he had received from Shameem.

The man nodded. 'And you came all by yourself?' Did he sound vaguely impressed? Sagar couldn't tell. He replied, 'Well, yeah, I mean ... Shameem was called as well, and he's not here.' The man nodded again.

He wasn't trying to intimidate Sagar. But at the same time, he wasn't letting him feel at ease either. Sagar didn't feel safe with him. His own mind was racing. Were these the guys after Aalmeen? Or were they just random men who had found an easy target? Should he even be talking to them?

If any friend of Sagar's had been around, the interaction with the man would have been different. Sagar would have felt less exposed. However, given that he was by himself, Sagar decided to be at his best behaviour—respectful and soft-spoken, saying *ahan haz, ahan haz*, yes, yes, to all the questions throughout.

The questions the man asked were peculiar—do you know where you are; do you know about this militant group; do you know about that militant group; have you heard about this commander; how about that one?

If the intention was to hurt Sagar, kidnap or kill him, he would have done it already. Sagar couldn't figure out the point of this walk and the questions being asked. Were the men vetting him? Playing with their prey? At least Sagar's humour was still intact because he could see the hilarity of this situation loud and clear.

They left the main road and started walking down narrow lanes. Until now, Sagar had a sense of where he was. But as the lanes got dingier, he started losing all sense of direction. The smaller the spaces got, the more Sagar's vision seemed to expand. He caught the tiniest of details that he would otherwise have ignored.

Thus, at one point, he came to notice one of the younger guys as he shifted his phẹran. It was as though he were adjusting a weight on his shoulder—such as the strap of a heavy schoolbag. Sagar momentarily saw a cylindrical bump near his shoulder before the thick phẹran material engulfed it again. Sagar froze. It was too narrow a bump to be a shoulder blade.

It was a gun. These men were armed. They were militants.

Whatever sense of humour Sagar had managed to hold on to now escaped. He saw that they were approaching an army bunker. A hypothetical scene started playing out in Sagar's head. If the army guys stopped and frisked them, the men accompanying him would open fire in defence. The army would retaliate for sure, and Sagar would become a casualty—collateral damage. If he survived, he would be arrested as one of them. There was no winning here.

Sagar wondered, 'If I start running now, how fast can I go? Can I conceal myself before the army notices? Can I hide before the guy lifts up his phẹran, pulls out his gun and fires?' Sagar's head started spinning. He could barely listen to what the man was asking him as they walked past the bunker, the beady eyes of the soldiers following them.

When they had passed the bunker and left it behind, Sagar's vision cleared and his ears started listening properly again. 'How do you know this girl? She is a Muslim, and you are a Pandit. What is your future here? Have you given it any thought?'

Sagar was about to answer when they took a right turn and came on to the main road. His body started trembling. Towering before him was a gigantic and monstrous building. Krishna Flour Mill.

'Do you know what this place is?' The man asked, watching Sagar closely. Sagar shook his head, feigning ignorance. In his mind, he was losing it bit by bit. His legs were jelly, and his mouth felt like sandpaper. He was ready to pass out. Everything that had been drilled into him was coming true. He couldn't help thinking, 'I played a dumb game, and this is the result. So stupid. They just want to torture the shit out of me. This is how I go.'

Just then, the man reached into his front pocket and brought out Sagar's ID card. His face gave nothing away as he said, 'Your father used to teach me. *Raṭh sā, garè gatshakh, salām dīzẹs.*' The man was telling Sagar to take his ID, go home and convey his salām to his father. 'And *never* be so stupid ever again. You won't be this lucky next time.' He handed the ID to a frozen Sagar. He then gave a Rs 20 note to one of the phẹran guys. 'Flag down an auto for him.'

Sagar couldn't believe the words he was hearing. All those rumours of ex-Biscoeites crossing over to Pakistan to become militants ... and here was an actual one, taught by Masterji. The man lit a cigarette and let out a thick cloud of smoke. Sagar was dying for a drag to calm his nerves, but he would not dare push his luck further.

As the phẹran guy went to stop an auto, the man turned to look at Sagar. 'Where's the other guy, Shameem?' Sagar shook his head to say he didn't know. He had been left speechless by this point, but still managed to string a few words together, 'So this wasn't about my girlfriend? That someone else likes her?'

The man gave him an amused look. 'This is not about girls. It was never about girls. We have a case coming up. We needed Shameem's father's signature in exchange for his son.'

Finally, Sagar got it. The plan had been to kidnap Shameem all along, and to get his father, the judge, to toe the line. Sagar had been made a pawn in Shameem's game.

Maybe Shameem had understood all of this when he got the call. He had roped in Sagar after deciding to be a no-show himself. He wasn't a judge's son for nothing; he knew to avoid a covert rendezvous.

Sagar had been played and sent here in Shameem's place. It was pure luck that this man was Masterji's ex-student. What were the odds?

The phẹran guy waved from a distance. The faraway purring of a waiting rickshaw broke Sagar's train of thought. He felt like he was sleepwalking right till he sat in the vehicle. The phẹran guy gave him a nod before closing the auto door behind him. It was only when he was halfway home that Sagar realized that he was still alive. His heart was beating fast, and his face was red. Today he had been saved only because of his father.

Sagar arrived home and hugged his father without a reason, even while being acutely aware that he would never tell him what had happened. A surprised Masterji patted his back warmly.

In the coming days, Sagar pieced together all the details of the incident. The man in the Khan suit was an area commander with the Hizbul Mujahideen. He had identified the girl Shameem was interested in; she *was* Aalmeen's cousin after all. He had called Shameem and asked him to meet, saying, 'You are following this girl, one of our guys likes her. Let's settle it in Zaina Kadal.'

Sagar and Aalmeen had not been involved in the story at all.

From the outset, the area commander had known that Sagar was the wrong guy. If he hadn't checked his ID card and seen Masterji's name, he possibly wouldn't even have bothered with the walk. He could've easily kidnapped Sagar for ruining the plan and secured Rs 10–15,000 as ransom. But when the connections became apparent, he simply decided to let Sagar writhe in agony until he managed to drive home a point—'Don't be stupid. Don't get into situations you can't get out of.' Sensing Sagar's fear—he could smell it, and he deliberately picked on it like a scab—he was certain that the lessons he offered would stick.

Sagar now saw that he had been so engrossed with the possibility that someone was interested in Aalmeen that he had failed to think logically or practically, relying instead on his first instinct—I need to go sort this out! Sagar ought to have learnt from this experience; instead, he got emboldened by the idea of being a hero.

It wasn't every day that one came away unscathed after meeting a militant. Sagar already had a reputation; now he was an urban legend. From wanting to be invisible in his early teens to becoming a public persona, Sagar Razdan had had quite the journey. The few guys who would follow Aalmeen occasionally also stopped doing it. No one wanted to get involved with Sagar.

When Sagar told Aalmeen about the encounter with the Hizbul Mujahideen commander, she was undeniably shaken. She broke down crying in the middle of Dreams. Sagar comforted her. 'Don't worry. I came out alive. I have the upper hand now.' She looked at him sharply. 'Don't be stupid.' Unknowingly, she reiterated the message that the commander had given him.

It took Sagar some time to get a hold of Shameem, who had been avoiding him. Finally, when he got him on the phone, Sagar said, 'If you dare cut the call, I will land up at your house right now and tell your father what you did. If I had died, it would've been all because of you.'

When Shameem had involved Sagar, he had heard about the fights he had won with his friends. He believed that Sagar would take his entourage along to the invited location and sort the matter out. On his own, Sagar could be soft-spoken, but with his friends, and their willingness to ignite an inflammable situation, he was certain to confront and was likely to emerge whole. Besides, when a fight broke out, people's connections came to the fore—the fact that they knew the police or the army or a militant organization. Matters would escalate till the crux of the issue would be forgotten. Shameem had been counting on his problem getting solved, too, through such an escalation.

Sagar left him with a warning. 'Never show me your face ... and forget about Aalmeen's cousin.'

From that day, Sagar realized that in Kashmir there was always someone in the background playing his own game. Sagar had been so focused on his identity as a minority that he had missed noticing a crucial fact—that *everyone* was trying to survive any which way, even if it meant throwing others under the bus. When the commander had indicated that Sagar could not afford to be stupid, he had actually meant, 'Play your cards well.'

This is not to say that Sagar had become cynical. There were people he trusted entirely. Bilal and Adil were two, and then, of course, there was Aalmeen. But there were others as well, and they came into his life from the most surprising of places and reaffirmed his faith in people. Sagar recalled one instance in particular. A random fellow had given Rs 500 to Sagar's regular Matador driver and had told him to rough Sagar up. 'That battè roams around every day with a Muslim girl ... teach him a lesson!' The driver calmly took the money, slapped him and told him to never show his face around the Matador yard again. Sagar knew it had nothing to do with the fact that he paid for all those empty seats; it had everything to do with the relationship he had cultivated with the driver.

So, too, with Maqsood, the chaiwala in Lal Chowk who not only made the most amazing tea but always kept his stall open for Sagar, even during Ramzan when everyone else was fasting. He would draw the curtains so Sagar could smoke and have his chai in peace without attracting dirty looks from passers-by. Maqsood was fond of Sagar and they had built a comfortable camaraderie. Maqsood could always tell if Sagar was sad or stressed—for, on such days even his best adrak-chai was no antidote. If Sagar did not respond to his questions, he would press gently, *'Sagar, kyā ḍalīl?'* What happened? And Sagar would bare his heart. Mostly the matter had to do with Aalmeen—not seeing her enough, not being able to talk the night prior because a cricket match was in session on TV precisely where the phone was kept, or not having enough money to buy a gift for her birthday. Without a word, Maqsood would reach into his front pocket, get a bundle of money out and place it in front of Sagar, his other hand deftly stirring the tea. He'd say, 'Take what you need and go. Buy her whatever you like. No need to pay me back.' Sagar would give him a big hug.

Sagar could now take Aalmeen to Dreams and tell her to look around and choose whatever she fancied; he'd buy it. Sagar never knew what to gift Aalmeen, so he was grateful she liked choosing presents on her own.

A LOT OF PEOPLE, from the owner of Dreams to Maqsood, had a soft corner for Sagar and Aalmeen. And they created safe spaces for them. They remained their champions in the midst of all the uncertainty that the future seemed to hold.

The future. That's what Aalmeen and Sagar spoke about the most. Whether their collective future actually would be *collective*. It was always the topic of conversation, right from the first day they started dating. They weren't oblivious to the complexity of their situation and knew the path ahead would be difficult. 'How can we do it? How can we make it happen for sure?' These were the questions that hung in the air, that occupied those long moments of silence and that greeted them during the Matador rides.

Muslim and Pandit romantic relationships were not common. Whatever they had heard of in the past suggested that these liaisons did not end well. Protests would inevitably break out and the couple would never live happily ever after. Whether there was any truth to these stories, or they were just cautionary tales, was hard to tell. The Muslims remained mum, and the Pandits who could have answered were not around in Kashmir.

Sagar could only talk to his friends, and they didn't know any better than him. Bilal and Adil couldn't step into Sagar's shoes and see his perspective. 'Being a minority, being in love with a girl from the majority community. What am I supposed to do?' Sagar often asked himself. He yearned for some guidance and missed having someone who had once been where he was right now.

Young love is an incredible thing. Sagar and Aalmeen, despite all the uncertainty around them, thought they were invincible. 'We will make it. We will be trailblazers. They will write stories about our love one day. You just wait and see.'

Besides the future, the second most important point of discussion for them was coordination. 'Today a guy was following me, so check on that; yesterday dad got suspicious about a boy calling, so don't call for a while; tomorrow is a hartāl, but tuition classes are still on. Will you come with me?'

'Of course I will.' This was Sagar's ready response to the last question. Now he had to figure out an excuse to leave the house during hartāl and make the journey to her tuition class and then back home. This was what Sagar lived for.

Sagar was obsessed with their day-to-day survival—when they were meeting, where they were going, what time he was going to call Aalmeen at night—that he didn't paid heed to his own future. What he wanted to do after the twelfth grade and where he wanted to study—these were issues he was yet to sort out. Sagar barely attended the tuition classes he was enrolled in and had no interest in the entrance exams. What good was an education if it would not help him be with Aalmeen?

One night, when Aalmeen's parents were at a wedding and she had the phone all to herself, Sagar told her his latest plan. 'I will become a militant, come to your house and ask for your hand. Your parents won't be able to say no to a militant. Soon we'll be married, I will give up my weapons, and we will leave Kashmir. Simple.'

Aalmeen listened calmly and said, 'That's certainly a possibility.'

'But?' Sagar groaned.

'I didn't say but ...' she replied.

'It's a silent but, I know it's coming, if not today, two weeks from now.'

Aalmeen chuckled. She obviously wasn't a fan of the plan.

Sagar made wildly imaginative plans every few weeks, and Aalmeen heard him out each time before being the voice of reason. Aalmeen was more mature than Sagar, and her outlook was much more realistic. She didn't wish to dampen his spirit, but she also tried showing him the inevitable consequences of his plans—consequences he seemed never to see. Sagar, on his part, seemed happy in his state of delusion—that is, till Aalmeen made him think. And when he did think, he could see no way out. He knew they could not be together. He hated seeing that.

'Once you are a militant, you are one for life. Even if you give up your arms, your name will be written in some book. The state will ask you to do things for it in return for letting you and your family live in peace. You'll have to give hāẓīrī to the army guys, maybe become a mukhbir. You won't even be allowed to leave the state then.' Aalmeen explained all of this logically after Sagar's 'I will become a militant' plan. 'Should I go on?'

Sagar was already feeling deflated on the other end of the phone. 'Why do you have to be so practical?' he grumbled.

Sometimes when he was waiting in the Matador during Aalmeen's Zaina Kadal tuition classes, Sagar listened to a particular song on loop, '*Tera Gham Mera Gham Ek Jaisa Sanam*' from the film *Ghulam-E-Musthafa*. It was a song that made him weep uncontrollably, for it seemed to articulate his future with Aalmeen. Sagar spent the majority of the time that he wasn't with her, thinking about a bleak tomorrow where he wouldn't have her company.

Besides the ideas that Aalmeen seemed to reject, the only other viable option for Sagar, if he wished to remain with his beloved, seemed to be conversion. If he were to convert to Islam and ask for Aalmeen's hand, technically there wouldn't be an issue. They spoke about this many times, but neither was convinced. Aalmeen—because, while she was religious and prayed for Sagar's safety, simply couldn't ask this of him. Sagar—because there were certain things that formed the core of his identity, and one of them was not believing in God. So, to convert when he wasn't spiritual in any way didn't make sense to him. This plan was a no-go.

Sagar, who shared a good rapport with Aalmeen's sister Bareen, would speak to her during his phone calls sometimes. She liked Sagar, but she was a realist. 'Listen, wake up. This is not going to last long. The sooner you both get it, the better.' She was trying to minimize the blow, but the statements landed like meteors on him.

Sagar's family had already learnt of his relationship with Aalmeen; they had stumbled into the truth a few months into his dalliance, after receiving expensive phone bills and confronting him. Already worried that Sagar got into fights, now they had another source of nervousness. 'He's going to get killed for sure,' they whispered out of his earshot.

There were two sets of stories they were aware of regarding Muslim–Pandit romantic relationships: pre-conflict and post-conflict. Pre-conflict stories were fairly simple. The families would give the couple an ultimatum. 'Do whatever you want to do but remember that you'll be dead to us.' The guy or girl would step back, not having the courage to go against the family. Or they would elope and get disowned by their kin.

Post-conflict, there would be a direct threat to the couple's lives and their respective families. 'You will be made an example of.' It was loud and clear.

After months of bunking his tuition classes, Sagar heard that his parents had finally decided to send him to Delhi to study computer science. They had gathered by now that Sagar wasn't going to choose a stream on his own and, thus, chose one for him. The reason Sagar was still dilly-dallying about this decision was because Aalmeen remained in Srinagar. She would spend another year in the city due to her twelfth grade. Post that, who knew where her parents would send her to study. Sagar fought his parents hard, declaring that he wished to stay back in Srinagar, but they forced him out of the Valley.

A part of Sagar was tired by now. He took a hard look at his life. He couldn't keep up with the rebellion, with the constant arguing with his parents. He knew that things would eventually go downhill with Aalmeen. Neither had come up with a solid solution yet. Besides, not one person had anything comforting or motivating to tell him about his relationship besides Aalmeen. The two of them were lost—the blind leading the blind. The weight of the realization was crippling for Sagar.

There was also this—with his parents, he could still manipulate them into letting him stay back. But he would never be able to ask Aalmeen to choose him above all else, if such a moment confronted them in the future.

The future. Once again, the future. He was just so tired of thinking about it. He couldn't keep mulling over it anymore.

So, Sagar decided to go to Delhi willingly.

Sagar could see the beginning of the end as soon as he took the decision. He knew the connection with Aalmeen would snap sooner or later once he was in Delhi. If he didn't see her every day during their Matador rides, nothing would be the same. Long-distance love wasn't pragmatic. As the day of his departure crept closer, he was in literal physical pain. 'This is not going to happen. Finish it before the pain gets worse,' he told himself.

Sagar chose to take all the blame and offer Aalmeen a way out. It was the only path that made sense to him.

A day before leaving for Delhi, Sagar called Aalmeen up. She answered—she had been expecting his call—and seemed far more excited than him about the beginning of his life in college. Sagar's heart flipped when he heard her voice as it always did. But what accompanied that sentiment was a sense of acute emptiness. He recited the words that he had been practising for hours. 'I don't love you, Aalmeen. I never did.'

'What?' she laughed at the other end, thinking he's messing with her.

He remained quiet.

'What?' she repeated. This time her voice seemed scared and high-pitched. 'Sagar? What are you saying?'

'I never loved you. It was all drama, make-believe. I don't feel anything for you. Please forget about me.'

Silence at the other end. He heard a few ragged breaths and then the click of the receiver. Aalmeen had ended the call.

In his head, Sagar reasoned that if Aalmeen hated him enough, it would be easy for her to forget about him and move on. He would be like a bad dream, a bad habit that she would never want to return to again.

Sagar wanted Aalmeen to be happy and get a new start to her life. In a year, she'd complete her twelfth grade. In five to six years, her family would get her married. If he parted from her now, as he had, she had much more time to be Sagar-free and stress-free.

That one-minute call was the last time Sagar conversed with Aalmeen. He never spoke to or saw his first love ever again.

BY 1997, SAGAR WAS in Delhi. He regretted his decision of ending things with Aalmeen many times. He called her hundreds of times; not once did she pick up. Maybe she heard the extended ring that came with long-distance calls and made it a point to stay away. Once or twice, her sister answered. 'Sagar, please, she's not going to talk to you anymore. Stop calling.'

Aalmeen's family would come to vacation in Delhi during the winters. Sagar knew that they had a flat in Lajpat Nagar. During subsequent winters, Sagar spent many days and weeks roaming the streets of Lajpat Nagar, through the pockets where he knew Kashmiris lived. He walked for hours in select lanes, hoping, praying to the God he didn't believe in that he would see her in a balcony or a kirana dukaan.

Sagar's plight was similar to Habba Khatun's—the Kashmiri mystic poetess who was married to the last native king of Kashmir, Yusuf Shah Chak. Chak was imprisoned by King Akbar and lived what remained of his life in captivity. Habba Khatun spent the rest of her life singing songs of longing for her beloved, asking him to come back, searching for him till the very end.

Sagar tried his best to find out where Aalmeen was going to college but learnt little. Maybe she made sure he could never find her. Maybe she had changed her name. Whatever it was, it worked. She disappeared without a trace—till there came a point where Sagar wondered if she had even existed in his life.

During this time, Sagar even started believing that there could be a God somewhere who kept them apart. Because he knew, if he got even a little glimpse of Aalmeen again, he would keep going back for more, and then some more—to that sweet, loving, heady relationship that they both knew had no future. At least not in this lifetime.

In the years to come, Sagar often thought about the last time he saw Aalmeen. It was sometime before their fateful last call. He had gone to Delhi for his initial admission paperwork and was returning a few days later. They'd decided to meet a day after he was back and had set up a time and place as well. Aalmeen was going to wait for him in Jawahar Nagar, and they would go somewhere together.

The day they were to meet, Sagar found out that Bilal was also back in town after many months. He had been getting entrance coaching elsewhere, and Sagar wanted to meet him and Adil before they went off to their respective colleges. In his bid to meet his friends, Sagar forgot about meeting Aalmeen later. He went off with Adil and Bilal and spent hours chatting with them. The infamous trio was back together. They laughed about the fact that Bilal was the one who had taken the other two to the tuition centre in Jawahar Nagar and never even ended up getting the girl. The only one who had successfully managed to woo a girl was Sagar.

At the mention of Jawahar Nagar, Sagar got a sinking feeling. He looked at his watch. It was three hours after the designated hour he was meant to meet Aalmeen. He stared at his friends in horror and told them what had happened.

'What are you still doing here? Go!' Both of them were firm.

Sagar ran to catch an auto. Ironically, he was meant to meet Aalmeen at the same bus stop where he'd seen her for the first time. He knew she wouldn't still be there, but he had to make sure. He got off the auto and ran to the Matador stop.

Aalmeen was still standing there, looking around, trying to find Sagar. Three hours later. Her eyes finally caught his—just like they had all those years ago. But this time she didn't look away. Instead, a big, fat tear rolled down her cheek, drawing a clean line across the grime that had accumulated after standing outdoors in the sun.

Sagar ran to her and told her what had happened. 'I lost track of time. I'm so sorry.'

Aalmeen nodded. She understood. She wasn't angry. She knew what the trio meant to Sagar.

But for some inexplicable reason, she couldn't stop crying.

Until this moment, if they ever had to meet, Sagar would have walked through a raging crossfire to see her just for a second.

And Aalmeen knew it. He would never have forgotten their date in a million years.

Sagar wondered why Aalmeen had waited those three extra hours—something she would never have done before. Fifteen minutes to half an hour—and she'd have been out of there. But right then, on that day, maybe she finally saw what was coming. The beginning of the end.

Aalmeen didn't say anything more. She wiped her tears, and they walked along the Jhelum till the sun set on the day and their relationship.

Sometimes when he closes his eyes, Sagar can still see Aalmeen clearly at the bus stop on that last day he saw her. She was wearing a blue kurta with small flowers embroidered in white thread; she had on a white salwar and a white chiffon dupatta. She had tied her hair in a ponytail, those rebellious flicks pinned in place. She had strapped on her backpack, nervously shifting the weight from one shoulder to the other. She was biting her lip slightly, an anxious frown creasing her forehead. Her eyes were searching. Searching for Sagar.

Like Sagar's eyes searched for her in Lajpat Nagar across many winters.

This image of Aalmeen over their last meeting is how Sagar chooses to remember her. The last image in the first place they ever met. Coming full circle.

3

KASHMIRI IN GAZA

Laila was born in Srinagar in the 1970s. Her father was an accounts officer, while her mother a teacher. Both had government jobs. Laila had a younger brother and the four of them lived in the Batmaloo area of Srinagar. Laila studied in Mallinson and her brother in Tyndale-Biscoe. Television wasn't allowed at home except for watching the news. Laila was a fan of Robin Cook's books, and her brother was crazy about Michael Jackson. Life was simple and uneventful.

This is until the year 1989. Militancy took wing in Kashmir, and the civilians started feeling the effects of it. As more and more young boys started crossing the border to Pakistan for arms training, concerned parents began sending their sons out of the Valley to study. 'Send him away so he doesn't die here'—this was the view of many parents.

Mufti Mohammad Sayeed was the Union home minister at that time, and Kashmiri students got a concession if they educated themselves outside Kashmir. Laila's parents were afraid that her younger brother would also cross over if he stayed back, so he was sent off. Laila followed suit soon after and started her bachelor's in biochemistry at Aligarh Muslim University (AMU).

Laila's first semester at AMU started in 1990. There were a lot of Kashmiris in the university, all getting away from the unrest back home. In her class of twenty-three girls, seven were from Kashmir. They instantly formed a small sub-community.

Laila's roommate was from the Maldives. For her college paperwork, her roommate had to get a mandatory HIV test done. Laila decided to tag along with her to the medical college on campus. While waiting there, a boy approached Laila and asked if she could help him fill a form. His named was Mahdi, and he was Palestinian. His English was weak, and he couldn't understand parts of the form. So, Laila decided to help him out.

There was a kind of calm about Mahdi that made her curious, but Laila was too shy to ask him more than what the form required. They went their separate ways that day, but Laila felt that the seed for something bigger had been planted. Laila didn't know what Mahdi was studying, and AMU was a huge university. She didn't see him again for a whole year.

In her second year at AMU, Laila ran into Mahdi in the bazaar buying fruits. There was instant recognition, and sparks started flying. It was as though they had been waiting for each other all this while. Mahdi waved at her, but Laila didn't know how to react. She got flustered and ran back to her hostel immediately.

After some days, a Sudanese girl, Rana, came to Laila's hostel and told her that Mahdi wanted to meet her. At that time, in AMU, the reputation of the Palestinian boys wasn't squeaky clean—to put matters mildly. They were always on the streets on their noisy bikes, hooting, shouting and teasing girls. They were known to be heartbreakers who dated and dumped girls whenever and however it suited them. They weren't considered 'serious lovers', and Laila was a very serious and studious girl. Naturally, she was sceptical about meeting Mahdi, but more than anything else, she was just plain scared. This was alien territory, and Laila had no prior experience or any idea about how to act, speak or dress in such a situation. Rana eased her fears by offering to chaperone her on the 'date'.

Mahdi and Laila met in a café under the watchful eyes of Rana, who was two tables away. Laila was bursting to say a lot, but no words emerged. Mahdi did most of the talking. She finally got to know that he was studying electrical engineering at AMU. He spoke of his big family back home in Gaza, of how much he missed them, and of how he hadn't been home in years. He spoke to Laila formally and respectfully, as one was supposed to. He was nothing like the Palestinian boys she had been warned about.

At the end of the meeting, Mahdi asked to meet her again. Laila wanted to see him, too. She wanted to know more about him, what he liked, what he disliked. But meeting him again was too overwhelming a thought for her. 'Can we write to each other instead?' He smiled and nodded. They exchanged several letters, and within a month, Laila was madly in love. Her friends started teasing her, calling her 'Lovelorn Laila'.

After a year of dating, Laila knew that Mahdi was the man she was going to marry. Aware of the Palestinian boys' reputation on campus, her close friends were very surprised that Laila was in love with one. They knew her to be diligent and respectable. They were shocked that she was considering *this* guy for marriage. That she would face the same fate as all the other heartbroken girls was clear to them, but they were too scared to tell Laila the truth.

Even if they had, chances were that Laila wouldn't have listened. That's how head over heels in love with Mahdi she was.

Laila was sure that she didn't want to marry a Kashmiri man. Most of the Kashmiri girls from her batch married non-Kashmiris eventually—men from Kolkata or from the Middle East. Apart from all else, Laila was against the way Kashmiri marriages were conducted; how matches were arranged based on physical appearances, educational degrees, property and the gold exchanged across both sides. There was a lot of pomp and show with little attention being paid to whether the two people involved would eventually click.

Laila wanted something more than the material things—she wanted an emotional connection. This took precedence over anything else. She had seen too many Kashmiri marriages where gold and dowry were the marker of a successful union, and after the wedding, the two people lived a dull life, rarely spending any time at all together. That was not the future that she envisaged for herself.

Laila, while she was sure that Mahdi was the guy she wanted to spend her life with, had no idea how to break the news to her Kashmiri parents. Laila and Mahdi made a promise that they wouldn't let go of each other even if it meant invoking the wrath of their families. They would get married in court if their parents didn't consent.

Three years passed this way, and Laila started her master's at AMU. As she sensed marriage pressure building during her phone calls with her parents, she finally plucked the courage to tell her mother about Mahdi. Her mother, as anticipated, went hysterical and did not give her approval. Laila tried to explain that Mahdi wasn't an outsider. He had lived in the subcontinent for many years and had assimilated very well. But her mother wasn't willing to listen. 'He is not a Kashmiri.' That was the end of the conversation for her.

As nothing fruitful came of the dialogue, in Laila's final year Mahdi went to meet her younger brother at his college in Manipal. He wanted Laila's brother on their side if things got ugly at home. Her brother was noncommittal. He left the decision to his father. By the time Mahdi came back to AMU from Manipal, Laila's father had already caught wind of the whole affair. Laila's brother had told him, and he was completely against the union.

The very next day, after her last practical exam, Laila found her father waiting near the hostel door. He had come to take her back to Srinagar. Mahdi caught a whiff of this, and rather than asking Laila to fight and stay back, he told her to go home peacefully and wait for him. So, Laila left, not knowing if she would ever return to AMU or see Mahdi again.

Before they went back to Srinagar, Laila and her father had a stopover in Delhi. He was working for the health ministry in Soura, Srinagar, at that time and had a meeting with Siemens in the capital to source oncology equipment.

While in Delhi, Laila tried to present her side of things to her father. She had always been closer to him than to her mother and was certain that she could make him see reason. But he was unwilling to hear her out. 'We will talk when we get home.'

Laila's father looked visibly ill and had been complaining of abdominal pain throughout the trip. He had not been eating much either. Assuming that this was caused by the stress her news had brought him, Laila didn't push him further and chose to wait. They would talk at home in Kashmir.

They reached Srinagar, and her father's pain still hadn't subsided. As ironic as his meeting in Delhi would seem now, two days later he was diagnosed with a secondary hepatic tumour. Laila's world crashed around her. She went numb. The doctors told the family that her father had a maximum of three months to live. Now, Laila couldn't even get herself to think about Mahdi or mention him. She was fighting a losing battle.

When her brother came back from Manipal, Laila's father made him promise that after his death 'under no circumstance is Laila to marry that Palestinian boy'. Laila overheard this, but her pain at the prospect of losing her father was so great that she remained silent.

Forty days after getting diagnosed, Laila's father passed away. He was only fifty-three. Everything turned blank for Laila, and all hope was lost. The rituals were a blur—the influx of relatives, the hundreds of cups of kahwè, the wailing, the wailing. Then all was silent again.

When she finally found her voice and spoke about Mahdi again, Laila was faced with total opposition. Her brother, who was honouring their father's dying wish, wasn't willing to listen. Her mother was as stubborn as ever.

News came from AMU that Laila had passed with distinction. She had missed spending her final days in college with all her friends. They had been planning a graduation trip for so many months. Laila wondered if they had gone for it without her.

Laila had wanted to pursue her PhD in Australia, but was in no state to do so after her father's death. The government had offered Laila a job as her father had passed away on duty. She didn't take it up, so it went to her brother instead. As he was in Kashmir now, Laila's brother was always hovering around, making sure she didn't do anything suspicious.

If Laila even uttered Mahdi's name, she confronted physical abuse and emotional blackmail. Her mother and brother would not tolerate the association. They wanted her to forget the boy.

But Laila did not. Laila's friend Sehar, who studied in a medical college in Srinagar, was her only support system and confidante. Through her, Laila was able to send titbits of information to Mahdi, who was still in AMU.

Laila fought for Mahdi for a year at home, taking all the blows that came her way. She told him to stay on in Aligarh, afraid of what would happen to him if he were to come to Kashmir. She couldn't bear to see any physical harm being done to him.

Laila's mother wanted to get her married off to her brother's son—Laila's cousin. When they came to see her, Laila's maternal uncle took one look at her and realized something was wrong. She looked gaunt and aloof. He took her aside and asked what was going on. Laila broke down and told him everything, crying in his arms. Her uncle went stiff for a moment, and then enveloped her in a hug. She cried louder, deeper, letting it all out.

Laila's uncle hadn't known about Mahdi. But now that he was in the loop, he took matters into his own hands. He calmed his adamant sister down and convinced her to give Mahdi a chance. He then summoned Mahdi to Srinagar.

Mahdi came with two of his best friends and met the family. The family softened, but only slightly. Laila's uncle championed them both. After fifteen days, Laila's mother grudgingly gave her assent to the union. Laila's relationship with her mother and brother was still strained, but they knew that there was no way to resist Mahdi's overtures since his relationship with Laila had now become a larger family matter.

In August 1996, Laila and Mahdi got married. In four days, Laila secured her visa to move to his hometown. Laila went before Mahdi and flew to Tel Aviv alone. From there, she joined Mahdi's family in Gaza. He had told her about his big family, but she had never anticipated their sheer number. So many women, men and children in the same big house. Her in-laws had over sixty grandchildren and thirty great-grandchildren. Quite unlike her own family, they were very happy about Laila and Mahdi's marriage.

Mahdi joined her after a month, and she conceived immediately. Her first daughter was born within a year of her marriage.

Things were calmer in Gaza at the time, and during her second year there, she delivered her younger daughter. Laila learnt Arabic and got a job with the Palestinian National Authority (PNA). She joined the national defence team as a quality control officer.

LAILA HAD BEEN WORKING for two years when the second intifada started in 2000 in Palestine. Gaza came under siege, and Laila saw a period of heightened violence unfolding in front of her own eyes. Having been sent away from Kashmir when the militancy had started, this was her first real encounter with a place of conflict. She felt a keen sense of kinship with the Palestinian people and the land. Their resilience gave her strength to survive.

In 2002, she had a son.

Laila's relationship with her own family was still difficult. In 2006, she went home to Kashmir with her kids. Laila hoped that on seeing her grandchildren, her mother would get placated.

Her hopes weren't entirely dashed, but there was still some tension between them.

While Laila was in Srinagar, legislative elections took place in Palestine. Hamas had won against Fatah and was unsupported by the West. After the two parties failed to reach a deal to share government power, the escalation led to the Battle of Gaza in 2007. Hamas overthrew the PNA government institutions in the Gaza Strip. As Laila worked for the PNA, she was out of a job.[11]

The PNA employees weren't allowed into their offices, and Laila stayed home till she secured involuntary retirement in 2017 as a lieutenant colonel. She joined an NGO for voluntary work as a project officer and became a translator of Arabic and English. She also joined a university in Jerusalem that was working on a project led by the UN. As a part of that, she studied the difficulties and challenges faced by adolescents of vulnerable communities, and especially by the Palestinian refugees living in Lebanon and Jordan amongst other places.

LAILA IS IN HER fifties now. Her kids have grown up. Though life in Gaza hasn't been the easiest, Laila has always been thankful that she got to choose it for herself. Mahdi and Laila had started their life together in Gaza with barely any money to support each other, but they made it work. Being united gave them the strength to fight all odds and build their home.

Laila and Mahdi still relate to each other the way they did on their first date—with happiness and curiosity and the conviction that they can depend on one another. They haven't let their love die on account of kids or domestic worries. Both have a wicked sense of humour that adds spice to their lives. In many ways, they balance each other out. Laila has always had a temper, and Mahdi is the only one who can rein it in.

Laila has seen a lot of marriages break apart—especially marriages in which Palestinians have married foreigners. They crumble due to family and societal pressure. If Mahdi and Laila have survived (even thrived), it is because from the time she was a new bride in an alien country, Mahdi made it a point to stand up for her. He didn't let his family interfere with their lives or their domestic tussles, because of which she never felt the pressure of her in-laws' expectations. He also eschewed patriarchal control—which in itself was a rarity since Palestine is a male-dominated society where women in the household seldom have a say in worldly matters. Not once did Mahdi try to subjugate Laila. She didn't have to ask for his permission because he was a man. On the contrary, she had full freedom to do whatever she wanted and raise their children in the way she wished.

Laila was supported by Mahdi when she chose to send their kids to a Catholic school—this despite the fact that the family was against it. She was supported, too, when she encouraged their kids to learn music and join sports academies—again, a total no-no for Mahdi's family. Today, one daughter has graduated as a doctor and another as a civil engineer. Their son is pursuing an engineering degree. All three are connected to their Palestinian roots as well as to their Kashmiri heritage. They speak Arabic, Hindi, English, Turkish and Korean, besides their mother tongue Kashmiri.

It's obvious that Laila is happy with the life she has had. It's obvious that she won't trade it for anything—this, despite the many wars in Gaza she has witnessed. The irony of moving from one place of conflict to another hasn't escaped her, even as she remains aware of the stark difference between Gaza and Kashmir—the Palestinians are caught in a religious conflict, while the Kashmiris are caught in a political one.

Today, because of the political climate, many have moved out of the Gaza Strip. In the past, each time Laila and Mahdi thought of leaving Gaza, they stopped short because of their jobs or because as their daughters grew older, they got selected into universities there. But now that their son is studying in Egypt and their daughters have graduated, Laila and Mahdi are finally free to move. And they are seriously considering the possibility.

While much has altered and continues altering in Laila's life, some things remain the same—her relationship with her family in Kashmir, for instance. Though they've made progress over the years, their association isn't as warm as it should be. There still remains some bitterness that she married a Palestinian. It's said that time heals everything, but that's not true for everyone.

'Maybe I still need time,' Laila says.

Note: Laila, Mahdi and their children have been forced to leave Palestine following the events of 7 October 2023 and after. Their home in Gaza has been destroyed by Israeli bombing. They have lost at least thirty members of their extended family, with many others injured and displaced.

4

PAPER MAPS

IT WAS DECEMBER 1986. Ahmad lived in Magam, which was on the way to Gulmarg, with his family. New to the ninth grade, fifteen-year-old Ahmad had curly black hair and sparkling eyes.

The winter vacations were upon him, and Ahmad was looking forward to three months of snow, sleep and solitude. But his plans were foiled all too soon when Inayatullah sir, the strict maths teacher from his school, was roped in to give Ahmad, his sister and cousin tuition classes through the winter. Inayatullah sir was Ahmad's father's friend and was doing this as a favour to him. Ahmad's father was a government schoolteacher known for his English classes—a fact that was a matter of pride for him. But he didn't want his children's academic prowess to stop with English.

With an air of disappointment, the kids accepted their fate.

Inayatullah sir would come to their house each day at 10 a.m. And three half-asleep children would be woken from their slumber to greet fractions and geometry instead of steaming hạrisè and nun-chai.

Ahmad's house was close to a renowned hospital in Magam. A doctor couple from Srinagar had just been posted there for the winter and had shifted, bag and baggage, with their family. They had a daughter named Zulaikha who was Ahmad's age. Ahmad's uncle worked in the same hospital, and when he overheard Zulaikha's parents' concerns about their daughter's academic growth, he offered her a place in Inayatullah sir's maths tuition class. They quickly grabbed the opportunity.

As in the past, the next winter morning, Ahmad peeled himself out of the warm covers of his bed and made his way down to the hamām—the room with a subfloor that held a wood-fired furnace to generate heat—where Inayatullah sir taught them. Hair dishevelled and eyes still puffy, Ahmad was thankful that sir didn't care about appearances. As he stepped into the room, he spotted a new addition to the group. Sitting there with her hair in a neat plait and wearing a nun-chai coloured phẹran was a teenage girl close to his age. He could only describe her as lovely. Zulaikha scanned Ahmad from head to toe, the corner of her mouth curling into a crooked smile. Ahmad suddenly wished that he were more presentable.

Inayatullah sir ushered him in impatiently. 'You're letting all the heat out, Ahmad. Now sit.' Ahmad sat down, subtly trying to flatten his hair. His sister and cousin giggled. Sir pointed at Zulaikha. 'This is Zulaikha, she ...'

'Zulfi,' the new girl butted in. 'Everyone calls me Zulfi.'

The other children turned to Zulfi, clearly impressed. No one cut off sir mid-sentence. A bit confused himself with the interruption, sir went on, 'Uh okay, Zulfi. Ahmad, she's in the ninth grade as well. Share your notes with her.'

Ahmad nodded, not looking at Zulfi. 'Yes, sir.'

Zulfi was sharp, enthusiastic and the most interested in maths out of the four children. She gave answers the fastest, and even helped the others out when they were stuck. Sir, who didn't offer compliments to anyone, grudgingly revealed that he was impressed. 'Good job,' he muttered, as if enunciating the words at gunpoint.

At the end of the class, Ahmad gathered all his old notes and handed them over to Zulfi. For the first time their eyes met. 'Thanks, I'll get them all back tomorrow.' He nodded, and she walked out. Ahmad's sister and cousin snickered in the corner. 'Someone's the smitten kitten!' Ahmad leapt at them, but they were too fast and darted out of the room.

Left alone in the hamām, Ahmad went to the window and drew open the curtains just a whisper. He peeped out to see Zulfi getting into her father's blue Ambassador car. She took one last look at the house, and Ahmad swiftly drew the curtains shut.

From the next day onwards, Ahmad would get out of bed ahead of time. Teeth brushed, hair combed, face washed and clothes changed. He would be the first one in the hamām every morning after wolfing down his breakfast. Zulfi would walk in five minutes after him and take off her woolly hat before she thawed in the warmth. Ahmad would offer her his kāngèr to get warm. She would take it graciously. Zulfi never missed a single class.

Over the next few minutes, before the others walked in, Ahmad and Zulfi would exchange some banter. She would tell him about how the Dal Lake in Srinagar was probably frozen over right now—'good enough to walk on'—and he would tell her about a majestic Kạni shawl he had seen in the neighbouring village of Kanihama that had taken the weaver a year to weave.

Gradually, Ahmad and Zulfi became close friends. They shared everything that had happened in their lives with each other without any hesitation. Zulfi started arriving earlier and earlier to the tuition class just to spend more time with Ahmad. And she was the highlight of Ahmad's whole day.

Ahmad knew they shared a special connection, but he didn't have a name for it. He had only seen these connections on TV, and they always seemed to be between adults.

Buniyaad was a TV serial that had started airing in 1986. Both Ahmad and Zulfi were fond of it. They would watch a new episode at night and then discuss what had happened the next morning. There was a character in *Buniyaad* referred to as Masterji who fell in love with a character called Lajoji. Zulfi was adept at drawing and had made a painting of the TV pair. One day, before class, she showed it to Ahmad. She had written his name under Masterji and her own name under Lajoji. Ahmad blushed. He now knew that Zulfi felt about him the way he felt for her.

Ahmad was dreading the end of the winter vacation. He knew that with the passage of a season, Zulfi's parents would get transferred back to Srinagar. Zulfi would have to move with them, and he wouldn't be able to see her every single day. The city was far away, and he didn't have the means to travel there or even a reason that he could offer his parents.

A few weeks before Zulfi was to leave, Ahmad stole the pencil that Zulfi made all her art with and kept it as a souvenir. Zulfi searched all over the hamām for it, while Ahmad pretended to help. He never came clean.

The feared day finally arrived in February. Zulfi was leaving for Srinagar the next morning. Even Inayatullah sir, not one for showing his emotions, could not be indifferent to his best pupil's departure. 'You should get 100 out of 100 in your board exams!' he said. Zulfi nodded.

Ahmad had been crying the night before. Today, when it was time to say goodbye to Zulfi, there were no tears left. They promised to write letters to each other. Zulfi scribbled her address on the back of his Maths notebook. Like the first day he had seen her, Ahmad watched Zulfi leave from his spot by the window of the hamām. This time when she looked back, he didn't draw the curtains shut. He kept watching till her father's Ambassador was a blue dot on the horizon.

FOR MONTHS AFTER ZULFI left, Ahmad kept stalling the writing of the first letter. He felt that the banter Zulfi and he exchanged in person could never get replicated in the written word. His reticence lasted a whole year. Zulfi hadn't written to him either.

Now that so much time had passed, Ahmad decided that his first letter to Zulfi had to contain some good news. So, he resolved to write to her after his twelfth board results. That was still two long years away.

Ahmad worked hard for those two years and passed with a distinction. That's when he retrieved his yellowing maths tuition notebook from his bedside drawer; he had preserved it carefully for Zulfi's address. He started writing her a letter. Ahmad felt that he wouldn't be able to find the right words for Zulfi, but they slipped off his pen like butter. He made it a point to emphasize his twelfth board marks just to impress her. He dropped off the letter in the red postbox he'd seen on Magam's main road and started waiting fervently for Zulfi's reply.

As if she had been waiting all this while, Zulfi wrote back immediately. Ahmad got her response within a month. She had lost his address during the move and had been too shy to ask her parents to get it from their friend—Ahmad's uncle. There was no talk of disappointment about the time lost. Both were ecstatic to have been reunited. Zulfi had passed her twelfth boards with distinction as well. She had scored 100 in her maths paper in the tenth grade, just as she had promised Inayatullah sir some winters ago. Ahmad made a mental note to tell Inayatullah sir, whenever he met him next.

The two kept writing to each other for a long time, but still could not meet because of the distance. Neither had an excuse to visit the other's house or locality. Whenever Zulfi saw the board for Magam on her way to Gulmarg for a picnic, she felt like asking the driver to stop. But she was never able to utter the words.

In one of his letters, Ahmad wrote that it was probably for the best that he didn't visit Srinagar, because in trying to find her house there, he would get lost. And pat came Zulfi's reply—a hand-drawn map of her house in Safakadal and another one of her maternal grandparents' house, her mātāmāl in Dalgate. Ahmad started carrying the maps in his wallet all the time, just in case. Even so, he couldn't shake off the feeling that he wouldn't be able to reach her.

SURELY IT WAS FATE that brought Ahmad to Srinagar. He secured admission for his bachelor's degree in electronics at the Government Degree College in Bemina. He started making the daily commute from Magam to Srinagar to get to his classes.

Before starting his course, Ahmad's mother had made him shave off the beard he had grown over the winter, so that he wasn't singled out.

It was 1989, and militancy was at its peak. Matador buses were regularly being checked by the army. Ahmad had gotten used to the routine—hands up with the ID card in one hand, to be checked by the soldiers. The hālāth were not good in Kashmir, and lines of stress were etched on everyone's faces. Ahmad's parents would get worried sick if their son came home even a minute later than usual.

In the midst of such uncertainty, Ahmad kept his feelings for Zulfi alive. Now that he was a regular in Srinagar, Ahmad knew that he could meet her—but he didn't just want to land up at Zulfi's house.

So, first, he poured his heart out in a letter, waiting for her go-ahead. He confessed his love for her from the time they were children. With the *Buniyaad* drawings fresh in his mind, he expected a similar response from Zulfi.

Ahmad waited for many days for her reply. When he finally got it, he was heartbroken to read a cold response. Zulfi emphasized in her letter that Ahmad should focus on his future and academics, just like her. At that point, she was studying journalism. She wished him a bright future but didn't say anything about it being a joint one.

Ahmad felt deflated but continued writing to her. More than in the past, he made it a point to update Zulfi about his academic life, so she knew that he was serious about his future—a future that he wished to share with her. He continued spelling out his love for her in those letters, hoping that one day she would reciprocate. Zulfi's responses were always kind and tender, but she never professed her love for Ahmad. Maybe over the years that they had been away from one another, she had grown up and grown out of the nascent feelings she felt for Ahmad—unlike Ahmad, who still carried the maps she had drawn for him.

Ahmad did not see Zulfi while he was in Srinagar. The frequency of their letters decreased gradually. College and academics took over their lives.

SEVEN YEARS PASSED, AND it was 1996. It had been ten years since Ahmad and Zulfi had first met at Inayatullah sir's tuition class. Ahmad was in Kashmir University in Srinagar now, pursuing a second master's degree.

On one warm day in July, he was in a Matador bus with his friend Abdullah, coming back from the university, when he saw Zulfi sitting by a window. She was looking out, the afternoon sun making patterns on her face. Even after all this time, Ahmad recognized her immediately. Zulfi momentarily looked around, and their eyes met for a brief second. She looked away, not showing any sign of recognition. Ahmad was excited and impatiently asked his friend what to do. Abdullah offered a tried and tested idea.

Ahmad sidled up to the bus conductor and paid for Zulfi's ticket. He then hid himself from Zulfi. The Lal Chowk stop arrived, and Zulfi got up. Ahmad was getting down here as well. She approached the conductor to pay for her ticket, and he shrugged and pointed to Ahmad, explaining what had happened. Ahmad jumped off the bus, not before catching Zulfi's confused frown. Abdullah gave him a thumbs up from the bus window. Zulfi got off and called out to Ahmad. She asked him angrily, 'Hey, you, why did you pay for my ticket?'

'My wish,' came the reply from a cheeky Ahmad.

Fortunately, Zulfi recognized Ahmad's voice. Her hand rose to her mouth in surprise, curling in the same crooked way it had when he had first seen her. As if in a matter of seconds, the two long-lost friends quickly filled the emotional gap in a way that the erratic letters had failed to. Both their faces bloomed like the first narcissuses of spring.

It was a dramatic meeting after a gap of years, but it was very short-lived. Zulfi had somewhere to be. Ahmad had been gathering the courage to ask her out for tea or coffee, but she rushed off with the promise of keeping in touch. She turned around midway and scribbled something on a piece of paper. She pressed it into his hands. Ahmad looked down at a familiar scrawl containing a landline number. He smiled.

Ahmad didn't have a landline at home and would phone Zulfi from the PCO. They didn't speak on the phone often, but just about enough that, one day, Zulfi invited him to come home to Safakadal. 'Even my parents will be happy to see you after so many years.'

Ahmad planned to go to Safakadal each time he had a break from university. But something kept getting in his way.

Once, he was on his way to Zulfi's house. He had reached Cement Kadal and was crossing the bridge when he saw a crackdown happening up ahead. Before he knew it, Ahmad was caught in it. He spent the whole day there and was only released when it was dark. He called Zulfi later from a PCO to apologize. 'It's okay,' she sighed.

ONE FATEFUL DAY, AHMAD got on a Matador with two of his friends from college. At Batmaloo, the bus was stopped by the army. They were all asked to get down. The IDs were scanned by the army personnel. To their shock, Ahmad and his two friends were asked to step away from the rest of the passengers. They looked at each other with fear.

They army men let the other passengers get back on the bus and sent it along. Ahmad and the two others were shaking in their spots. It was never a good sign to get singled out in an army check. The three young men were blindfolded, piled into a car, and taken to the nearby military camp. As they rode in the dark van, Ahmad prayed that he would be able to see Zulfi again. 'Even if it's the last time, God, keep me alive for that.'

Once in the camp, they were led out of the car and taken into a cold room. The air smelt damp and musty. They sat there for a long time, shivering and still blindfolded. Ahmad didn't dare utter a word to his friends, not sure who else was in the room with them. After some time, he heard footsteps approach and men whispering. A moment later, he felt someone's warm hand on his head. Ahmad felt a chill go through his entire body. He was being singled out.

Ahmad had been in enough crackdowns to understand what this meant. At some point, a mukhbir would come in and point to the man with affiliations to the taḥrīk. Today it was Ahmad. Through his blindfold, Ahmad puzzled out the blurry figure of the man with his hand on his head, now gesturing as if to say 'this one'. He left the room. And then, there was silence again. Ahmad cried silently, his blindfold soaking up the tears.

After fifteen minutes, the blindfolds were taken off. The three boys squinted, their eyes adjusting to the dreary room. The army guys who had taken them from the bus stood in a corner, talking. One of them approached the three and pointed to Ahmad. 'You ... get out of here.'

Ahmad's eyes widened in shock. A soldier poked him from behind, compelling him to stand up. Ahmad looked at his two friends, who were staring back at him with fear in their eyes. He opened his mouth to protest, to ask for their release as well. But the words froze. Another poke in his spine and he staggered forward. With uncertain footsteps, he walked to the door, unable to look back at his friends another time.

As Ahmad got to the gates of the army camp, the soldier guarding the exit chuckled while opening it for him. 'Get some sweets to distribute on your way home.'

Ahmad caught the last Matador going towards Magam. He got home and went straight to his room without food or water. He wept all night like a child, the gatekeeper's words echoing in his head, as they would for many years to come.

When Ahmad returned to college a few days later, his two friends were nowhere to be seen. Two days later, their dead bodies were found—one in a church, the other on a road. Racked with survivor's guilt, it was a while before Ahmad could speak about the episode.

Ahmad didn't reach out to Zulfi for quite a long time after that. The incident had rattled him to the core, and something inside him told him that the two of them were not meant to be. Ahmad had always felt inferior to Zulfi as her family was more well off than his. And then there was the matter of him being Shia and her being Sunni—not always the easiest of matrimonial unions. Their correspondence slowly dwindled again.

Ahmad finished his master's degree in linguistics in Kashmir University. Four years after that chance meeting in Lal Chowk, Ahmad and Zulfi bumped into each other again, this time at the university. Ahmad had barely attempted to keep in touch, and Zulfi had stopped asking him to come home. But when they saw each other, none of that mattered.

It was autumn, and the chinars in Naseem Bagh had changed into delicious colours. This time neither Ahmad nor Zulfi was in a hurry to be anywhere. They spent almost five hours walking through the university. They talked about all their life experiences, just as they had when they had first met as children. Ahmad told Zulfi about all that had happened in the army camp—something he seldom discussed with people. Zulfi listened with patience and empathy, and Ahmad finally felt like he could forgive himself for being the sole survivor that day.

Zulfi had never chastised Ahmad for professing his love for her. Nor did she this time, when out of nowhere, he told her directly, 'I love you, Zulfi. I want to be with you.' Ahmad could tell by the look on her face that she had harboured a similar feeling in her heart for many years, but like always the words that escaped her mouth were the same. 'You just concentrate on your future, Ahmad. Build something for yourself.'

This time she added something else. 'We'll see.'

They rode the Matador together. As Ahmad got off at Batmaloo, Zulfi promised that she would meet him again. She waved to him from the window. Ahmad sighed and went along his way. He knew at that very moment that they would never see each other again.

IT WAS A FEW months after Zulfi's meeting with Ahmad in Kashmir University that her father arrived at his home in Magam with his daughter's wedding invitation. As tea was served to him, he pointedly said, 'My daughter is getting married and moving to California. It is in America.' He emphasized 'America'.

Somehow, Ahmad knew that the words were directed at him. A clear warning—'Don't try anything.' And Ahmad didn't.

Zulfi completed her master's, got married and moved to the US. Ahmad's parents attended the dāwath, but he stayed home that day. Zulfi didn't call or write to Ahmad before the wedding or after.

Ahmad often thought of Zulfi's father's visit to their house. He was a doctor of a high stature. For him to personally invite them to her wedding was odd. He had certainly come to make a statement. In which case, had Zulfi spoken to her parents about him? Ahmad hoped that her 'we'll see' hadn't been a false promise. Even if Zulfi had not succeeded in securing her parents' approval, her father's visit still brought a smile to Ahmad's face.

Ahmad was married soon afterwards. Many years later, he heard through the grapevine that Zulfi had become a professor in a reputed university in the US. She had two children. Ahmad started a small business in Kashmir and had a son. When he sent him to Inayutallah sir for tuition classes, he was amused to hear sir still telling any student who would listen about Zulfi. 'My best student till date, she got 100 out of 100 in maths.'

On winter mornings that are reminiscent of the one in 1986 when he first met Zulfi, Ahmad often looks at the small pencil that he stole from her many, many moons ago. Ahmad smiles thinking of all that was, all that couldn't be, and all that will always remain.

RĀTH

yesterday

5

VISA

ZARA WAS PURSUING HER master's and PhD in Rochester, US, in the late 2000s. Her research was in the field of biomedical genetics, and she was nearing the end of her degree. While she was born in Saudi Arabia, Zara was Kashmiri by birth and spirit. As her father was posted as a physician in Saudi Arabia, she had done most of her early schooling there.

In August 2008, Zara and her two brothers were to get married in Srinagar—it was planned as a triple wedding. At this point, Zara only had her last year of research pending. Around July, she left for Kashmir during her college vacation. The plan was to get married and come back to finish her PhD in Rochester.

Zara had an Indian passport and would usually renew her student visa each time she visited Kashmir. This time as well, she reapplied at the US embassy in New Delhi and went onwards to Kashmir to get married.

Zara's eldest brother was born in Kashmir and had grown up with his grandparents. It wasn't uncommon back then for newly married couples to keep their young children at the grandparents' home till the parents figured out their careers and livelihood. While her parents made a living in Saudi, Zara and her second brother were born. They came to Kashmir every year for vacation and to meet their elder brother.

It was when Zara was in the tenth grade that the family decided to move back to Kashmir. The year was 1996, and militancy was still an everyday reality. Zara remembered hearing gunshots through the door at her mātāmāl in Safakadal. The siblings would snuggle up close and try to fall asleep.

It felt like the unrest would not end, and after a few years, the family decided to move out of Kashmir and to the UK, where Zara's father had secured a job. Zara completed what remained of her schooling there and shifted to the US for college. Eventually, her parents moved back to their house in Nishat, Srinagar, even as Zara continued studying in the US.

While Zara was pursuing her master's, talks of her marriage started. Her parents began actively searching for a groom in Kashmir. Zara had lived the majority of her life outside the Valley. While she was Kashmiri at heart, her outlook wasn't always aligned with that of someone who had grown up there. The early matches didn't amount to anything, and her parents soon realized that Zara wouldn't find a perfect fit in Kashmir. Since Zara's academic interests and work kept her in the US, they decided that it was better to look westwards.

There was another reason for her parents' change of heart. Zara's mother had just been diagnosed with colon cancer. The news hit the whole family like a thunderbolt and left Zara especially shaken. Zara's mother, who had always been adamant about her children marrying Kashmiris and staying true to their roots, stopped looking at the nitty-gritties. 'They should just get married into good families and to a good person,' she said.

Finding a Kashmiri bachelor in America wasn't easy. It was like sifting for a ring in rice. It was an arduous process that didn't bring Zara's parents immediate (or any) results. They finally asked their family friends in Washington DC if they knew Kashmiris living there. The reply was immediate. They didn't know of other Kashmiris with eligible sons, but they did know of a good family of Hyderabadi Muslims. They had a son, Rehan, who was looking for a bride. 'The parents moved here when they were young. All the kids were born here, so they are "fully" American. They may not be Kashmiri, but they are very good people.'

'Good people' was just what Zara's mother sought. So, with no Kashmiris in sight, and with their friends vouching for Rehan, Zara's parents told her about him. Zara, who by now had become exasperated with the marriage process, finally felt her interest being piqued. A boy in the US, so she wouldn't have to move continents after getting married—it seemed like a win-win proposition.

In a few weeks' time, Zara was in DC. Along with her aunt, she met Rehan and his family. Rehan himself lived in Baltimore and worked as a health services administrator in the Maryland Department of Health. Zara and Rehan hit it off immediately to her surprise. Both shared a common past—that of being away from the places that their parents were from. They understood the complexity and awkwardness of being somewhere in the middle of that cultural spectrum. It was this understanding that brought them closer. They met a handful of times, and Zara warmed up to Rehan and his family fairly quickly. After the fifth meeting, Zara had a call with her parents. She could hear the eagerness and hope in their voices. She put them out of their misery right away. 'Go ahead and fix it,' she said. They were both beyond thrilled.

Zara and Rehan's families spoke to each other over the phone to seal the deal. The dates were fixed—with just one condition since Zara's brothers were getting married as well. 'We want all three of our children to get married in the same place. In our home in Kashmir.' Rehan's parents agreed. 'Of course,' they said. 'We haven't visited Hyderabad in such a long time. This is a happy excuse to do that.'

So, it was settled. The three siblings would get married in their house in Nishat in August. The respective in-laws and to-be spouses would fly in as the wedding date approached.

EVER SINCE ZARA HAD landed in Kashmir in July after her visa stopover in Delhi, she could tell that the atmosphere in the Valley was tense. She soon learnt about the Amarnath land row that had gripped the state.

The Amarnath pilgrimage took place every summer in Pahalgam in Kashmir. Thousands of pilgrims would make their way to see the lingam of Lord Shiva, in the form of an iced stalagmite, in the Amarnath mountain. In May 2008, the government decided to transfer 99 acres of forest land to the Shri Amarnathji Shrine Board to set up temporary shelters and facilities for pilgrims.[12]

Since Kashmir has a Muslim-majority population and Jammu is largely Hindu, demonstrations began immediately in Kashmir against the transfer, even as protests started in Jammu in support of the agreement. Initial opposition to the land transfer was based on concerns about the region's delicate ecological balance, but it snowballed into something much bigger. It triggered an anxiety that this was the beginning of a change in the demographics of the Valley. Men and women poured out into the streets in great numbers; there were non-violent mass protests. Calls for azaadi started echoing through the roads after a long time. *'Hum kya chahte? Azaadi!* What do we want? Freedom!' Curfews and lockdowns announced by separatist leaders and stone pelting became a regular occurrence. Though the state government revoked the land transfer in July, the anxiety continued; times remained fraught when Zara's wedding was right around the corner.

Zara had been through the unrest during her brief stint in Kashmir in her late teens. The uncertainty of those times came rushing back to her. More than the wedding, she was worried about Rehan and his parents who would be visiting Kashmir soon. They weren't familiar with the Valley, and she prayed that nothing untoward would happen while they were there.

As Zara anticipated, her in-laws were perplexed by the strained political climate in the Valley as soon as they arrived. On the way from the airport, their car had got stuck in a wave of protests, and they were jittery by the time they reached Zara's residence. They hadn't experienced the kind of military presence that Kashmiris bore witness to daily—a sight that even Zara had yet to come to terms with. Zara could feel their nervous energy. So, when they announced that they'd leave the moment all the functions were done, she wasn't surprised at all.

The wedding date crept closer. The decorations were up, the shāmiyānè was hoisted, and the house was bustling with people. But Kashmir remained in a state of limbo. Srinagar was operational on some days and curfew-ridden on others. A ḍhīl was called so that civilians could move about and complete their chores. But these hours of normalcy were short-lived.

In the days leading up to the triple wedding, a massive curfew was imposed. For reasons of safety, Zara's mother had decided to take out the wedding jewellery from the bank locker a week before the big day. Now that the banks were closed, Zara couldn't get any of her jewellery out. Her mother was alarmed and blamed herself for the faux pas. After calming her down, Zara chose to wear whatever she could find of her mother's jewellery at home.

This was just the first of many challenges. The make-up artist bailed, so Zara had to handle her own make-up. The mehandī artist didn't show up, so an amateur aunty from the neighbourhood had to take over. Even the photographer who turned up wasn't Zara's first choice; he ended up taking the most unflattering photographs of everyone.

Surprisingly, the nikāh itself was peaceful and proceeded without a hitch. On 9 August, in a relatively calm Srinagar, the three couples got married. As though the city had relaxed only for the joint wedding, in the days after, a spate of curfews kept bringing lives to a standstill.

Zara, who was just beginning to get to know Rehan, had been waiting to get away from her bustling wedding house and explore the city with him. Rehan, who had only been to India once to visit his parents' hometown, Hyderabad, had also been looking forward to sight-seeing and travelling around Kashmir with his wife. But everything was closed post the nikāh. And except for visiting the Mughal gardens, the newlyweds weren't allowed to venture out anywhere.

Delhi offered a slim window of opportunity. Zara and Rehan had to travel to the capital to submit additional wedding documents to the US Embassy for Zara's visa. They discussed applying for a marriage visa instead of the student visa. But since the student visa was in all likelihood already being processed, they decided it was best not to cause any kind of bureaucratic confusion. 'I've done this so many times. The visa will come in a few weeks,' Zara said.

With that out of the way, Zara and Rehan started travelling. They did a small Delhi tour, catching everything from Humayun's Tomb to the Qutub Minar, and also took a quick excursion to the Taj Mahal.

From Delhi, Rehan left for the US. Zara came back to Srinagar to wait for her visa. 'See you in a few weeks,' she said as she hugged him goodbye.

IN DELHI, ZARA HAD been confident about securing a visa. But as days turned to weeks, and there was no intimation from the US embassy, Zara started getting anxious. In faraway Kashmir, she had no way of visiting the embassy herself, and if she called, they'd always offer the same vague answer, 'Ma'am, we cannot provide any information at this point. Please call next week.'

At the other end of the world, Rehan was feeling uneasy as well. But he tried reassuring Zara. 'It could just be a random check. Maybe they flagged something in your documents. I'm sure it'll be resolved soon.'

Zara and Rehan soon figured out the cause for the delay. Post 9/11, there had been an anthrax scare. A spate of letters containing spores had been mailed to US officials. Everyone was on high alert, security had been beefed up, and visa laws were (expectedly) getting more stringent. Government agencies were urged to carry out extensive background checks on people trying to come back to the US. To complicate matters, those affiliated with the sciences, especially with the biomedical field, were under scrutiny. It didn't help that Zara, besides being a biomedical genetics student, was also born in Saudi Arabia and had a Kashmiri address on her passport. She ticked all the boxes that made for a 'suspicious' visa applicant.

Zara was distraught. This was supposed to be the start of the rest of her life with Rehan. They had made plans of spending time in Baltimore before she went back to study in Rochester. Now, those dreams were broken.

Soon, Zara's non-American PhD friends were back in Rochester after their break. None of them had been denied re-entry. They had received their visas on time. Zara missed not only their camaraderie but also the classes she so enjoyed.

As another month passed, Zara submitted a leave of absence to her college. She had already missed quite a lot, and even if she made it back within this semester, she wouldn't be able to catch up. Rehan drove to Rochester and cleared out Zara's apartment. He carried everything back to Baltimore, including her pet cat Muffin, who had been looked after by Zara's friend while she was away in Srinagar. Now, the cat—who loved sitting on Zara's textbooks—had to get used to a new home in another city in America. Rehan told Zara over a phone call, 'He's sitting on my books now!' Zara sniffed, 'What a traitor!'

Since she had assumed she would be in Kashmir only for a few weeks, Zara hadn't invested in a cell phone. Now it became imperative to get one to talk to Rehan. This was easier said than done. To buy a SIM card, one needed ID proof, and the only identification Zara had was her passport, which was still with the

US embassy. So, Zara had no choice but to rely on her father's cell phone. Zara and Rehan scheduled conversations, and he would call her since it was cheaper for him. As her father needed the phone for work as well, Zara couldn't speak when he was busy—and he was busy often.

This wasn't how Zara had wanted things to be. In the nascent stages of their marriage—that too an arranged one—when they were supposed to be getting to know each other, Zara and Rehan had to sustain their relationship through timed and timid conversations. They were denied the ease and spontaneity they so desired. It didn't help that Zara's brothers and their wives were glowing with marital bliss and the joy and ease that comes with proximity.

Zara could take it no more. During her second month in Kashmir, she coaxed her father into getting a BSNL broadband dial-up connection installed in the house. It was an unreliable network, but it was better than nothing. Zara and Rehan could IM one another—the only form of communication that the broadband connection would support. Skype or video calls were out of the question; limited emoticons worked sometimes. 'If you miss how I look, you always have the wedding pictures,' Rehan would tease her. It had become common knowledge now that they both hated their wedding ceremony photos.

One day when there was a grenade blast in Srinagar, the internet promptly gave way. Zara wasn't able to keep her online date with Rehan. He sent her message after message but got no answer. Agitated, he finally called Zara's father. Zara told Rehan what had happened. Except now, Rehan was even more agitated—about not just the blast but the fact that Zara was conveying the news so casually. How could he know that Zara wasn't taking the episode lightly? She was simply turning into the average Kashmiri, desensitized after decades of violence.

Back in Baltimore, people started asking Rehan the same question. 'Didn't you just get married? Where's the missus?' He didn't know what to tell them. Rehan had a vague understanding of the Kashmir conflict, but it was barely enough to describe the complexity of the situation he found himself in. In truth, Rehan's knowledge of the Valley was informed by one film, *Mission Kashmir*—the only film he had seen that was set in his wife's homeland. And like most Bollywood films, it failed to paint a complete or a balanced picture.

Between erratic internet chats and abrupt calls, Zara and Rehan had been unable to have a prolonged conversation about the land and politics. After the grenade blast and Rehan's response, though, Zara realized that it was time to have 'the talk'. She had to explain to her American husband where she came from—have this most difficult conversation across seas and continents and when their marriage was still young. Regular relationships had growing pains; here, two people had been thrown into the deep end of the pool without floaters.

As well as she could, Zara explained to Rehan what it meant to live in Kashmir; what hailing from this land signified. She told him that the conflict wasn't rooted in the present moment or the recent past; it could be traced right back to the independence of India and prior to that as well.

Rehan tried making sense of the information he received. He educated himself. And then, like so many others, when he read of the human rights violations that had happened and continued happening in Kashmir, he slipped into a phase of deep denial. 'This can't be true. This can't be happening. Especially to your people and in your land.' Zara heard him out.

She could not provide him any comfort because she had none to give.

The grenade blast wasn't the first or the last disaster to strike the Valley. And it wasn't the last time that the broadband connection died. Finally, Zara offered her brother's ID as proof and got a SIM card and a cell phone of her own. She could be in touch with Rehan now regardless.

'WE CANNOT PROVIDE ANY further information at this point of time.' The line that the US embassy offered Zara was now embedded in her mind. It would resonate through her waking and sleeping hours. She dreaded it, but circumstances were such that she had to hear the statement every single week.

Every. Single. Week.

Each Tuesday, an Excel sheet would be released on the embassy's website. Battling a slow internet connection, Zara checked to see if her name appeared—eagerly in the early weeks and tentatively later on.

Her name didn't appear.

A sense of hopelessness engulfed Zara. She kept getting updates from her fellow students about the course—after all, she was still on several email chains started by her professors. As her peers continued with their research, Zara felt a rush of panic—like she was standing on an empty platform with the train long gone.

Meanwhile, Zara's research advisor kept offering suggestions that she felt were tone deaf. 'Why don't you join the Journal Club? You can make good use of your time.' Journal clubs were meetings in which people gathered to study scientific papers published in research journals. 'I'm sure you can do it online,' he tried egging her on.

Zara didn't know how to convey to him the impossibility of her situation. Here she was with an internet connection that was barely hanging by a thread. How was she supposed to have long conversations regarding scientific papers online with other students? That's when Zara realized that her advisor simply didn't have an understanding of where she was coming from. He had no context about Kashmir, nor did he know what it felt like to be under the scanner because of one's background. A man of scientific and academic pursuits, he barely knew what was happening in his own country, let alone in other parts of the world.

It was late November now. The chinars in Kashmir that had turned a fiery red in autumn slowly started shedding their leaves. Winter was here. Zara hadn't brought winter wear with her; she only had her wedding trousseau, a few other garments, and the childhood winter clothes that her mother had preserved. Zara started getting ready for the oncoming winter by buying some woollen essentials. Back in Baltimore, Rehan got ready for a bitingly cold season alone. They both felt like they were being punished for no crime they had committed.

The visa didn't arrive.

THE CALENDAR YEAR CHANGED to 2009. Hibernating at home, Zara had become listless. Both Rehan and Zara would try to hide their frustration during phone calls, but they weren't fooling anyone. Their strained voices and forced laughter had started becoming apparent, but both tried to ignore what was entirely obvious to the rest.

As the season shifted and the world outside thawed, Zara decided that she needed a distraction—a constructive one at that—to keep her sanity intact. In March, it would be over six months since her wedding, and she could not endure a slow, painful, directionless wait any longer.

One day, over morning chai and tsoṭ, while she happened to be rifling through the *Greater Kashmir* newspaper, Zara saw teaching opportunities in the classifieds section. Something struck her right then. She had a degree in biology. Surely she could teach at a school.

None of the teaching positions advertised in the newspaper were for the subject she had trained herself in. Nonetheless, Zara started applying to the schools in the Valley, hoping that, as they opened from their winter break, one of them would seek a biology teacher.

There were those who'd see her decision to secure a job as a sign that she was giving up and accepting her fate. But Zara's parents perceived things differently. As did Rehan. Both agreed that this was a good move—'You can't be in your head all the time!'

Zara updated her CV, printed out multiple copies and went to the various schools in Srinagar. It wasn't as easy as she had thought it would be. Most schools were at full capacity with teachers, and the others raised their eyebrows at Zara's slight American accent. 'We don't think you'll be a good fit,' they said. 'The way you speak will prove distracting to the students. They won't understand what you are saying.' Zara tried assuring them that if the need arose, she could explain in Urdu, too. But the school administers would shake their heads and hand her CV back.

Finally, when Zara had almost given up on her venture, an administrator in one of the last schools she visited asked, 'Why don't you give Convent a go?'

Presentation Convent Higher Secondary School—or Convent as it was famously called—was one of the most prestigious all-girls schools in Kashmir. When Zara told her parents that she was giving Convent a shot, they exchanged bemused looks. 'Don't get your hopes too high! It's Convent, after all!'

Zara refused to get dissuaded and went to meet the administrator at Convent the next day. The stars must have aligned themselves in her favour because it turned out that the senior biology teacher in the school was going on maternity leave. Convent was in dire need of a substitute teacher. The flustered administrator looked at Zara as though she were an answer to all her prayers. 'Can you start on Monday?' she asked eagerly. Zara took up the job at once.

As she walked out of Convent that day, Zara observed how the teachers there dressed; she would soon have to emulate them. Their attire had been meticulously put together, with the dupattas perfectly matching their suits. Zara didn't have too many suits or even matching dupattas. All she had was her wedding trousseau, and she certainly couldn't wear that! After announcing the good news to her astounded parents, she raided her mother's closet. Selecting a few of the clothes she already had, and some of her mother's garments, Zara put together a few outfits that she could mix, match and repeat.

Now that she had started fretting about her new job, some of the stress related to the visa dissipated. Zara started feeling the familiar tingles she experienced before the start of a new semester—only this time, she was the teacher, not the student.

The administrator had informed Zara that they had a school bus along the Nishat route. People around the neighbourhood knew where the Convent students waited for buses and pointed Zara in the right direction.

On Monday, Zara was at the designated stop with a bunch of curious schoolgirls. An old State Road Transport Corporation (SRTC) bus, moonlighting as a school bus, creaked to a halt in front of them. 'Bus Number 13: Nishat' was written in bold letters on a makeshift card stuck on to the windshield. Zara got on with the children. A small girl was kind enough to point to the seats up front. 'Those are for the ma'ams,' she said. Zara smiled to convey her gratitude. As more girls clambered in, their expressions conveyed their surprise. 'Who is the newbie?' they seemed to ask. The teachers, too, took notice of Zara, and after exchanging niceties, expressed some curiosity about her accent. When Zara told them about her visa troubles, they clucked their tongues in sympathy. Zara smiled. She had made some new friends that day.

The Convent girls were at once naughty and nice, and always receptive. Zara had never imagined teaching. And yet, now that life had propelled her in this direction, she found herself looking forward to the twinkling eyes of her students as she walked in. She loved all of it—so much so, she wished to go the extra mile to make her students happy.

Zara had always been adept at note-making. In Saudi, her classmates would always copy her notes. She now tapped into that special prowess by laying out lesson notes for her students on Microsoft Word. When she'd give them printouts the next day, they'd look at each other with wide wonder-filled eyes. 'What happened?' Zara inquired. A girl spoke up. 'Ma'am, everyone else makes us write lessons down.' Another mumbled, 'Till our hands hurt.' The class burst into giggles. As for Zara, she was pleased—how desperately she wanted to ease the kids' burdens. As news spread about Zara's lesson notes, she overheard barbed comments. A fellow teacher and friend let her know, 'Some of the other teachers think you're trying too hard to be cool ... what with all the printed documents!' Zara worried and asked if she ought to change her approach. Her friend shrugged. 'You *are* cool. So be it.'

With each passing day, Zara started thinking less about her visa situation. She'd still check the Excel sheet every Tuesday, but the rest of the time would fly by in teaching chapters on respiration and human excretion and asexual and sexual reproduction.

Zara's parents could tell that she was calmer now. Even Rehan on their calls would say, 'You sound like you are having fun.' Zara would grin and admit, 'Yeah, I really am.'

By July, Zara had worked at the school for four months. She had become close to the students. They had ceased being a mere 'excuse' to keep visa worries at bay. Through them, and by teaching them, Zara had regained hope—hope that despite the uncertainty, there was good in the world. She could see such good in all the girls she taught; in their future.

In another month, it would be Zara and Rehan's first wedding anniversary—a fact that troubled Zara so greatly that she had started ignoring the J&K bank calendar hanging on the wall.

However, as with her Convent job, it was time for the stars to align again. A month shy of her first wedding anniversary, Zara's visa arrived. She returned that day from school to see her beaming parents holding the envelope from the US embassy containing her passport with the visa. Zara was over the moon! All of them chatted excitedly, even as Zara called Rehan to tell him the news.

'I'm booking your flight now!' he yelled.

Zara didn't stall.

The next day, she told the school that she was leaving and said goodbye to her students and the friends she had made over those four months. As she left Convent, she experienced a bittersweet feeling. A couple of months ago, Zara would have packed up in a jiffy without a backward glance. Now, she quavered, for she felt truly connected to Kashmir—and all because of the kids who looked up to her, joked with her and treated her like their friend; who had given her life so much love and purpose. The thought of leaving them made Zara feel downhearted.

But there was someone waiting for her. There was someone she was waiting to start the rest of her life with.

Over the next call, Rehan was still pinching himself. 'Is this really happening? Are you really coming?'

'Yes!'

ZARA LANDED IN BALTIMORE a little before her first wedding anniversary. Both Rehan and Zara were part-giddy, part-shy—they were meeting each other after so long! Slowly but surely, they rediscovered their love for one another.

Rehan's large family—which had been most curious about his elusive bride—held a much-delayed wạlīma for Zara. Zara's mother flew down specifically for it, even though she was ailing. While she was staying with them, Zara told her about her plans to re-join the PhD programme in Rochester. The couple was now adept at sustaining a long-distance marriage, and Rochester was but a few hours away from Baltimore.

'How about med school?' her mother suggested.

'Me, a doctor?' Zara laughed it off.

Zara got back into her programme at Rochester, but her advisor had moved to North Dakota. She tried to cope without him, but it was more complicated than she had imagined it to be. Her fellow students had moved on with their theses, she was lagging behind, and without her advisor, she felt unable to get back to the rhythm she needed. Her advisor suggested she consider North Dakota, apply for a fresh round of grants and complete her research there. But Zara was too overwhelmed by the idea of moving yet again and to a new place. Besides, her mother's cancer was advancing, and she didn't know when she'd have to fly back to Kashmir. Too much was in flux, so finally, Zara gave up her research project in Rochester and moved to Baltimore permanently.

Zara's mother passed away in February 2011. Zara joined her siblings in Kashmir for the final farewell. All three of them supported their father who had been her primary caregiver. Inhabiting the Nishat house felt unreal without their mother's presence. Any moment, Zara was convinced, she'd walk through the door ... and it would all be a dream. Sometimes, Zara would hear her mother's voice, 'You should give med school a shot. I know you can do it.' As the voice echoed, Zara realized that with her mother's departure, her will to help people in need of medical support had increased manifold. She wanted to give others hope, life, care.

As soon as Zara got back to the US that year, she started looking up medical schools. She was already trailing behind the average student on the med school path. She was nowhere close to beginning her pre-clinical studies—let alone completing them. So, she joined a school in the Caribbean and completed her pre-clinical requirements in twelve months flat. She came back and began medical school in the US.

When Zara looked back, it felt as though there was a pattern to her life. In Kashmir, she had, without ever meaning to, become a teacher of biology. Now, in medical school, biology was the subject that she was wedded to. It was all meant to be.

Zara would become a certified psychiatrist.

TODAY, ZARA LOOKS BACK at the year of separation from Rehan as the period that established the foundation of their relationship. They learnt the value of communication and of keeping in touch under the most challenging circumstances—what with unpredictable internet access and the time difference. In many ways, they were *forced* to communicate—there was no other option. They couldn't see each other; they couldn't feel each other. There were no video calls, and there was barely any way to send pictures back and forth.

They also mastered the vital art of having tricky conversations. Zara and Rehan came from such different backgrounds that they had to work hard to find common ground. They learnt to speak, listen, understand and support each other; to thrash things out when they disagreed; and take time off when the conversations got too hard. They had the most gut-wrenching chats long-distance—about Zara's mother's chemotherapy and about the political disarray in Kashmir. These were big topics that couples typically took their time with and eased themselves into; Zara and Rehan had to discuss it all then and there.

That year, in essence, made them stronger, wiser and more resilient. They knew if they could survive this, they would survive life.

So, by the time Zara and Rehan met almost a year later, much of the hard work that builds relationships had already been done. A year of perseverance had got them closer.

Zara often thinks of a ritual Rehan and she had stumbled into during those calls from Kashmir to Baltimore. They'd play a game. Both of them would close their eyes and picture the other person. 'No cheating, okay?' They'd conjure up the other's face and hold on to it for as long as they could. It was harder than it sounds. The first person to lose the image would lose the game.

Neither of them ever lost the image.

That's how they felt close. That's how they felt alive.

6

HOME IS WHERE THE HEART IS

Bushra is from the Bagh district of what the Indian government refers to as 'Pakistan-occupied Kashmir' (PoK). It constitutes the western part of the Kashmir region and has been the subject of dispute between India and Pakistan since the Indo–Pak war of 1947–48.

Bushra grew up in Bagh with three brothers and a sister. Her paternal grandfather was Kashmiri, originally from Pattan in the Baramulla district of Jammu and Kashmir. During the Indo–Pak war of 1965, he fled across the ceasefire line that would later be called the line of control (LoC). He married a woman from Bagh and settled down there. Like him, many families had been split across the LoC by this war and the preceding war of 1947–48. He had two brothers who continued to live in Pattan and had land there as well. But with no means of speedy communication, they lost contact. Many split families would dedicate songs to each other on the radio at frequencies both sides could catch.

While growing up, Bushra had been told the story of her grandfather settling in Bagh but had never asked more questions about her family's roots. At home they spoke Pahadi—which was her grandmother's tongue—and Urdu, which was easier for her grandfather. Her grandfather passed away in 2003 when she was still in school, so any curiosity about their family on the other side of the LoC dimmed with his demise.

That was until 2005, when an old man landed up at their doorstep asking about Bushra's grandfather. This man was his brother, Bushra's grand-uncle. Earlier that year, India and Pakistan had started the Srinagar–Muzaffarabad bus service as a confidence-building measure following peace talks between the two warring nations.[13] Many families who had been separated for decades took this bus to meet their loved ones across the LoC. One of them was Bushra's grand-uncle from Pattan.

The old, weary man was distraught to learn that his brother had passed away just two years ago but was happy to find the thriving family he had lost contact with. The link that had been broken started rebuilding. Like so many others in their position, Busha's family now had the opportunity to talk on the phone and send letters to their formerly lost relatives.

As communication burgeoned between Bushra's grand-uncle and her family, in the next few years, a marriage proposal came for Bushra all the way from Pattan. Her grand-uncle lived close to a family whose son had crossed over from Kashmir to Pakistan in the 1990s. He, along with many young boys and men, had made the journey for arms training during the height of militancy in Kashmir. Several of these men had left militancy but weren't able to come back home legally, so they stayed back and made a life for themselves in Pakistan. Others, who didn't leave militancy, also operated out of there. Many such Kashmiri men also lived in Muzaffarabad near Bagh; they had come as teenagers or twenty-year-olds and were now grown men.

The boy in question—the one Bushra's grand-uncle was talking about—was named Burhan. After living in Pakistan for more than a decade, he had moved to Muzaffarabad. Burhan's parents—who hadn't seen their son in over a decade—on finding out about Bushra's grand-uncle's connections in Bagh, extended their son's hand in marriage to Bushra. They knew their son may never be able to come back home to Pattan, so thought it best for him to settle down in Muzaffarabad.

Burhan's family sent the rishta from Pattan to Bagh. Bushra's family relied on the grand-uncle's word that they were a good family and accepted the marriage proposal quickly. Bushra's chacha went to Pattan to fix the rishta soon after, the bus service making it a possibility. The family didn't know anything about Burhan when they accepted the proposal, but they were happy to make a new relation amidst their old roots in Pattan.

Bushra's wedding clothes and jewellery, cosmetics and gifts were all sent over from Pattan. This was 2008, just after Bushra's matriculation. She was only seventeen years old and barely knew anything about the world. Bushra and Burhan's nikāh took place soon after. Though Bushra's parents were aware that Burhan wouldn't be able to legally move back home to Kashmir, they made him give it in writing that he would not leave for the Valley in the future with their daughter. They didn't want him to take her far away from them. He assuaged their fears; he gave it in writing that he would remain close.

Freshly married, Bushra and Burhan moved to Muzaffarabad. Affection blossomed between the two slowly, and soon enough Bushra was head over heels in love with her husband. In her eyes, he could do no wrong. If it was the two of them against the world, she would always be his shield, his protector. She would take his side in any argument, no matter what, no matter against whom.

Bushra didn't know much about Burhan's past. All she grasped was that in the 1990s, when the situation had been dire in Kashmir, an eighteen- or nineteen-year-old Burhan—along with a bunch of boys from his village—crossed over to Pakistan. Whether they went of their own accord or were taken by someone was unclear to her, and Bushra didn't feel it necessary to enquire further. How did it matter anyway? It was all in the past. Burhan and she had their newly married life to look forward to.

Before getting married, Burhan had been with the militant outfit Hizbul Mujahideen. Once he married Bushra, he left the Hizbul Mujahideen and started his life afresh with her in Muzaffarabad. Many of the Kashmiri men, who had crossed over in the 1990s or later, all lived with their wives and children in the same area. It was a close-knit community, and they were supportive of one another. Burhan and Bushra owned a fruits and vegetables shop that sold cold drinks and groceries as well. They were genuinely happy to be there. In 2009, Bushra gave birth to a son. The couple was overjoyed, and it felt like nothing possibly could go wrong.

In 2010, the then chief minister of Jammu and Kashmir, Omar Abdullah, announced a rehabilitation policy. Under it, the Kashmiri men who had crossed over to PoK and Pakistan for arms training would be welcomed back to Kashmir—as long as they were ex-militants who had given up arms and were choosing to come back home.[14]

As news of this policy trickled into Muzaffarabad and other areas, there was a flurry of activity and anticipation. So many Kashmiri men had been away from home for over a decade; they hadn't met or seen their parents, siblings or friends. They had made peace with the fact that they would never legally be able to go back home and even if they found a roundabout way to get there, they wouldn't be able to live normal lives as ex-militants. But here was a policy which was not just inviting them back, but their wives and children as well. They were also promised training in skills and trades to facilitate re-integration into society. They jumped at the idea of it. How much they yearned for the scent of their homeland; for connections deeper than letters and phone calls; for a meeting with their loved ones in the flesh.

The policy document designated four points of return—through JCP Wagah–Atari or through the Chakan Da Bagh or Salamabad crossings at the LoC or through the Indira Gandhi International Airport. The document said that only those militants who had crossed over to PoK and Pakistan between 1 January 1989 and 31 December 2009 and their dependents would be eligible for consideration.[15]

All the boys who had left Kashmir over the dates mentioned were now grown men—men who were married and had children. While the policy mentioned that dependents were welcome, would they truly be accepted by the government? No one was sure. The only way to find out was to take a plunge and go to Kashmir.

In their excitement, many of these men started getting ready to leave; they sold their businesses and shops, not wishing to look back. But there was one big problem. Many of the wives did not want to leave their homes.

While Bushra had heard a few stories of women leaving willingly with their husbands, the bulk of the narratives she had come across involved women being blackmailed into coming along. The husbands always had the upper hand, threatening to take the children away to Kashmir with or without their wives.

Unable to separate from their offspring, the women had no choice but to tag along.

By 2012, Burhan started nudging Bushra—who had given birth to their second son—to leave. While Bushra loved Burhan dearly and trusted that he would never lead her astray, she was deeply hesitant about leaving home. But then, she heard of a woman—someone from her own neighbourhood—whose husband had taken their two-year-old son and left for Kashmir; she was now a broken shell. As Bushra watched her despair, she was left shaken. She had two sons with Burhan under the age of three. If Burhan whisked her boys off to Kashmir, how would she survive?

Bushra started making her peace with the idea of leaving Muzaffarabad. Burhan assured her that she would be able to come back in five to six months' time. This mollified Bushra; she wouldn't be away from her home for very long. Besides, she felt for Burhan, for how deeply he missed his home and his parents.

When Bushra told her parents of her plans, her mother was the first to dissuade her. This was a new and unknown place. What if she struggled to adjust? But at that point, all Bushra could see was Burhan and her children. She told her mother that *this* was the relationship she had chosen, that they themselves had chosen for her, and she would honour it till the end of the world. Her mother sighed in distress.

Bushra's parents were not just upset that she was leaving but also that Burhan had not kept the word he had given them during the nikāh. But they couldn't do much. In their world, a daughter was a husband's responsibility after marriage; they had no right to protest beyond a point.

Before leaving, Bushra hugged her mother goodbye extra tight. She whispered, 'I will be back soon. Wait for me.'

Bushra traversed the road leading from her parents' house in Bagh, which she knew like the back of her hand. She told herself that she would be running down this path soon enough to hug her mother again.

In a few months, everything was ready for their departure. Burhan got Pakistani passports for all of them. Bushra's elder son was almost three years old, and the younger one had turned six months. By the end of 2012, they left along with the lady whose son had been taken away from her, and another family that had roots in Kupwara. Burhan led the way. They reached Nepal by air. From there, using the porous border, they drove into India by car and reached Patna. Then they took a train from Patna to Jammu. At Jammu, Burhan's brother and some other family members came to receive them. They drove to Srinagar together.

Ex-militants returning under the policy had to surrender at the Jammu and Kashmir Police's Counter Intelligence Kashmir (CIK) at Humhama in Srinagar. They had to declare that they had come back under the rehabilitation policy and wanted to live a normal life in Kashmir. They would be kept in jail for a few days and then let go.

Burhan made his way to CIK and surrendered there, while his brother took Bushra and the kids home to Pattan. Everything in Pattan felt unfamiliar to Bushra; she didn't know how to act or what to do. She had never had in-laws as such, and now she was meeting her husband's family in a wholly different cultural context. Her in-laws spoke Kashmiri and knew but a smattering of Urdu. Bushra who only knew Urdu and Pahadi, was unable to follow most conversations and felt lost and scared. She could only wait for Burhan to come back to teach her the ropes.

After three to four days, Burhan was released by the police, and he came home. A flood of feelings washed over him as he walked through the door.

Burhan's homecoming was celebrated. His parents were delighted to see their long-lost son. Burhan, on his part, was like a small child in his mother's arms. Bushra was happy for him, and happy for her in-laws, though a profound sense of alienation didn't leave her. And how could it? She couldn't communicate anything more than a few sentences. And she was stuck in her room with her children, while Burhan rediscovered the world outside.

In the weeks to come, Bushra tried hard to find solace in her young children and in Burhan. She attempted to embrace Pattan as one of her homes. Besides, this was only a pit stop in the journey of her life, she told herself. Soon she would be back home in Muzaffarabad and be able to visit her mother in Bagh.

A few months in, Bushra started to get restless. She was missing her home intensely. Burhan could stay on for as long as he wanted in Pattan—she was clear—but she wished to be home with her parents and siblings and have sprawling conversations in a language she knew.

Bushra finally asked Burhan for her passport and her children's, too. She could take the bus and go back to Muzaffarabad. Burhan tried stalling and finally said that he didn't have the passports. Bushra was confused. 'What do you mean? You had them all along. I want to go back!' Burhan remained firm, not disclosing anything. When she prodded him further, he revealed, 'I threw the passports away in Nepal.'

Bushra couldn't believe what she was hearing. This man—the one she had trusted with her life and loved more than anyone else in the world—had lied to her, had let her down. He had tricked Bushra into coming to Pattan, knowing all along that he didn't intend to let her go back to Bagh. As this thought sank in, something within Bushra broke. It was her trust in Burhan. He was as cruel as the man who had taken his kid and abandoned his wife. She could never see Burhan the same way again.

'I followed you blindly,' she told him, enraged. 'All so that you could be reunited with your family. I've been living in one room like cattle since I've come here, not asking for anything, not complaining. And now you tell me this? You've shown your true colours. You've betrayed me.'

Burhan didn't meet her eye because he knew deep down that what he had done was unjust. Swayed by his love for his home, he had snatched Bushra's away from hers.

Things would never be the same again between the two. Burhan and Bushra argued every day. It was always about the same thing. 'I want to go back. I want to go back. Make it happen. In whatever way, make it happen.' Bushra's in-laws were sympathetic but couldn't do anything to assist her. The language barrier didn't help. The quarrel went on for so long that months passed unnoticed, and Bushra didn't even realize that it had been a year since she had come to Pattan.

There were times when Bushra tried accepting her fate. But she failed, overcome with pangs of separation from her family and land. It didn't help that her in-laws perceived her differently and unlike the other Kashmiri daughters-in-law. During functions, her sisters-in-law were offered respect and attention; they were told to handle formalities and attend to guests. Bushra was only ever looked at with a mixture of sympathy and scorn. 'Things are done differently here. You won't know how.' Bushra would bristle and think to herself, 'How will I know until you guide me?'

Then, there were her encounters with ordinary Kashmiris. While there were many good souls, there were also those who lashed out at her. 'Didn't your parents find anyone from Pakistan to marry you off to? Maybe you were a burden to them. Maybe they wanted to get rid of you.' The remarks cut deep.

When Bushra would speak to her parents or siblings, her sense of dislocation would deepen. Her voice would choke with sadness. She had not told them about all that had happened since she had reached Kashmir—she didn't want them to worry—and so, they believed that Bushra was staying longer than had been planned of her own accord.

To pass time and make some money, Bushra took up small jobs as a tailor. Burhan did menial work in the meantime. The rehabilitation policy had promised training and skill development, but not one of the men who had come back seemed to have secured a job.

Bushra pleaded with Burhan to get the documents made again. She didn't know anyone in Kashmir, and he needed to help her. Burhan was reluctant to assist, so he sent her on a wild goose chase. He told her to get her ID card made, assuming that the paperwork would dissuade Bushra from trying to make her way back to Bagh.

But Bushra was resilient. She was in early twenties, and while she may not have had many life-altering experiences, she had a fire inside her fuelled by one dream and one dream only. Home.

Bushra got her ID card made in Kashmir but learnt that it wasn't enough to travel with. So, she got her Aadhar card made, then a PAN card and even a State Subject document. Everything took time; no process was simple. But Bushra had her papers in order. What she *really* needed was a passport. And that was tricky as she had to be an Indian citizen to apply.

Bushra finally decided to apply for a passport online. But she was asked for her birth certificate to prove her nationality. She was in a fix. So, she went to the Pattan police station to get her birth certificate made in Kashmir. They told her, 'Go ask the tehsildar.' After a long time, Bushra caught hold of the tehsildar and told him about her problem. Instead of empathizing with her predicament, the tehsildar scolded Bushra. 'Why did you come here? What you ask for just cannot be done. It's too risky!'

Now, it was 2014. Burhan and Bushra would barely even look at each other. They didn't eat together and spoke in monosyllables. Bushra was firm in her stance that Burhan had betrayed her. And Burhan remained firm that he had no interest in helping Bushra return home.

When Bushra got worried calls from home—her parents had started suspecting that something was wrong—she kept updates vague, and her parents chose not to overstep. They started keeping things from Bushra as well. They didn't tell her that her elder maamu had passed away (and so had her elder khaalu). And when Bushra's elder brother got married, she had to watch the proceedings on her tiny phone screen; it was pure torture. 'I feel like someone has left me alone in a jungle to fend for myself. Who do I ask for help? What do I do?' Bushra thought.

IN 2014, BUSHRA HEARD about a Pakistani woman who had taken her life in Kashmir. She was like Bushra and had been brought from Pakistan by her Kashmiri husband under the policy. What must she have gone through to take such a drastic step? Bushra's heart went out to her; she gathered the details of the village she had lived in and went to give tāziyat. There, she was surprised to find several dozen women from PoK and Pakistan, all mourning their departed sister. Tragedy brought these women together—almost all of them were here because of the policy. Amongst all these mourning women, Bushra finally felt less alone.

Bushra met Saira Javid there; she was from Karachi. She had been trying to go back to Pakistan for years now. Bushra poured her heart out to Saira, who nodded empathetically. Phone numbers were exchanged, and a new bond of friendship was formed. Bushra found out that Saira and other such women were actively protesting to create awareness about their cause in Kashmir and the lack of rights they and their children had. 'Either give us and our children citizenship or deport us to our country!' This was the common sentiment.

Through Saira, Bushra found out about the term 'pushback'—state measures to ensure that refugees and migrants are forced back across the border after they've crossed it. Bushra wrote to the deputy commissioner's office in Baramulla, asking him to give her a 'pushback'. After years, she finally felt hopeful that something could happen in her favour. She didn't need to find a way to get an Indian passport to travel out; she just needed to prove that she held a Pakistani passport and get deported home.

After some preliminary verification, Bushra was sent back to the CIK office in Humhama, where Burhan had surrendered years ago. To her shock, they told Bushra that they would actually be slapping a case against her and everyone in her contingent who had travelled to India. Bushra was flabbergasted. What fresh hell was this? 'Why will there be a case against us?' she asked. They told her that Burhan, Bushra and the others had come to the country illegally. 'Illegally how?' she asked. 'We came under the rehabilitation policy!' They said that Bushra had taken the wrong route into the country. There were four designated points of return to India, all detailed in the policy documents, through which Kashmiri men and their families had to travel. Nepal was not one of them. In other words, they had entered the country *illegally*.

'If we had entered via the wrong route, why did you accept my husband's surrender? Why didn't you arrest him then and there? Why didn't you just deport us at that time? After all these years, you are saying that we are living here illegally?' Bushra lost her temper. The officials were in no mood to listen.

Bushra left the CIK office more dejected than ever. Any hope that had birthed in her after meeting Saira was now crushed. It was 2016. The state government had changed, no longer led by the political party that had passed the policy. Bushra and countless other women stuck in Kashmir were caught in a web of bureaucracy and red tape.

In 2017, a challan was issued against Bushra and all her fellow travellers—Burhan, the woman who had come to Kashmir to be reunited with her child, and the other family going to Kupwara. Bushra soon found out that this sort of FIR was filed against anyone who applied to get deported if they had entered India through Nepal under the policy.

Due to the challan, Bushra's application to get deported got halted. She went to the Pakistan High Commission and applied there, too, to get deported. The Pakistan High Commission wrote to the Indian Ministry of External Affairs (MEA), petitioning them to send Bushra and other women like her back as they were Pakistani nationals. The MEA replied that since Bushra had an active court case against her, they could not deport her just yet. Only when she was cleared of all charges would that happen. The Pakistan High Commission conveyed this to Bushra. She was back to square one.

Before Bushra had come to Kashmir with Burhan—when she had still been unsure about her decision—she had spoken to a woman who had made the journey before her for advice. The woman had told Bushra that she had no reason to hesitate; life in the Valley was idyllic. Bushra had asked her when she planned to return to Muzaffarabad, especially since her intention had been to make the journey back in a few months. The woman had deflected the question. 'I will celebrate Eid back home for sure,' she had said. Bushra's decision to leave her homeland with Burhan had been motivated in no small measure by her dialogue with this woman.

Now, it turned out that the woman she had trusted had lied to her at the behest of Burhan and her in-laws. Both had pleaded with her to paint a rosy picture. 'We desperately want to see our son,' her in-laws had wept. And the woman could not refuse their entreaty.

Bushra blamed the woman for leading her down a path of no return. And she decided—and it was a decision she made good—that if placed in a similar position, if asked by other women from Bagh or Muzaffarabad if they ought to come to the Valley, she would tell them clearly, 'This place is not for us.'

TIME PASSED. BUSHRA'S KIDS were in school. Burhan and she were still barely speaking to one another. He had started running a hotel and had a fruit business on the side. The jobs promised under the policy were a distant dream—doubly so, now, because the route they had taken to India was suspect.

One day, Bushra and Burhan's fight got out of hand. Words were said that could not be retracted. They were as good as divorced. Bushra didn't want to live with him any longer. She left the house, taking her children with her. She sought refuge with Saira who lived in Kupwara. Saira had a clothes boutique that doubled up as a beauty parlour, run entirely by Pakistani women. Saira took Bushra in as an employee. Bushra started working as a tailor there and lived on rent in a building nearby.

Bushra joined Saira in her protests to bring notice to the cause of women from PoK and Pakistan stuck in the Valley. They held rallies, press conferences and had long conversations with officials and politicians. 'If you announced this policy, why didn't you see it through?' they asked. 'You chose to call us here; then why do you insist on viewing our status as illegal? And if we are "illegal", why are you still accepting more families coming in through Nepal? Why aren't you sending them back and telling them to enter the correct way? We are stuck in any case; why should more people be caught in a legal tangle? Why haven't you sanctioned Nepal as a possible entry route?'

The fact was that those returning to the Valley usually avoided the designated points of entry to evade Pakistani security agencies who kept a close watch on them and also to avoid getting arrested by the Indian security forces.[16] After all, many worried that the policy was a ploy to get them all caught. The men, who entered via Nepal with their families, destroyed their Pakistani passports, crossed the porous border between Nepal and India and finally reached the Valley.

Bushra and Saira wanted someone to take responsibility for the false promises made under the policy. 'Where are the jobs guaranteed to the men? Where are the papers and documents they need?

'And what happened to giving the wives and children rights? We can't vote, we can't travel, we are branded as the partners of ex-militants, our children are labelled as ex-militants' kids. What future do we have? We don't have Indian passports; our children can't travel out of this country for education or employment. If you can't make us Indian citizens, if you cannot accept us, at the very least deport us to our homes where we have rights. You can't call the men back if you cannot take care of their families!'

Bushra's reading of the situation wasn't wrong. In 2017, the legislative assembly accepted that no one had been able to return through the four designated points in India under the rehabilitation policy launched in 2010. The government added that 377 ex-militants along with 864 family members had returned from Pakistan via Nepal and Bangladesh since 2010.[17] Roughly 350 Pakistani women had come to Kashmir under the policy. None had been 'rehabilitated'.

In many countries, if one stayed in it for a certain amount of time, the government could grant citizenship. Saira had come to Kashmir with her family in 2007—before the rehabilitation policy had even started—through the Wagah border. She had an Indian visa. But her documents had been discarded by her husband and she had no way of returning. She had a case registered against her—under Section 14 of the Foreigners Act—for remaining in India for a period exceeding the visa duration. Despite having lived in Kashmir for a decade, she had not secured

Indian citizenship for herself or her children. What she longed to do was return to her homeland with them.

While Saira could still be called a foreign national as she was from Karachi, it was much less reasonable for somebody from PoK to be called a 'foreigner'. In 1994, a resolution of the Indian Lok Sabha and the Rajya Sabha described the entire territory of Jammu and Kashmir—including PoK—as an integral part of India. In fact, the Jammu and Kashmir Assembly had 24 seats reserved for the region.[18] Legally, someone from PoK could not be arrested under the Foreigners Act. So, when women like Bushra were slapped with cases for being 'foreign nationals attempting to illegally enter India' and were refused official documents, it was cause for concern.

The Rehabilitation Policy of 2010 has now been stopped.

BY 2019, BUSHRA GOT a legal divorce from Burhan.

Bushra ran her house on her own through the Covid-19 pandemic years, taking care of her children all by herself. She had a maintenance case against Burhan; she needed money to raise their children. The courts were closed during the pandemic, so there was no question of a hearing. Burhan refused to offer money on his own and had no desire to ask after Bushra or their two boys.

Suddenly, in 2022, Burhan landed up at her home in Kupwara and took the kids away. He was adamant. 'My kids will not live like this. God knows what can happen to them here!' Burhan asked the boys who they wanted to live with, and to Bushra's alarm they chose their father over her. And just like that, Bushra was left all alone.

Bushra could hardly believe it. Back in the day, she used to curse the men who had left their wives behind and come to the Valley with their children. But Burhan—he had taken the kids away from Bushra after she had brought them up, after she had taught them right from wrong. Which situation was more cruel? Was there even a contest? Bushra whispered, 'He got everything. He got his parents, his inheritance, his children after they were raised. What did I get? I was left empty-handed. I lost my parents, my watan—my land. And my kaum kabila—my entire tribe.'

In all the years Bushra had been in the Valley, she always put her bravest foot forward while speaking to her family back home. It had been well over ten years of separation; well over ten years since she had felt her mother's warm touch or laughed herself silly with her sister. She could watch them sometimes on video—'I can't hug them, but at least I can see them,' she'd console herself—but not once did she reveal her exact circumstances.

However, now, it was impossible to keep the truth under wraps. Bushra's protests with the other PoK and Pakistani women had gone viral on social media, and her family found out all that had happened to her. Bushra came clean. Her mother was the most heartbroken. 'You were in trouble, and you didn't tell me. We could have helped you. We could have got you out of there somehow.' Then, after a long pause, her mother said, 'I'm coming there.'

Bushra protested. She didn't want her mother getting stuck like her in Kashmir; nor did she want her to see how she was living. 'She won't be able to take it, and she won't be able to leave me. If she does leave, she'll believe she is abandoning me,' Bushra thought to herself. 'I can't let her see my hālāth.'

And so, the no remained a no.

BY 2023, SAIRA HAD been fighting her case for over eight years. It finally ended, and she made her arrangements to go back to Pakistan. She and her children were deported. She went without her husband. Saira was only one out of hundreds of women who 'lucked out'. Bushra held on to the hope that this could be her story, too.

Of course, not all the women who had come to Kashmir from PoK and Pakistan wanted to go back. There were some whose children had grown up, had studied in Kashmir, had married within the Valley. These women wanted nothing more than for the government to accept them and grant them citizenship. However, even this possibility grew slim when in 2024, the Indian government announced the implementation of a controversial citizenship law that aimed at granting Indian citizenship to six persecuted religious minorities—Hindus, Sikhs, Buddhists, Jains, Parsis and Christians—who had come to India from Pakistan, Bangladesh or Afghanistan before 2015.[19] Missing from the list of potential beneficiaries were Muslims from these nations—Muslims like Bushra and other women like her, some who had been living in Kashmir for thirteen to fourteen years and were waiting to get accepted as citizens.

BUSHRA NOW LIVES WITH another Pakistani family in the same building near the boutique where she still works. Her case regarding her illegal entry into India is ongoing. The pandemic had made the wheels of justice stall, but now, with hearings happening almost every three months, Bushra finds herself going to Pattan routinely for the hearings. The others who entered India via Nepal with her are also making the rounds of the court.

Bushra's older son is in the ninth grade and the younger one is in the fifth grade. Their school is in Pattan, so they stay with her over weekends and vacations. She is grateful that she can see them once in a while and harbours the hope that when the time comes, she will be able to take them back to Bagh with her. 'They are Pakistani nationals, after all, like me,' she says. They were born there, like her. They hold Pakistani passports, like her. Even if their passports were thrown away or destroyed, some record somewhere details their origins. 'I want my kids and myself to be deported at all costs. That's all I want,' she murmurs.

Recently, when Bushra was denied permission to take the Srinagar–Muzaffarabad bus to visit her family for a bit and return, she could not help but wonder—what would her life have been like had she refused to come to the Valley in the first place? She recalled her conversations with other women like her, and she realized that no matter her decision, she'd have been trapped. She'd have been blackmailed and lied to; and she would have lost. 'I don't know where I went wrong,' Bushra sighs. '*Humhe bas Allah pe bharosa tha, doosra shauhar pe.* In God I trusted, and then my partner. I was naïve.'

The irony of her situation doesn't miss her. 'The men came back because they missed their families. They had been away anywhere from twelve to twenty years, and blind love pulled them back. The lure was so great that they took their wives with them. And now we, the women, are in the position the men once were in. We long for the motherland. We have taken each other's places,' Bushra confesses. Then, after a pause, she says, 'I wish I had listened to my mother.'

Bushra plays the dual role of a daughter who is away from her mother and a mother who has been pulled away from her children. She longs for them both. In all that she has been through and continues to go through, there is a single thought that keeps Bushra going. It is the thought of home. It is her deep love for her homeland. And above all else, it is her yearning for her beloved mother.

Bushra's mother tells her of a dream she often has; in it, Bushra has returned. She has walked down that familiar path leading home; she hasn't told anyone of her arrival. When Bushra's mother opens her eyes, she thinks Bushra is there. She goes to check. She doesn't know whether it is a dream or reality.

Bushra says, 'I want to make her dream a reality. The first thing I want to do, once I walk down that road, is hug my mother. Because she is waiting for me. And then, I must meet my father, my three brothers and my younger sister. They, too, are in wait.'

After all that has happened to Bushra, her parents have become cautious about her younger sister's marriage. Even though she is getting rishtas, her mother will not commit to anyone. Bushra smiles. 'I tell them my sister is barely of age. Not to get her married early like me. Let her grow up a little, learn the lay of the land. And do not give a daughter's hand in marriage to a musafir—a wanderer—ever. Every musafir has to return home at some point.'

TWELVE YEARS OF BUSHRA's life have passed in wait.

Sometimes she closes her eyes and imagines that this isn't really her life. That she is sixteen or seventeen and that her wedding is yet to happen. She is in Bagh, young and carefree, with her parents and siblings.

Bushra remembers everything. The light in the house, the smell of that home. She takes a deep breath in her dream. She remembers the roads, all the alleyways. She can map them out in her head. All the nooks and crannies. She remembers the walk to school. Seventy kids from one mohalla alone. She recalls her brother's friends calling him from the outside, '*Zayed chal, daer ho jayegi*. Come fast, Zayed, it's getting late.' All the siblings quickly stuffing breakfast into their mouths and leaving. And from the tiniest of kids to the oldest of them—everyone emerging like a swarm of bees, buzzing wildly for a few minutes.

And then, the din settles.

She imagines them returning. She can see her mother waiting at the door. At 2 p.m. sharp they have lunch together. Her Ammi refuses to eat till the kids come back. At 4 p.m. they wait at the door for Abbu. As soon as his footsteps are heard, the afternoon chai is put to boil. There they are, having it together.

All of it is repeated the next day. Over and over.

How she wishes to be back.

Her life now is wildly different. Every night, as it gets dark, Bushra sits alone in her room. 'When light breaks, I think a new day has come. May Allah give me a ray of hope.'

She goes to the boutique and works the whole day. She comes back in the evening to an empty house. She sits by herself again, waiting for light.

Bushra remembers the last hug she gave her Ammi before leaving Bagh; the words she had whispered, 'I will be back soon. Wait for me.'

'My mother still remembers it,' Bushra says. '*Meri Ammi mere intezaar mein baithi hai*. She is waiting for me. Waiting to never let me go.

'They say that times gone by cannot return. I understand all my happy memories won't come back ... but I pray that the bad ones don't either.

'The good times may never return. But surely ... surely I can.'

AZ
today

7

AMBULANCE

IN THE SUMMER OF 2019, Khawar and Iqra had been engaged a few years. Both of them were doctors. Khawar was doing his senior residency in general medicine at Shri Maharaja Hari Singh Hospital (SMHS) in Karan Nagar, and Iqra was pursuing her MD in psychiatry at the Government Psychiatric Diseases Hospital in Rainawari. While they worked in different hospitals, they were governed by the same educational institution—Government Medical College (GMC), Srinagar.

While growing up, Iqra had often heard people refer to the Psychiatric Diseases Hospital as 'mental hospital' or 'pagal-khaana'. The term was loaded, carrying the full weight of societal stigma—as a result of which Kashmir produced only a few psychiatrists every year. Psychiatry was not a branch that was favoured by most medical students, nor was it one that common people viewed with a high degree of regard. This was problematic for many reasons—not least because, after witnessing endless cycles of unrest, many Kashmiris had post-traumatic stress disorder (PTSD) and, given the shame and humiliation attached to mental health, the condition often went undiagnosed.

Iqra was passionate about her field of work. To her, it was unforgivable that mental health was dismissed since it wasn't a 'physically noticeable trauma'. She wanted to shift public perception about mental health and ensure that the psychiatric sciences were granted respect.

Iqra and Khawar shared a symbiotic relationship. Iqra—the eldest of three sisters, and with an ailing father—was well aware of the unspoken responsibility she carried at all times. It was in Khawar's presence that she could be vulnerable, that she dared to fall apart without feeling guilty. He not only offered her a valuable medical second opinion when she needed it, but he also gave her mental and emotional support. Iqra, on her part, kept Khawar accountable and steady in his academic pursuits.

By the end of July 2019, something started feeling amiss in Kashmir. There was a flurry of activity, with desperate attempts, largely by locals, to hoard food, medicines and fuel. With the Amarnath pilgrimage cancelled, all the tourists had been ushered out of Kashmir. Khawar and Iqra were caught in this maelstrom. In a place where people could disappear over their morning bread run to the kāndur, anything could be expected. And now, it seemed likely that some kind of a political upheaval was around the corner.

On 4 August, late at night, Khawar and Iqra were on the phone. They were probably not the only ones. Rumours were spreading like wildfire, and nobody could sleep. Phone and internet services were supposedly going to be snapped at midnight. 'Article 370 will be removed and there will be a war' was the most perturbing of messages going around.

A common saying goes, 'In Kashmir, the news can be wrong, but the rumours are always right.'

Over the past few days, approximately 38,000 additional troops[20] had been deployed to the Valley. Schools and colleges had been shut down and regional political leaders like Omar Abdullah of the Jammu and Kashmir National Conference party (JKNC) and Mehbooba Mufti of the J&K People's Democratic Party (PDP)—both former chief ministers of Jammu and Kashmir—had been placed under house arrest. After the coalition of the PDP and the Bharatiya Janata Party (BJP) had broken down in mid-2018, Jammu and Kashmir had been under governor's rule for the eighth time in its history. Unable to form an alternate government after the collapse of the PDP–BJP alliance, President's Rule was imposed in the state subsequently.[21]

On that night of 4 August, Khawar and Iqra were anticipating the call dropping any moment. A routine conversation now seemed like a privilege. What was going to happen? Were Kashmiris going to survive? As they spoke, they could hear aircrafts flying overhead. As the sounds got closer and louder, the atmosphere on the call got tense.

'I have a strong feeling that I'm going to die,' Iqra's voice quivered. Khawar shushed her and offered comfort. He promised to meet her the very next day, come what may.

Exactly at midnight, the call dropped. Phone networks, cable TV, Wi-Fi—all of it collapsed at once. What 5 August would bring was still a mystery. All that the people of Jammu, Kashmir and Ladakh could do was wait.

The next morning, Khawar started his day on schedule. He hoped to meet Iqra at her hospital or near her house. But as soon as he left for hospital duty, he was stopped by the armed forces at a barricade. No one was allowed to move ahead. Khawar was sent back home. Srinagar had become a ghost town; there was not a civilian in sight. That's when the reality of the situation sank in. This wasn't just a communication blockade; it was a physical one.

Iqra lived in Peerbagh, near the Srinagar airport. She experienced even higher security arrangements than Khawar, who lived in Soura, as the airport was controlled by the Indian army. Khawar soon realized that he would not be able to drive down to meet Iqra or even walk to her workplace or residence. With troops everywhere and with concertina wire blocking roads, it was mission impossible.

Both Iqra and Khawar stayed home that day. Thankfully DTH television connections were still working, and both had access to it. So, they watched as the home minister of India presented the fate of the state of Jammu and Kashmir to the Indian Parliament under the Jammu and Kashmir Reorganization Act.

THE 5 AUGUST 2019 announcement by India's home minister, which in the future would just be referred to as 'Article' by the Kashmiris, saw Articles 370 and 35A—those that gave the state of Jammu and Kashmir a special status in the Indian Constitution—getting scrapped. Jammu and Kashmir was bifurcated into two union territories: Jammu and Kashmir as one, Ladakh as the other. This happened even as a majority of the population in Jammu and Kashmir lay in a shroud of fear, with no information.

Article 370 was the foundation of Jammu and Kashmir's accession to the Indian Union at a time when the former princely state had the choice to join either India or Pakistan after independence from the British in 1947. The Article was added to the Indian Constitution in 1949 and allowed the state of Jammu and Kashmir a certain amount of autonomy. It exempted the state from the Indian Constitution and granted it jurisdiction to make its own laws in all matters except defence, foreign affairs and communications. It established a separate Constitution and a separate flag and denied property rights to outsiders.

Article 35A was introduced through a presidential order in 1954 to continue the old provisions of territory regulations under Article 370 of the Indian Constitution. In other words, it forbade outsiders from permanently settling, buying land, holding local government jobs or winning educational scholarships in the region. The Article, referred to as the Permanent Residents Law, also barred female residents of Jammu and Kashmir from property rights in the event that they married a person from outside the state, extending to their children.[22]

Both these articles guaranteed a certain degree of autonomy to the people of Jammu and Kashmir, who had been promised a plebiscite by Jawaharlal Nehru under a UN Resolution passed in 1948. The plebiscite—that would allow the people of the region to choose if they wished to be with India or Pakistan or become independent—has yet to be carried through.[23]

The original Article 370 has been diluted and eroded many times since its inception.[24]

Interpreting the Permanent Residents Law as one that discriminated against Kashmir's women and denied them equal rights,[25] as well as prohibited Indians from buying land there, the BJP government pushed for its abrogation.[26] The party had, in fact, been asking for its removal for several years.[27]

For many of those in Jammu and Kashmir—a region that had been ravaged by conflict—the Permanent Residents Law provided security to civilians, so they would not fear displacement. With it being struck down, people from the rest of India would have the right to acquire property in Jammu and Kashmir and settle there. Kashmiris feared the move would lead to a demographic transformation of the region and their own slow erasure.

'They want Kashmir, and not Kashmiris'—this was the common sentiment all around.

The ones who had access to TV news disseminated information about all that had happened in the Parliament on 5 August. Slowly the fate of the erstwhile state acquired definition. On 9 August—the Friday following the abrogation—after jumma nẹmāz, the BBC reported that thousands of protesters had taken to the streets in Soura against the government's decision. These included many women, whose coming out to protest was in direct opposition to the government's reasoning that the abrogation was for their sake. The media outlet claimed that it 'witnessed the police opening fire and using tear gas to disperse the crowd.'[28] The Indian government maintained that the protest hadn't taken place.

In a matter of days, Soura had become the hub of Kashmir's anger.[29] It had turned into a fortress—constantly under siege as youngsters dug up roads and blocked them with logs, making it difficult for the security forces to enter.

KHAWAR, AS WE KNOW, lived in Soura.

Iqra's heart sank when she saw the news. More so, as Khawar would always stand up to authority if the situation demanded it. Iqra used to coax him to lie low. She'd urge him not to pick fights. She'd tell him to keep alive his instinct for self-preservation.

If not for his own sake, he had to do this for her. As the eldest daughter in her family, she had learnt the value of patience, and she knew how to maintain the calm. Khawar, on the other hand, had always been a little volatile. For Iqra, this was cause for worry. After all, anyone who protested could easily be rounded up and jailed under the archaic Public Safety Act (PSA) in Kashmir—a non-bailable offence. Iqra was crippled with fear each time she wondered how Khawar was, after seeing the protests in Soura.

Bạḍ Īd or Kọrbān Īd (Eid al-Adha) was coming up. Iqra hoped that the phones would restart that day. Maybe Khawar's family would send hers some meat from the sacrificial lamb, as was tradition. Maybe someone from Khawar's family would come with it, and she'd be able to send a message to him. But Bạḍ Īd came and went, and there was no sign of the lockdown easing.

Indian Independence Day, 15 August, was around the corner. Maybe the phone lines would open up then? Surely the Indian government would want to make an extravagant show of Kashmir before the world on this important day? Again, Iqra was left disappointed.

With no other date to look forward to, the future started looking particularly lonely and bleak.

Weeks passed without news or any form of communication between Iqra and Khawar. Their hospital duties had resumed, so they had work to keep them busy. But deep in their hearts, they ached. Two people, who had been living like a single unit for the past four years, who were engaged, who were dependent on each other for so much more than just love, suddenly didn't even know if the other was alive and breathing.

To make matters worse, Iqra's father's health had started deteriorating. Iqra agonized as she took his vitals each day. How desperately she wished to communicate with Khawar. She'd ask herself how Khawar would act in her situation, what medical course of action he would prescribe, what words of comfort he would give her. This provided her strength and a clearer idea of the treatment to follow.

Khawar, on his part, was growing increasingly agitated as well. Many times, he thought of sneaking out late at night or in the wee hours of the morning to meet Iqra, hoping to make use of the lax security at these times. But his responsibility to his family steadied him. What would they do if they found an empty bed and no way to contact him?

Both Iqra and Khawar waited.

DURING THIS TUMULTUOUS PERIOD, doctors weren't allowed to take their own vehicles or use public transport. So, both Iqra and Khawar travelled in hospital ambulances to work, passing multiple security checkpoints on their way.

Srinagar was still under heavy security, and no one knew what the coming days would look like—and it seemed the security forces didn't either. The CRPF soldiers who lined every street due to the heavy deployment didn't really know why they were there. It had been weeks, and like most civilians, they had no contact with the outside world. 'We thought we were sent on election duty!' they grumbled. These men—who to the average Kashmiri were the 'other', the 'oppressor'—were as clueless as the rest of the populace. They were merely doing what everyone in Kashmir was—living day to day.

Given that Khawar and Iqra's hospitals were governed by the same medical college, they shared an ambulance manager.

But as their commute routes were different, they didn't bump into one another. Sometimes Iqra's ambulance would stop outside Khawar's hospital, but not long enough that she could go look for him. Even if she were to step into the hospital compound, as landlines weren't working, it would be hard to track Khawar down in a few quick minutes. Furthermore, Khawar practised general medicine, which was an emergency specialty—in other words, he had hospital duty every day. Psychiatry, on the other hand, wasn't viewed as an emergency branch. Therefore, Iqra's duties spanned fewer days a week. With so many arbitrary factors at play, the probability of them meeting was slim.

It irked Iqra to no end that her field of work was viewed as 'not an emergency'. Scores of Kashmiris at that point in time were cooped up in their homes without communication and human interaction; they were anxious and lonely and oftentimes traumatized. The impact of such confinement would have long lasting effects on their being and behaviour. To still think that mental health wasn't an 'emergency'—to Iqra the stance was absurd and borderline offensive.

One day, while in the ambulance on her way home, Iqra started thinking about an unusual episode she had witnessed. Earlier that day, she had seen a young girl leave a letter with a shopkeeper outside her hospital. Given the care with which the letter had been sealed and handed over, Iqra assumed that it was for the girl's lover. Iqra imagined a young man arriving at the shop and the shopkeeper handing him the note. The joy spreading across his face. It warmed her heart to think about them.

That's when it struck her. 'I can send Khawar a letter through the ambulance chain!' Iqra almost jumped up in her seat with delight.

Ambulances used to go from the Psychiatric Diseases Hospital to SMHS Hospital with patients every couple of days. This was Iqra's chance to reach out to Khawar.

Iqra had always been 'old school'. In a world of 'okay, K, see you, bye', she would send long texts spanning sixteen lines. She'd beseech Khawar to write to her, convinced that when he did, he exhibited his most vulnerable self.

Now, she put her writing prowess to full use. The words flew off her pen, and all her pent-up feelings found articulation. This time, letter writing wasn't simply a romantic gesture. It was a necessity, a means of survival. When she was done, Iqra sealed her missive, taped it, stapled it all across for extra safety and gave it to the ambulance driver. She knew that there was a huge possibility that the letter would get lost in transit, but she had to make an attempt to have it delivered. It was the only way of putting her mind at ease. She instructed the driver to hand it to the Chief Medical Officer (CMO) at SMHS and tell him to give it to Dr Khawar. In case no one could find Khawar, the letter had to be returned to her.

When her friends and batchmates saw her giving the letter to the driver, they teased her. '*Oho, ye toh bohat aashiqui chaa rahi hai!* There seems to be romance in the air!' Iqra shrugged it off. 'No, this isn't "aashiqui". I genuinely don't know where Khawar is, and I need to see him.'

The ambulance driver was unable to find the CMO. So, after holding on to the letter for three days, he finally handed it over to a peon at SMHS with instructions that he give it to Khawar directly.

A few more days passed. The peon with the letter had been searching for Khawar for some time now without success.

The landlines were still down, so he could only look through word of mouth. In a hospital complex where earlier just about anyone could be found within seconds, now it had become impossible to track down a doctor. Three days after the letter had been delivered to the peon, Khawar happened to change his regular route. He left from the emergency gate of the hospital rather than the main gate. Luckily, that's just where the peon with the letter was posted.

The excited man ran up to Khawar and exclaimed, 'Sir, I've been looking for you for the past three days!' Before a bewildered Khawar could ask the man if everything was all right, the peon pressed Iqra's letter into his hand. He explained that an ambulance had come from the Psychiatric Diseases Hospital with transfer patients and the driver had given the letter to him. It was all conveyed with a shrug, as though this were a perfectly regular episode on a perfectly regular day.

A simple letter had taken almost a week to navigate a distance of 4 kilometres and reach its recipient. But here it was, finally, in Khawar's hands.

On the outside, the envelope read: Dr Khawar Khan—Registrar, SMHS Hospital. Khawar recognized Iqra's handwriting right away. As blood raced to his heart, he almost dropped the envelope. With trembling hands, he opened the first piece of correspondence he had received from his fiancée after what felt like a lifetime.

Besides pouring out her heart in a long letter to him, Iqra had written of her father's medical condition as well. She had offered all the details—haemoglobin: 7; creatinine: 2; still getting fever, still on drugs. Khawar was so overwhelmed that he felt Iqra was right in front of him, conveying all her news.

Khawar wrote back to Iqra immediately and gave his letter to the same peon. The peon again waited for four days for the Psychiatric Diseases Hospital's ambulance to come and handed it to the driver. As Iqra wasn't on duty every day, the ambulance driver waited till she was on call. Almost ten days after Iqra had dispatched her letter, she received Khawar's response. One letter cycle had finally been completed.

IN KASHMIR, THE MẠNZIMYẠ̄YR—the matchmakers—would go to the houses of the to-be mahrin' (bride) and mahrāz (groom) on big religious occasions. On one such religious day, Iqra didn't know if the mạnzimyōr would be visiting. Since phones were yet to revive, there was no way of knowing.

In any case, Iqra had written a four-page letter to Khawar. She hoped to drive to his house and have it handed over. Iqra had heard that doctors could drive their personal vehicles now if they showed their medical cards to the army at regular checkpoints. She had no idea if this actually worked or whether ease of travel was entirely dependent on the army man's mood. But she was willing to give the plan a shot.

In Kashmir, the bride could not enter the groom's house (and vice versa) before the wedding, so Iqra knew she'd have to send someone else to personally deliver the letter after driving to Khawar's house. She roped in her cousin brother for this. Iqra even dabbed perfume on the letter for dramatic effect.

But just as Iqra was planning to leave, the mạnzimyōr arrived with mithai and phirni from Khawar's house. Iqra was convinced that her plan was foiled now; there'd be no time to drive back and forth. That's when the mạnzimyōr surprised her. He took Iqra aside and whispered, *'Doctor sahab, ek minute, ye un doctor sahab ne aapke liye letter bheji hai.'* He revealed to her that Khawar had used his services to send her a letter. Iqra was thrilled. Now it was her turn. She unabashedly pulled her letter out and gave it to him. He smiled and took it. The matchmaker had truly lived up to his title that day.

Iqra and Khawar had amassed a pile of letters. A huge fan of the TV show *Friends*, Iqra started labelling her mail by borrowing the prefix—'The One'—from the *Friends* episodes. And so it went ...

Letter 1: The one which is the first, but certainly not the last

Letter 2: The one which was overwhelming

Letter 3: The one with the postcard

And so on ...

This went on for three months; twelve to thirteen letters were exchanged through the ambulance service. The letters were more than sheets of paper; they were emotional bonds. They held two people together who hadn't met since the lockdown and who could no longer be just-a-text-away. They helped Iqra deal with the stress of attending to her ailing father. Even if Khawar's medical advice reached her days after she sought his views, his letters, at the very least, helped her know for certain if she had made the right medical choices. For each, the process of writing was in itself cathartic.

The exchanges weren't always long. Sometimes they were small, scribbled notes on tissues saying 'I love you' and 'I miss you'. Sometimes they held parcels with two chocolates. Sometimes the ink would be smudged because Iqra happened to be crying while writing.

The messengers also kept changing. From peons to the parking attendants, everyone was clued into Iqra and Khawar's small postal system.

Close to the four-month mark of not having seen each other, Khawar was in the CMO's emergency room writing a letter to Iqra. He had heard that the Psychiatric Diseases Hospital's ambulance was coming with transfer patients in a few hours. What Khawar didn't know was that Iqra was going to be in that very ambulance.

When she arrived, Iqra decided to look for Khawar. She just had fifteen minutes before the ambulance headed back after transferring the patients. Call it intuition or just pure luck—her gut told her that Khawar was in the hospital premises that day. She went to Khawar's ward and asked for him. He wasn't around. She had a list of places mapped out in her mind and walked to the next one. He wasn't in the triage ward. Two places down. Time was running out and so was the list. On a whim, she decided to check the CMO's office. Even if he wasn't there, she could tell someone to inform Khawar to wait in there at 4.30 p.m. (she had to return to SMHS the same day).

She ran.

Iqra was wearing a yellow chikankari salwar kameez. In her own words, this is how Iqra felt she appeared to onlookers—'all filmy, dupatta flowing, hair flying dramatically like Paro in *Devdas*'. The people watched agape as Iqra rushed through the hallways—not unlike the Sanjay Leela Bhansali heroine she imagined she was. She finally entered the CMO's emergency room. And there he was. Khawar. In the flesh.

Iqra lost track of time and place, and she ran over and hugged Khawar. Neither of them spoke for a long time. There were patients and doctors all around. But Khawar and Iqra were so overcome with the fact that they were finally *seeing* each other that they noticed nobody and nothing. Finally, after what felt like hours—but really amounted to only a few minutes—they peeled themselves off each other. In Kashmir, couples don't just hug in public. But to their surprise, everyone had gone back to work, not paying any attention to them. No one even raised an eyebrow. They seemed to understand exactly what the two of them were feeling.

Iqra and Khawar had just two minutes to talk. Iqra didn't know how or where to start and stammered a few words. Khawar calmed her down and said, 'It's okay, just the fact that I saw you is enough, you don't have to say anything.' They set up a time and place to meet again. Khawar and Iqra left work that day, finally feeling complete after a long time.

They made every attempt to meet again. Most of their pre-planned dates fell through due to work engagements—and there was no way of letting the other person know—but they kept making new plans nonetheless.

A FEW WEEKS LATER, the lockdown started relaxing, especially for doctors. Iqra had to go to the All India Institute of Medical Sciences (AIIMS) in Delhi to get her father's reports reviewed. At that time, some officials in Kashmir had been given satellite phones (that connected via radio link through satellites orbiting the earth rather than via terrestrial cell sites that regular cell phones use). Someone in Khawar's hospital had a functional satellite phone, and Iqra managed to convey the message about AIIMS to him. Worried that Iqra was going to AIIMS alone, without anyone to emotionally support her, Khawar told her that he would join her the very next day. In case there was something concerning in the reports, someone had to be objective enough to know what to do next.

Iqra left for Delhi, still unsure if Khawar would make it the following day. She had no idea what flight he would take. The satellite phone wasn't reachable anymore.

It was a guessing game now. Iqra looked up the Srinagar–Delhi flights. She calculated Khawar's work timings in relation to the flight timings. Some seemed too early, others too late. The flight at 1 p.m. could potentially work for him. She tracked the flight and went to the airport at 3 p.m. She waited outside. One hour turned to three, and she started losing hope.

It wasn't just love that compelled her to wait. Iqra realized that she really didn't want to go to AIIMS alone. It was an overwhelming place if you didn't know people. It wasn't like Kashmir where everyone knew everyone; where you could find a personal connection with anyone you met. She had come to Delhi putting on a brave face, but it finally dawned on Iqra that she yearned to be taken care of, especially after months of being a caretaker.

Iqra sensed all the doubts and anxieties she had suppressed surfacing.

She closed her eyes and started thinking of things to calm her. She visualized the Bādāmwạ̄r orchard near her hospital. How beautiful and serene it looked in the beginning of spring. All the trees would be laden with the pink and white almond blossoms till the rains would come, and then the earth would be carpeted with flowers. She thought of herself walking in the orchard the following spring with Khawar by her side.

Khawar. Maybe Khawar wasn't coming after all.

Her eyes opened. The reverie broke.

Iqra was ready to give up and go back to her hotel. She started gathering her things when someone tapped her on her shoulder. She looked up.

It was Khawar looking as amused as ever. 'Nice place for a nap. How long have you been here?' Iqra leapt up and hugged him in response. She was happy that they weren't in Kashmir and didn't have to feel conscious about what the onlookers would think. In this sea of strangers, they felt at peace.

In the cab, they clasped their hands tightly, not letting go. Only once did Khawar move away to give her his boarding pass from the flight. On it he had written her a letter.

The pilot had just announced, 'We are at 13,000 feet ...' And Khawar had drawn out his pen right then.

'I am writing to you from 13,000 feet ...' So it began.

A fitting last letter to the series that the two would never ever forget.

Note: Iqra and Khawar got married in the summer of 2021.

8

I WILL WALK TO YOU IF I HAVE TO

THE DATE HAD BEEN decided a long time ago. Beena and Sakib were going to get married on 24 August 2019 in Srinagar.

By the end of July, everything was on track. The photographer had been booked, the make-up artist had been given the dates, the fabrics for Beena's trousseau were with the tailor, and Sakib's house was getting renovated—barring his own room, which was going to become theirs soon. They had decided to renovate the room together in the last days leading up to the wedding so that it would reflect both their tastes. The wedding cards were fresh off the press. They were yet to be distributed.

Sakib had started a new job with the marketing department of Airtel in June and was going to fly to Srinagar on 9 August, a little before the wedding. It was cutting it close, but he was getting inducted into the company on 5 August in Delhi, so he needed to stay back. Beena was following a hybrid work model; she was employed with a non-profit called Naandi Foundation based in Hyderabad. As the wedding drew close, Beena reduced her professional travel requirements. She was in Srinagar already, helping her mother get everything ready for the big day.

Beena's father had passed away before she was born. Her older sister, Fizalah, and she had been brought up by a single mother. Always having lived a life that was slightly unusual, Beena wanted a wedding that was as 'normal' as normal could be.

Around 3 August, things started getting frantic in Kashmir. Rumours were flying amok about the abrogation of Article 370. Beena had been in Kashmir in 2016 when the Hizbul Mujahideen's young commander Burhan Wani had been killed in an encounter by the armed forces.[30] In the months-long curfew and hartāl following his death, her landline and BSNL network phone were both working; even the broadband connection was up. So, she expected something similar this time around, too; things could certainly not get worse. She told her colleagues that even in the worst-case scenario, she would have the BSNL number, and they'd be able to contact her. At the time, Beena was working as a communications and PR lead for one of Naandi's social enterprises—the launch of Araku Coffee in India. Fortunately, she had done her handover; she was, after all, supposed to go on leave soon.

Beena and Sakib were on the phone on the night of 4 August like many other couples. They were discussing what the next day had in store for Kashmir. Their families were worried, especially about the wedding. Sakib assuaged her fears. 'Don't worry,' he said. 'I'll be there. It's not like they'll stop everything.' Beena agreed. 'Of course, that would be crazy!'

On 5 August, when Beena woke up, she learnt that cell phones, landlines and Wi-Fi were no longer functional. Even cable TV had been cut, barring some DTH connections. As the day progressed and news broke of the abrogation of Article 370, Beena's heart sank. This was much more terrifying than 2016. This lockdown didn't seem to have a certain end in sight. Her hopes of having a normal wedding or any wedding at all started dimming.

'All this drama when I never even wanted to get married,' she grumbled.

BEENA AND SAKIB HAD been the best of friends before any talk of marriage had come up. They had a lot of warmth and love for each other but had not been officially dating. Neither had fathomed that their friendship could be any more than what it was.

When the ten-year friendship mark came around, their families started egging them on to make it official. Beena was against this. She had always thought of Sakib as her younger brother—she was two years older than him—and on occasion had even introduced him to people as her 'chota bhai'.

'That's incest,' she protested when her mother tried to convince her.

Apparently, the two families had come together and hatched a master plan. It was the classic 'you spend so much time together, so why don't you get married' spiel that was doled out to the unsuspecting Beena and Sakib.

The awkwardness of the entire turn of events (not to mention the shock!) meant that Beena and Sakib couldn't bring themselves to talk to each other for a month.

Eventually, the families sent friends and relatives to counsel them both. Beena had never been a fan of the idea of marriage as she wished to stay with her mother and support her. Given that Fizalah was already married, Beena had no desire to see her mother living alone. She saw marriage as a form of abandonment.

But her mother was having none of Beena's arguments. And Beena soon realized that there was no way out of this.

If marriage was a necessary evil, she reasoned, and if she did have to marry, what could possibly be more prudent than choosing someone she knew very well? And who did she know—and who knew her better—than Sakib?

The two were engaged in 2017. It was a 'best friends–arranged marriage' situation.

The turn of the relationship came with its own set of challenges and growing pains. The two of them had spoken informally for a decade—they had always referred to one another as 'tu'. Suddenly they weren't sure if they had to converse with greater etiquette. Was 'aap' a more appropriate term?

So profound was their confusion that the first few times they met after the engagement, Beena couldn't even look at Sakib directly in the eye. Sakib was taken aback, 'This is just wrong!' he protested. A few seconds of awkward silence followed. Finally, they both burst out laughing at the absurdity of it all.

The friendship they had nurtured helped them tide over every perplexing change, each impasse, till they re-established the rapport they were used to. The banter returned, and they eased into a new chapter of their lives. It was a chapter neither of them had envisaged in their wildest dreams when they had met for the first time as teenagers.

NOW, BEENA WONDERED WHEN she would speak to Sakib next.

As for Sakib, he found himself in a huge corporate building in Delhi. He and many newbies like him were being informed about the company philosophy and work culture. They were sitting in a glass cabin. Behind him, outside, was a big TV mounted on a wall; it was visible through the glass doors. The news channel had a grim anchor offering breaking news updates. Sakib was looking at a presentation and not paying attention to the TV screen. Suddenly there was a huge cheer outside, and he turned around. His eyes caught sight of the TV screen. Bold letters screamed, 'Articles 370 and 35A abrogated'. Sakib immediately felt an invisible gaze on him. At that exact moment he knew—this is not good.

Sakib excused himself to make a call. He knew the phone lines in Kashmir were down as he had tried to call Beena and his parents in the morning and had found all their phones unreachable. Now he wondered, 'Who do I call?'

He phoned his cousin in Bangalore and vented. 'What should I do? I'm getting married in nineteen days. Or at least I think I am. Should I even go?'

His cousin calmed him down, 'Let's just wait it out.'

Sakib went back to his office in a daze and sat in his chair, his mind racing. Everything felt uncertain, and he was no longer sure how he would be getting home.

It was as though the last few years had been leading up to this moment. He was the paithai bānè—the eldest born—in his family, even amongst all his cousins. His was the first wedding of their generation. Everyone was excited about it. Perhaps all the nervous energy and anticipation surrounding the big day had somehow jinxed it? Sakib pushed the intrusive thought away.

Sakib's phone started buzzing with messages from his friends from Bangalore, Delhi and overseas, who had booked their tickets for his wedding. 'What's the scene, man, is the wedding on?'

He replied, 'If I find out, I will tell you.' As he wrote this, he broke into a grim smile—all at once amused by the situation. Then he went back to fretting. On seeing his pale face, his boss asked, 'Why are you so worried?'

Sakib explained the situation, and she heard him out patiently. Then she plainly stated, 'If you sit here and wait, you will never get married. Just book yourself a flight and go!'

'But I was supposed to go on 9 August,' a diligent Sakib protested.

She stopped him midway and smiled kindly. 'Just go. Get married.'

Sakib packed up his stuff and looked up flights to Srinagar. There were no flights available on 5 August, and most of the flights for 6 August were cancelled, barring one. He booked himself on that.

On the first day following the abrogation, when Beena wasn't sure where Sakib was, and whether he would come back to Srinagar, she missed their banter. She was transported back to a time in 2014 when floods had engulfed the Valley. Both of them had been in Kashmir. Due to the flooding, none of the phones were working. The only way to catch a signal was to climb up to a height. Beena had climbed a tall structure near her house and called Sakib to check if he was alive. His area had been inundated, with water reaching the first floor. She was concerned. Thankfully, she got through, and he chuckled, 'I thought *you* were dead!'

In 2016, even when there was severe curfew in Kashmir, they managed to remain in touch.

Now in 2019, when she had no idea what was going on, only one thought dominated Beena's mind—'I think God saved all the craziness for this wedding!'

Sakib was certainly going crazy in Delhi, buying last-minute things for the wedding. He had assumed he'd have a few days to shop before heading back, but now that he was leaving the next day and entering a zone under lockdown, he had no option but to make his own purchases—besides the things that his family had demanded—post-haste in Delhi. At some point, he decided to look for dulha chappals—the sandals traditionally worn by grooms. In his muddled state of mind, he ended up purchasing a pair of sneakers instead. It only hit him later at night when he was packing, 'Why did I even buy these?'

The next day in the flight, there were only three people, including Sakib. One was a Kashmiri doctor who hadn't heard from his family, and the other was an army man.

At that moment, Sakib felt that something as significant as a wedding felt altogether insignificant when one considered the bigger picture. This was the thing about being from Kashmir—perspective was all. He looked at the empty seats around him and thought of all the people who would kill to be on this flight, just to find out if their loved ones were okay, if they were alive.

SAKIB LANDED IN A deserted Srinagar airport. He lived in Rambagh, a ten-minute car ride away. But the five cabs in the parking lot asked for Rs 5,000 to drive the distance. Sakib was shocked that after coming back, he was being looted by his own people. But then again, there was no one coming to Kashmir any longer. These cab drivers were watching their daily wages plummeting to zero. They were trying to earn what they could. Sakib could see this, but he could not dole out such an unreasonable amount for a short distance in good faith.

He decided that it was best to start walking. At least he'd be home in thirty minutes.

As he started his journey, he saw his father's friend driving by. He spotted Sakib and stopped his car. He asked, 'Beta weren't you getting married?' Sakib replied, 'Uncle, why do you think I'm here?' Sakib hitched a ride with him, thankful for small mercies as he had four big bags stuffed with wedding shopping—things his mother, sister and cousins had asked for, which they couldn't find readily in Kashmir, besides his own purchases.

His father's friend could only drop him till Barzulla Chowk, where concertina wire fencing stopped vehicles from moving ahead to Rambagh. Sakib got off with his multiple bags and walked the last kilometre-and-a-half.

He got home to his surprised and relieved parents and to his younger sister Saiyba. They were dismayed that they hadn't known he was coming—they would have picked him up—and amazed that he had walked the distance dragging along four trolley bags.

After Sakib had settled down, his father came straight to the point. 'What should we do, tell me? We live in Kashmir. Things may calm down eventually, but who knows when. Are you going to bring your life to a standstill because of that?'

Sakib's father told him he had a plan. Early next morning he would go to Beena's maamu's place. He would tell her maternal uncle that the wedding would happen on the scheduled day. 'We weren't sure if you would fly down, but now that you are here, let's do this. Whoever comes, comes.'

So, the next day, at 4.30 a.m., Sakib's father left for Beena's uncle's house. This is how the people in Kashmir now managed to get around—late at night after 8 p.m. or early in morning before 7 a.m.—in a bid to beat high security.

At this point, Sakib hadn't spoken to Beena for almost seventy-two hours. He had no clue about what was happening with her or her family. His family was paranoid and didn't want him travelling anywhere far from home. Besides, since traditional Kashmiri culture forbids a mahrin' and a mahrāz from landing up at each other's houses before the wedding, Beena and Sakib couldn't visit one another to ask about the road ahead. Even in dire circumstances, tradition took precedence over the necessity for information.

On 7 August, the day Sakib's father planned to visit her uncle, Beena was yet to have clarity about the wedding that was supposed to occur in a fortnight. The cards hadn't been distributed, and now there was no way to distribute them as Srinagar had heavy blockades everywhere, barring people from travelling. Beena knew that Sakib was scheduled to be back on 9 August. But as flights were getting cancelled, civilians were restricted from driving during curfew, and taxis were quoting exorbitant prices to take civilians through a ghost town, Beena felt that Sakib wouldn't be able to make it back to Kashmir, and that the wedding would in all probability get postponed.

As these thoughts swirled through her mind, Beena's maamu landed up at their house looking delighted. 'You know what happened at 5 in the morning?' he asked excitedly. Not expecting an answer, he rambled on. Sakib's father had come knocking in the wee hours of the morning. He didn't know the exact address, so it was only after knocking on several doors that he had managed to reach Beena's uncle. All to tell him that the family would be visiting Beena's house the next day at 5 a.m. to decide what to do about the wedding. Again, the banality of all these traditions hit Beena. They couldn't just come to her house, they had to send a message first. Though, in a way, she was grateful. If her in-laws were visiting at 5 a.m., the last thing she wanted was for them to find her dishevelled or asleep.

The next morning at 5, as cups of tea were passed between bleary-eyed people, Beena's father-in-law told them that Sakib had come back. Beena was startled and relieved. 'But he was to return tomorrow!' He told her all that had transpired.

Then Sakib's father came to the point. There were barely two weeks left for the wedding and many arrangements had already been made. Sakib was home. Moving ahead with a less-than-perfect wedding was better than not having one. They could deal with the obstacles they encountered on the way and improvise. Beena's mother, who had been contemplating postponing the wedding to the following summer, was at first sceptical. But then she reminded herself that this was Kashmir, you never knew when the situation would sour; who knew what a future date would bring?

The consensus finally was to have a smaller ceremony with fewer people. Given that there was no way to distribute the cards, they decided to rely on word of mouth. Beena, who hadn't spoken to Sakib since 4 August, would now in all likelihood only see him at their nikāh. The thought in itself was bizarre.

AUGUST IS PEAK WEDDING season in Kashmir, and gradually stories emerged of grooms being beaten up on their way to the bride's house, or of cars with brides going back with the bārāt being halted and stone-pelted by both the police and the protesters. There were other heartbreaking stories, too—of a pregnant woman who had to walk to the hospital while in labour; she subsequently lost the baby because she couldn't reach in time.

In the midst of so much fear, ambiguity and stress, Beena and Sakib started putting together the final pieces for the wedding. With no phones, a conversation that would have spanned a few minutes now stretched across several hours or days. Beena realized how much they took phone interaction for granted. But then, wasn't it fair to expect some modes of communication to work, she wondered. And was this even fair—a people locked up with no means of speaking to the world, much less to one another?

Every step of the way, Beena and Sakib faced challenges. Beena hoped that all those people whose services she had booked didn't assume that the wedding had been called off. There was no way of informing them one way or another, and to visit them with updates meant having to figure out their whereabouts. Besides, venturing out wasn't even safe. Beena lived in Soura, which had been one of the more volatile neighbourhoods in Kashmir following the abrogation. It had seen major protests and was heavily barricaded; shops were closed and the denizens were compelled to keep vigil at night. Beena felt like she lived in a fortress.

Then, there was the problem of securing jewellery. Beena's wedding jewellery was in the bank locker, and the bank was closed. Through word of mouth, she established the bank manager's approximate address. Beena and her mother went house to house till they found the manager, accompanied him to the bank and got hold of the jewellery they needed. In all of this, Beena missed meeting Sakib. It turned out that he had tried visiting her home (without informing his parents, and cheekily breaking the Kashmiri tradition) while Beena had been at the bank. After all this time—Beena could scarcely believe it—an errand had kept her away from him.

Before she could dwell on this, there was a problem involving her wedding clothes. Beena's tailor had half of her outfits, and she found out he had left Kashmir. This wasn't entirely surprising since non-locals had been asked to leave by the government before the abrogation, and terrified, the non-Kashmiri tailor must have fled. Beena's clothes were locked up in his shop in Rajbagh. Beena scoured the entire neighbourhood to find out who owned the building with the shop in it. She finally found the owner and told him her story; he had heard wilder ones by now. He unlocked the shop for her, and Beena got the clothes that were hers. Thankfully, the tailor had stitched them before leaving.

Sakib wasn't as lucky. He had told his dad to leave out his room during renovation, and now it was completely bare. The rest of the house was done up, but his room came with four whitewashed walls and little else. Beena and he were supposed to choose the wallpaper and buy the furniture together just before the wedding. Now, not only did he have no way of buying the wallpaper and furniture—not a single shop was open—but he also had to second-guess what Beena would like. His family had given away all the old furniture, so there was also no way of making do till the tide turned. With great difficulty, he found a vendor who sold wallpaper, but the nervous vendor was only willing to open his shop at night. At 10 p.m., Sakib went to the shopping complex his shop was in, climbed the wall to get in as the main gate was locked, and watched as the vendor quietly opened his own shop like a thief. Sakib selected the first wallpaper design he saw, eager to get out of that place. They sneaked out as stealthily as they had come in, eager not to draw any attention.

Now it was time to put up the wallpaper. Kashmiri labourers were notorious for not doing this job neatly, and non-Kashmiri labourers who were adept had fled the Valley. 'Push comes to shove, we will do it ourselves,' Sakib's father said. He had become rather enthusiastic about do-it-yourself projects, but Sakib wasn't sure that taking his help was the best course of action in this situation.

He found two labourers in a nearby village who could do this job, but they were afraid to travel to Srinagar. Sakib's father worked for the police and sent a truck with two guards in it to get the labourers in safely. All so that they would wallpaper Sakib and Beena's to-be room. The labourers completed the job in one day and were escorted back home the same way.

The next problem for Sakib came in the form of meat. Kashmiri weddings are nothing without a traditional feast—wāzèwān—and given the huge number of the guests attending most weddings, the wāzèwān cannot be cooked in a kitchen. Most wedding households demarcate an area in their gardens or backyards for the wāzè—the cooks—to prepare the wāzèwān over a wood fire. The wood fire also imparts a distinct smoky, umami flavour to the meal. So, for the wāzèwān to be cooked properly, one needs the wāzè, utensils, firewood and, most importantly, lots of mutton. Not one of these was certain for Sakib and Beena's wedding.

Sakib's family had expected over 450 guests to show up—this was before the abrogation. Now they weren't at all sure who would attend. Still, if the close relatives were counted, at least 40–50 guests were guaranteed. The family had to organize meat for each of them. The vendor in charge of sourcing meat refused to commit to deliveries as the state highway was allowing in goods sporadically. It took a while for Sakib's family to identify a pujj—a butcher—in another village and procure mutton from him.

Next in the order of business was the bed. At 5 a.m., a few days before the wedding, Sakib went to the Babdem area behind Maisuma; it was known for its walnut wood furniture. The shopkeeper refused to open his shop during the day. 'Boys come and throw stones at us and break the glass,' he complained. Once more, Sakib's father's truck had to come to the rescue. The shopkeeper was informed that it would drive in at night, and the bed could be loaded into it. Sakib paid the man Rs 5,000 extra to sweeten the deal. The shopkeeper consented to the plan, and the bed arrived at Sakib's house at 2 a.m. It would have been a most peculiar sight for any neighbour who happened to peep through their curtains at that hour—a king-sized bed being hoisted out of a truck in the middle of the night. Nothing to see here.

As the wedding date approached, Sakib's family was informed by the imām that the nikāh document had been updated. So, a new one would have to be procured. Sakib tried sourcing the new document, but all the places he visited were still carrying the old one, which had apparently ceased being relevant or applicable. Surely after all the work done to get this wedding on track, the most crucial of documents wouldn't fudge their plans! After hours of searching and asking and reaching out to others who were also getting married, Sakib managed to get hold of a valid nikāh-nama.

BARELY A FEW DAYS before the wedding, Beena went with her cousin to 7/11 in Sanat Nagar. Sanat Nagar, unlike Soura, was a relatively peaceful neighbourhood and, therefore, the supermarket was open. She was walking through the aisles to buy some last-minute essentials when she heard someone shout out her name—'Beena didi!' She looked around to see Sakib's younger sister Saiyba running towards her. Before they could even greet each other properly, Saiyba told Beena that Sakib was there as well. The two women went to look for him, and there he was in one of the aisles looking for nothing in particular, waiting for his sister and cousins to finish their shopping.

'Bhaiya! Beena didi!' Saiyba screamed. Sakib looked up to see a radiant Beena.

Beena and Sakib, who hadn't spoken for almost twenty days now, had less than twenty minutes to catch up. Nothing significant could be said, especially with Saiyba around. They just smiled and told each other that they were fine and would get through this. *'Baaki saari baatein shaadi pe kar lenge,'* Beena smiled. 'We'll speak at leisure at the wedding. Next time I see you, you will be my husband.'

Just like that, their time with each other was over. They parted with the promise to meet on 24 August. Call it serendipity or chaos—but they had met. Now they could get married in peace.

As Sakib became a dim figure in the distance, Beena remembered the bedroom and their plans to renovate it together—choose the upholstery, the wallpaper, the furniture. They hadn't been able to do any of it. Sakib must've had to do it all on his own, second-guessing her likes and dislikes. If only she knew then the lengths he had to go to. All of it would be a surprise now. Beena couldn't wait. She couldn't wait to pull Sakib's leg for his wallpaper choices.

THREE DAYS BEFORE HER wedding, the wedding photographer landed up at Beena's house. It had taken him four hours to find it. He had come just to tell her that he would show up at the wedding. Having known a host of uncertainties so far, Beena was thankful for these small kindnesses.

Then there was the question of the make-up artist. Two days before the wedding, Beena and Fizalah—who lived across town and had found out much after her family that the wedding was back on track—were wondering if the make-up artist would come as planned. Fizalah felt she would. Beena believed she wouldn't—for she had been booked before the lockdown. The sisters found a backup, just in case. They didn't know it then—but the backup would prove invaluable. On the wedding day, when the make-up artist would fail to make it even at 2 p.m., it would be the backup artist—a neighbour's sister-in-law—who would come to the rescue. Funnily enough, the original make-up artist would show up, but at 6.30 p.m.! She would admit to losing her way and couldn't be faulted too much under the circumstances.

Finally, it was time to get the mānzirāth—mehandī raat—organized. In Kashmir, young girls from the groom's side visit the bride's house on mānzirāth, carrying henna and a cake. Recently, during another wedding in Beena's neighbourhood, a young mānzi-kūr's—mehandī girl's—car had faced stone pelting. She had arrived with glass shards in her hair and blood on the cake. On hearing this, Beena and Sakib cancelled the ritual completely. There was no way they would make Saiyba go through this.

But a bride needs mehandī, and Beena had booked professional artists for the night. However, given how volatile Soura was, the artists, non-local men who were at a much higher risk of being pelted with stones, refused to visit. They suggested Beena drop by at their studio. Afraid that their car would get attacked, Beena's cousin took her on his motorbike. It took a few hours to complete her bridal designs, and that's when she realized that she couldn't go back on a motorbike—for the mehandī would get ruined, not to mention what an odd sight she would make. So, she waited till 11 p.m. at the studio, and once things were calmer in Soura, she was brought back home in a car. Every plan asked for a certain degree of inventiveness. For Beena, the dream of the perfect wedding had long gone. Now she simply hoped to get by with an uneventful one.

In Sakib's house, in the meantime, friends and acquaintances had started showing up. They took on all his pending work, so he could finally relax. Three scouts organized themselves along a 1-kilometre radius near Sakib's house looking out for trouble. Even Sakib's intern from two years prior landed up after walking a distance of 30 kilometres. He said, 'Sir, I remembered it was your wedding. If times had been normal, I wouldn't have come. But given the situation outside, I thought you'd need all the help you can get.' Sakib was touched beyond measure. This boy would end up working harder than anyone else, taking care of the guests and looking into all arrangements. With the help of Sakib's friends, the wedding was up and running.

The wedding ceremonies were finally here. From Beena's side—because the cards hadn't been distributed—only Beena's uncles and their families came. None of her friends did because sending girls to Soura was considered too dangerous. Sakib's contingent was larger and more diverse because his area wasn't as volatile.

A day before the wedding, Beena's mother started complaining about an eye irritation. Beena checked her vitals, and they were all fine. Assuming that it was on account of stress—her mother had just fought with the caterer—nobody paid much attention. But the discomfort started getting worse, and on the wedding day, she couldn't see anything from her right eye. As her own optician couldn't be contacted, she was taken to the hospital directly. This was at 7 p.m. Beena obviously couldn't go in her bridal attire. When her mother returned, no one told Beena anything. It was only later that she found out what had happened—that due to the fight with the caterer, her mother's blood pressure had shot up, and that had led to her retina getting detached. She would need an operation soon.

Under regular circumstances, the bride's family gets a call from the groom's side that the wedding procession has left for their house. In this wedding, there was no such luck. All that Beena's family could do was wait. Beena, who had been ready since 5 p.m., had to stay put in one place so her outfit wouldn't wrinkle. With no phones for entertainment and barely any friends around to chat with, Beena prayed that Sakib would hurry up. He finally arrived at 10 p.m.

The celebrations were quiet so they wouldn't attract any attention. The wedding ceremony and rituals went by in a blur. The nikāh-nama was read, and the guests were fed. Before she knew it, Beena was in the car with Sakib—newlyweds on their way home after a quick wedding in turbulent times.

Just as the car started, a relative from Beena's side decided to break the silence. They got out one of those golden karaoke mics and started singing the wanè-wun that is traditionally sung during the bride's rọkhsạtī. It wasn't a wise idea as it attracted some people and they came to attack the car the bride and groom were leaving in. Beena screamed at the driver to get out fast. The car zoomed off, even as Sakib laughed, 'Whose genius idea was the mic?' Beena just shook her head in shock and amazement. She couldn't even call her relatives and yell at them for their stupidity.

Just then, something struck Beena. Kashmiri houses traditionally have floor seating for big occasions. Since Beena's lehenga had a can-can skirt underneath to make it voluminous, she couldn't sit cross-legged on the floor. 'Is there a couch that has been arranged?' she asked. In the past, small details of this sort could've been communicated easily via a phone call; but now, they seemed like great obstacles to overcome. Sakib obviously couldn't call ahead to organize a couch, so when they reached his residence, there was a scramble for the right kind of furniture. 'So near, yet so-fa,' Beena laughed. 'Glad to see your lameness is still intact,' Sakib quipped.

In Kashmir, some days after the wedding, the bride has to go back to her parents' house with her husband for a ceremony called phirsāl. Before that, Beena's cousins had to visit Sakib's house for a post-wedding ritual called khabri gatshun. But when the cousins kept showing up every other day after the wedding for khabar, Beena started getting suspicious.

When she returned home for phirsāl, it all came together. Beena learnt of her mother's eye condition and that the surgery was scheduled for the very next day. She almost collapsed, overwhelmed with guilt and worry. If she could, she would have contacted doctors outside Kashmir and ensured that the surgery happened someplace safe. But given that the option didn't exist, and that attending to severe retinal issues couldn't be delayed, Beena decided to make do. 'I will be there tomorrow,' she announced, ignoring her mother's protests.

When Sakib and Beena were making their way back, their vehicle was stopped by the army at a barricade near Iqbal Park. There were four army guys checking every car. It was 11 p.m. When it was their turn, they were asked to switch on the light inside the car. The army men saw two newlyweds in elaborate outfits squinting because of the sudden light. One army guy was undeterred by this. He had a DSLR camera and said he needed to take their picture for 'documentation'—he was recording everyone coming and going. Sakib, always ready with a wisecrack, said, *'Sir main pose leta hoon, aap phir uthao*!' He wanted to be ready with a pose before the man clicked. This was to help cheer Beena up, and she cracked a smile. The army guy took the photo. Sakib whispered to Beena, 'Our official Government of India photograph.' She guffawed, even as the army guy told them to move ahead.

WHENEVER BEENA LOOKS BACK to the time leading to the wedding, she remembers the last call she had with Sakib on 4 August. She was crestfallen about what was coming and the uncertainty of it all. She was the last person who would obsess over make-up or photographers. But her wedding was important to her, especially because, given the unusual nature of her early years, she yearned for stability, for a life she could have control over, and especially for 'normal' things. She wasn't seeking dhoom dhamaka, pomp and show. She was seeking the ordinary.

It was the very thing that was denied to her. When she griped about this to Sakib, he tried to cheer her up. He told her that what they were going through was nothing. In the late 1980s, when his parents were getting married, one couldn't even beat the meat for gọshtabè—served as the last wāzèwān dish at a wedding—in peace. Given that the meat and fat had to be pounded by the cook for hours till it turned pulpy and smooth, and that the noise could be misconstrued in a zone of conflict, it was a hard thing to achieve. As no wāzèwān trạm' was complete without the gọshtabè, it had to be done.

Beena laughed at the image, then said, *'Wo waqt aur tha.'* That was another time.

Sakib then turned serious. He told her to forget about the wedding—because at the end of the day, it wasn't about a wedding, they were building a marriage.

Then he said the one line that Beena would remember forever; a line that she cherished and that still gives her goosebumps; a line she remembered during those days of uncertainty leading up to the wedding. It's the line she tweeted before the Wi-Fi got cut, and the line that she saw, weeks later, had been retweeted hundreds of times and had even been featured in a Buzzfeed article.

Sakib said in a soft voice, 'I will walk to you if I have to.'

9

ROOHANI

ASAD WAS BORN BIOLOGICALLY female, and his parents named him Rabia. He grew up in Srinagar, and from a young age he knew that he was in the wrong body—that this was not where he belonged. Now in his twenties, Asad identifies as a transgender man.

Asad had always been more interested in toys and paraphernalia 'that were for boys'—video games, cars, bikes, you name it. He had no interest in the dolls that were bought for him. Not that a boy couldn't play with dolls, but since Asad, even as a four-year-old, believed that certain toys threatened to identify him as a girl, he rejected them. When he went to kindergarten in an all-girls' convent school, he came back and told his parents, 'Everyone's a girl in my school, I'm the only boy who has gotten admission.' They just laughed, writing this off as an innocent childhood observation.

As Asad grew older, his body started transforming. He was aware that his body was female, but his 'rooh', his soul, was not. In other words, he sensed that he was a man trapped in a woman's body. He'd cover his head in a hijab, but he maintained that such things were superficial. To those he trusted, he revealed his true identity. And by his twenties, in closed circles, he adopted the name Asad.

Amongst those he trusted, there was one who *truly* saw him—Haika.

Haika was Asad's girlfriend. Haika and Asad had met many years ago at an entrance exam coaching centre. She had cleared her medical entrance tests and gone off to study medicine in Islamabad, Pakistan. Asad had taken up journalism in Amritsar.

Asad had lost his mother and brother as a child. His father remarried his mother's cousin a few years later and had a son from that marriage. Asad was on good terms with them, and his father was his rock. But only Haika *really* understood him. When they used to meet in public, while referring to Asad, she seldom used verbs like 'karegi', unconsciously using the verb 'karega' instead. In a language where verbs changed to match the gender of the subject, Haika's manner of speaking touched Asad. Still new to love, he would sometimes ask her if she missed having a masculine frame to hug or if she would've liked him to be taller. But Haika always shook her head and said: '*Mujhe teri rooh pata hai*. I feel your soul.'

IN AUGUST 2019, ASAD was in Srinagar. He was back home from college to prepare for his exams that were scheduled for December. He had marked himself as a non-attending student for the semester so as to study remotely. Haika was back in Islamabad. By now, they'd been together a few years.

Asad and Haika had recently quarrelled. It had been about something mundane, and typically such disagreements simmered down in a day or two. But neither Asad nor Haika had the luxury of time. As rumours started spreading that the internet could shut down, one of Asad's close friends Insha—a journalist herself—told him to make up with Haika at once. It was 4 August, and Insha was sure that the communication lines would collapse like dominoes by midnight. Given that Haika and Asad talked via WhatsApp—it was cheaper than placing an international call—an internet shutdown would make communication impossible.

Asad wasn't terribly concerned. Even if there was a blockade, it would be lifted in a few days as always. And this would serve Haika right for fighting with him.

An exasperated Insha argued that Asad and Haika couldn't go a single day without talking to each other. She wasn't exaggerating. The two would talk every night. They would fall asleep to the sound of each other's voices, their phones lying next to them. The call would get cut only when one of them woke up in the morning or if the batteries died.

'Make up right now or you'll repent later. I'm in no mood to hear you whine in a week's time,' Insha said. Whatever was coming—Insha was sure—wouldn't blow over in a few days.

Asad finally conceded. But knew that Haika was as obstinate as him.

When he called to tell Haika about the impending internet blackout, she took the news as casually as Asad had at first. Since Haika lived in a college hostel and had loads errands to run—there were groceries to be bought, clothes to be washed, a room to be cleaned, the list went on and on—she told Asad she'd catch up later. Asad tried reasoning with her, even spouting Insha's lines—'You must take the rumours seriously or you'll regret it!'—but Haika, assuming that all of this was a ploy to get her to talk, pushed back. 'Stop crying wolf. Let me finish my work. I'll talk to you when I have a moment.' Click. The phone went dead.

Asad gave his best see-what-I-have-to-deal-with look to an amused Insha.

'You two are really meant for each other!' Insha declared.

While Haika was grocery shopping, back in Kashmir, Asad started scrambling, like all other Kashmiris, for odds and ends, hoarding food, medicine and fuel in anticipation of whatever was coming.

As the rumours became stronger and darker, Haika's friends and family reached out to her. Her father asked her if she had enough money or if he should send her some before the internet collapsed. Her mother told her to lie low and not get into any trouble in a bid to reach them. She urged her not to post anything political on social media and to eat on time. Haika had a sinking feeling in the middle of a crowded bazaar in Islamabad. 'So Asad wasn't joking after all!' she thought and started running back to the hostel.

In Srinagar, it was getting dark. Haika still hadn't called. She clearly wasn't back at the hostel. Asad was getting antsy. He called her in panic, reiterating the gravity of the situation. 'You obviously don't care,' he told her bitterly. Haika, already frazzled with all the running, got mad. Tensions were running high. All they wanted to say was that they loved each other, but in the anxiety of that moment, they blurted out things that in hindsight felt callous. Haika yelled at Asad, calling him a moody, immature child. Asad accused her of being unsympathetic. As soon as Haika stepped into her hostel room, Asad's internet snapped and the call dropped.

Asad's area in Srinagar was one of the first to experience an internet shutdown. His cellular network was still working, but Kashmiri numbers had been barred from making calls to Pakistani ones. He called Insha instead to check if her internet was still working. It was. He told her to call Haika. 'Ask her if she's happy now!' He was so angry with this woman he loved, this aggravating person who pushed all his buttons. He also knew that he would do anything to hear her voice right about now. Haika, on the other side of the border, felt guilty as hell.

At midnight, all cellular services in the Valley died. Everyone, including Asad and Haika, believed that this would pass. After all, in the past, whether a politician died or a prime minister visited, the outages had always been temporary. Kashmiris weren't new to basic communication services being snatched away. By that extension, they weren't new to the idea that the services were treated like candy being dangled before a rebellious child. Eventually, the child would get his candy. Eventually, the services would get restored.

The next day—5 August—saw the abrogation of Articles 370 and 35A. Now, all the pieces started falling into place. Kashmir would plunge into a long period of isolation, with no means of communicating with the outside world.

All Asad wanted was to hear Haika's voice again. The Indian government had proven its point; now please could he talk to her? He could very well have been screaming in an echo chamber—for all he could hear was his own voice bouncing back.

DAYS TURNED INTO WEEKS. Asad was getting depressed, not just because of the enforced isolation and his inability to reach out to Haika but also because of himself.

Even though homosexual relationships had recently been decriminalized in India, few in Srinagar accepted Asad for being queer. In the conservative Kashmiri society, he was still called Rabia. Haika and a few close friends were the only ones who supported him and gave him confidence.

Asad knew that in Kashmiri society being queer was perceived as being 'against the law of nature'. The most visible group he recalled being *openly* part of the Valley's LGBTQIA+ community comprised of the mạnzimyạ̄yr—the marriage matchmakers. Known to dress distinctively in male clothing in public, with the hint of a colourful dupatta or manicured eyebrows, these transgender people helped heterosexual marriages come to fruition. The mạnzimyạ̄yr would also sing and dance at weddings, this time in traditionally female attires. But beyond these limited details, surprisingly little was known or said about their sexuality—as though the mạnzimyạ̄yr's profession alone granted them social acceptance and a place in the world; as though their desires didn't count. There were younger transgender people in Kashmir who did not want to be limited to the mạnzimyōṛ profession; some had become make-up artists. Now with traditional matchmaking dwindling, and a lack of support from the government, combined with social stigma, most people from the transgender community were finding it hard to find work. Besides them, the queer community in Kashmir was seldom vocal or visible.[31]

Interacting with Haika and his friends regularly would help Asad reaffirm his gender identity. Now, cooped up indoors with no one to talk to, he felt as though he was growing smaller, shrinking. He couldn't share his feelings with his family. His stepmother was kind, but she wasn't *his* mother. His father, while a pillar of strength, was also unpredictable in these matters—what if he institutionalized Asad? What if Asad, therefore, never got to see Haika again? That was a risk he was not willing to take.

Maybe his mother would've understood. Maybe. But she was gone.

So, here, too, was why Asad really missed Haika—she offered him the motherly love he so desperately missed. She told him, 'Don't you dare say that you don't have a mother. You have me.' Even though she was younger than him, she was affectionate the way he imagined his own mother was.

Now, the only person Asad trusted with his life didn't know how he was doing. And vice versa. His close friends, including Insha, were inaccessible. He couldn't afford to share his identity with anyone new. Even if he wished to, his parents weren't about to let him leave the house—after all, they maintained that he was a girl, so they had to be protective of him. The loneliness was killing Asad slowly.

What kept him alive was knowing that at some point this would end; that he would be able to speak to Haika again.

IT WAS SEPTEMBER NOW. Bạḍ Īd had come and gone. People had started queueing up at police stations to call those living outside the Valley. Asad was sure that Haika's family, too, had reached out to their daughter. He just needed confirmation that Haika was well.

Asad couldn't queue up to call her himself. He knew that he'd be quizzed—especially in the middle of a police station—if he asked to speak to someone in Pakistan. He wouldn't know how to explain his reasons for calling. He couldn't risk getting detained or worse, any news getting back to his parents.

So, Asad took a different route. He requested his friend Sahiba, who lived close by, to take him on her scooter to Haika's house. The two set off covertly, and to avoid the army patrolling the streets, took narrow alleys. Eventually, they got to Haika's house. Her mother was in the garden when she looked up and saw Asad's familiar face. She knew him as her daughter's good friend, and to watch him was to solidify the memories of her daughter. As Haika's mother ushered Asad and Sahiba in, Asad asked if she had spoken to her. He waited with fingers crossed for the answer. Haika's mother shook her head sadly. She hadn't been able to as yet. 'But ...'—Asad's ears perked up now—'a cousin of hers went to Delhi and spoke to her. She is fine.'

Asad was relieved. Trying not to sound too enthusiastic, he said, 'I miss her too.'

That's when he decided that he would travel out of Kashmir to talk to Haika. He told Haika's mother of his plan. She smiled. She didn't know anything about the depth of Asad and Haika's relationship, but any news from her daughter would be welcome and appreciated.

Asad was sure that he was the only one going crazy and missing Haika. She probably didn't long for him as much. After all, she had always been the carefree one, the person to take things in her stride. She had a lot of sabr, a great deal of patience, willing to space out her thoughts and words and balance them out. Asad, on the other hand, was be-sabr—hasty and anxious; he was a whatever-you're-thinking-say-it kind of guy. Even though Asad was afraid of finding out that all the angst was ek-tarfa—

one-sided—it was still a chance he wanted to take. He needed to get out of Kashmir.

Asad decided to use a fail-safe way to convince his parents—the pretext of a solid education. Asad's exams were in December in Amritsar, and it was September now. If he had known that there would be a lockdown in store, he would have never opted to be a non-attending student that semester. Now, all the study material he required to prepare for his exams was online, and he couldn't access it because of the internet blockade.

Asad knew that his father wouldn't let him leave Kashmir in the current political climate. Even if he managed to travel in peace, there remained concerns for his safety and that of all Kashmiri students outside the Valley. Under normal circumstances, a cricket match between India and Pakistan could imperil their wellbeing. Now, post 5 August, the threat was much bigger. There were stories of Kashmiri students in other parts of the nation getting verbally harassed on the streets; or being beaten up by mobs if they retaliated; or getting driven out of universities if they posted against the abrogation online. There was talk that most Kashmiri students felt like someone was going to come for them if they aired their opinions.

This sense of being in danger of persecution wasn't new to Kashmiris. Be it the khọftan phạkīr post Indian independence or the ikhwạn' in the 1990s, Kashmir had a long history of surveillance and eavesdropping; of having dissent crushed through it. Technology had just made the scrutiny more obvious.

Asad was aware of all the danger. Nonetheless, he took on the challenge of seeking his parents' consent to travel.

Asad began by telling his father that he needed to go to Amritsar to gather his study notes. His father was staunchly against this. If Asad travelled, he wouldn't be able to contact him. Asad had a ready retort—that his father had an acquaintance with a working BSNL satellite phone, and if anything happened, Asad could be called. It was a matter of three days, and he would be back before his parents knew it. His father still refused. So, Asad resorted to emotional blackmail. He broke down before his father and cried—his future was getting ruined; he was going to fail. 'The college won't make exceptions for Kashmiri students!' But his father coolly told him that he was overreacting. At that point, Asad wondered if his father would've had a similar response if he viewed him as a boy; after all, sons in Kashmir were given a lot more freedom and were treated more leniently.

Asad had a final trump card to play. He went to his grandfather to tell on his father. His grandfather summoned his son and ordered him to let Asad go, his future depended on it! His father listened with lowered eyes but wouldn't reconsider.

His father, now extremely annoyed, took Asad to a travel agent to put the fear of God in him. The travel agent, probably trained by his father, said what he had to. 'It is not safe to fly in these uncertain times!' Asad argued that students were flying out to Bangladesh and other countries, he only needed to go to Punjab—which was in India the last time he checked. He understood that making an overseas call from Kashmir wasn't straightforward right now; but placing a call from Kashmir to Punjab wasn't an impossibility! The travel agent couldn't defeat such logic. Asad, at the end of his tether, asked the agent to book the tickets; he would pay for them with his own savings. The agent looked at Asad's father for permission. The father was mortified since his plan seemed to be backfiring. Quietly, the father paid for the return trip to Amritsar. On one condition: Asad would have to travel by plane.

For Asad, this was an absolute nightmare. He was terribly afraid of flying. His heart thumped in his chest every time he did, and he always felt that each flight would be his last. He resorted to travelling by cars or trains whenever he could, even if it quadrupled his travel time. But this time around, he had no choice. His father didn't want to risk a long-winded road trip. It was air or nothing. Asad pictured Haika. He gulped and agreed.

So, it came to be, Asad left for Amritsar. He was happy beyond measure. He was finally going to speak to Haika! The world was beginning to make sense again. No airplane journey could scare that feeling away.

But suddenly, his excitement was tinged with trepidation. Asad wasn't unaware of stories of break-ups because of the abrogation and the breakdown in communication; couples who had been dating for years had drifted apart. Someone he knew had chosen to get engaged to a woman who wasn't his beloved; if the end of the world was close—and it seemed close—it was better to be married than not. Asad wasn't sure if his love stood a chance. The thought kept troubling him before take-off. Would Haika be surprised to hear from him? Would she be aloof? What if something had changed during the hiatus and she didn't love him anymore? What if?

As soon as the plane took off, Asad froze in place. The flight was only an hour long, but every moment was excruciating. Asad's nails dug into the armrests, his eyes were tightly shut throughout. He recited verses from the Quran to calm himself down. He didn't open his eyes even when the flight attendant asked if he wanted water. Not till they hit the tarmac again. That's when his eyes flew open and he scrambled to turn on his phone. All around him, eager Kashmiris followed suit.

This was the moment of truth. He was as excited about getting the internet back as he was afraid of it. Now he'd find out if Haika had thought of him. If she had missed him at all.

But not a single beep emerged from any of the Kashmiris' phones. Were all their mobiles jammed, having been without a signal for so long? They gave each other nervous smiles and waited, hoping that their fate hadn't followed them out of Kashmir. But the signal didn't return even when the plane came to a standstill, nor when the seat belt sign was turned off, nor when they disembarked and were ferried away in the airport bus.

It was only after Asad had collected his luggage that his phone began coming back to life. Suddenly, it started beeping non-stop. A barrage of messages flooded in. TING TING TING TING TING. And it was her. ALL HER.

Asad breathed a sigh of relief.

No one else had messaged him but Haika. Hell, no one else mattered.

Asad had been writing to Haika each day of the lockdown, aware that the messages wouldn't reach her. He wrote for his peace of mind—good morning, good night and everything in between. A month of silence, and his faith had started getting shaken. She still loves me; she loves me not. Over and over and over.

But outside the Amritsar airport, as texts flooded his phone and his heart, he knew that she had missed him equally, if not more. She had messaged him every single day, telling him all that she was thinking, all that she was hoping, all that she was doing. Her messages to him would have displayed a single tick—sent but not delivered—still she went on writing, hoping that Asad would read them all one day.

And here he was.

His own messages rushed off to her in one big wave of warmth and love.

In that moment, a tiny part of Asad felt grateful for being away from her.

'I can't live without you. I can't imagine life without you. You are the most important thing to me.' They must have said these things to each other a thousand times. But during the abrogation, the words had become their reality. They reaffirmed what they felt, they reaffirmed their love.

Asad got into a cab. Shy, as if talking to a middle school crush, he dialled Haika's number. He waited. The call didn't connect. So, he called her roommate, Simran.

Asad and Haika had many people in their lives who had tried to dissuade them from their relationship. Simran was one such person. She was the last person Asad would've called, but he had no other choice. He was yearning for Haika's voice. Simran picked up, her voice cold and cutting. After what seemed like an eternity of pleading, she handed the phone to Haika. He immediately clicked on the 'request video call' button. She accepted. The moment they saw each other, they burst into tears.

Asad tried to keep himself together in front of the cab driver, while also keeping Haika from falling apart. Haika kept saying his name again and again, as if trying to make it sound real. She relished saying out loud the name that she had only whispered over the last month. Hearing Haika say 'Asad' in her voice was bliss.

Asad kept telling her that he was right here. The words poured out effortlessly. 'I came only to see you. For three days, only for you. Just to make sure you're okay. Nothing else matters. I know your exams are coming up, and I knew you wouldn't be able to study without knowing how I was, so I came. Don't worry now. I went to your house, everyone is fine. Your mother misses you. They've all told you not to worry. It'll be okay.'

Haika told Asad that she'd get back to her dorm and call from her own phone. Asad nodded and smiled. He'd already got what he had come for.

Asad plugged in his earphones and started listening to the voice notes Haika had sent him, which were loading one by one. He listened to her voice breaking as she told him about her day. She said that it wasn't easy, she would cry like someone had died. She really knew now that she couldn't live without him, even for a second. 'I didn't know you were so important in my life. Now I know. I'm sorry for taking everything for granted. I'm sorry I didn't believe you that day before the Article.'

Asad started thinking of their journey so far. They'd been together since January 2014. But then had separated for a while because people like Simran had pulled them apart; and because Asad assumed that Haika felt about him the way they did. Asad hadn't heard her out at that point.

If not for that break, they wouldn't have been so close right now. Some things are written, this being one of them. He had apologized and asked her to take him back. In 2016, they had found their way back to each other.

Asad was supposed to stay with a family friend in Amritsar but changed plans to get more privacy. He went to a hotel instead. When his father called via the satellite phone, Asad didn't mention the hotel, knowing that he would get worried.

When Haika got back to the dorm, she called Asad immediately. 'How did you travel?' she enquired. 'By flight. Only for you,' Asad said. Haika was floored knowing what that meant.

Talking to Haika was thrilling. It felt like they were relearning things about one another. Everything seemed like a pleasant surprise. The way she sneezed, the way she stirred her tea furiously, the way she fiddled with her hair—tying and opening it again and again. It was all an education—one he had no problem attending multiple classes of.

Haika didn't go to college for those three days that Asad was in Amritsar. Just so she could talk to him. He told her not to skip her classes, to talk to him only during the breaks, but she refused and kept saying, '*Bas teen din hain. Ab ek saath rehna hai!*' We only have three days, she reiterated, and we need to be together.

They remained connected via phone continuously, devouring each other's voices, filling their eyes, their souls with images of one another. Even when Asad went to his college to get notes as a valid proof of his visit, they didn't cut the call.

'Don't go. Stay another day,' Haika pleaded with him on his last night, afraid that once he would be back in Kashmir, she wouldn't know how or where he was. Asad smiled. 'I want to stay forever.' They stayed up the whole night talking.

At 3 a.m., Haika told Asad to sleep so he could get up in time for his flight. 'Anyway you get scared, I don't want to add to your anxiety.' Asad chuckled. He would rather stay awake now, so he could pass out during the flight and avoid the whole ordeal.

They spoke all through, right till Asad reached the airport and was on the plane. They didn't hang up even when the plane was taking off. Miraculously, it didn't get disconnected. They were both greedy, and Haika blurted out whatever she could within that time. 'I am with you. Take care of yourself. Eat on time. Sleep on time. Don't think that I've run away or abandoned you. Don't jump to conclusions like you always do. I'm here.'

It was almost ten minutes into the flight's ascent—and they got disconnected. Asad immediately drifted off to sleep, his heart and mind full. His flight back was much smoother. He only opened his eyes when he had landed back in Srinagar.

Back in Srinagar, some landline phones had started working. Asad didn't have a landline in his home, but his uncle did. He had pre-emptively given the number to Haika. She had been trying every day, till one day the call connected. The first call on that phone was actually from her.

But there was another hurdle to cross. Haika couldn't make international calls every day as they were too expensive. Asad couldn't call her as calls to Pakistan from Kashmir didn't connect. So, he looked for a friend within India who could help him out. Asiya was studying medicine in Agra. Asad would call her first from his uncle's landline, which would connect only after ten to fifteen tries. Then Asiya would make a WhatsApp call from her roommate's phone to Haika. Asiya would then keep the two phones together on loudspeaker so that they could speak to each other. She'd leave the room to give the lovebirds some privacy. Asad and Haika spoke this way a handful of times, but the calls on the landline were erratic and dropped every five minutes. Besides, there were too many variables to factor in, and too many gadgets to line up. They were denizens of the year 2019. But they had been transported back decades and were relying on complicated trunk calls. Both knew this mode of communication was unsustainable.

So, they moved to Skype, where calls could be made to a phone number via the internet. Haika opened a Skype account. She could now call directly on Asad's landline. But such Skype calls came with limited minutes. One had to buy a pack for Rs 1,000 and only with an Indian bank's card. A thousand minutes for a thousand rupees, valid for one month, no carry-overs. If one ran out of minutes, one couldn't buy more in the same month. This bizarre scheme was unsustainable, too.

What Asad and Haika were going through wasn't the craziest thing that people in Kashmir were doing to communicate. Many couples were taking pictures of the letters they'd written to each other and sharing them via Bluetooth. Others were sharing APK (Android Package Kit) files of phone applications via Bluetooth. These files would let the user install the application on to their phone without having to download it from the internet. Some of these included Bluetooth-enabled messaging apps, where in a stipulated area range, people could message each other. Those lovers who lived close by could enjoy messaging like the old times. But most had to make a commute. Many a boyfriend visited his girlfriend's neighbourhood, and once in the area range, messaged her while standing in the lane right outside her house, hoping she checked her phone and his journey would not prove futile.

As most avenues of communication proved ineffective after a while, Asad was frustrated. '*Waise hi tension kam hain humhe?* As though we don't have enough to worry about already!' Asad whined to Haika.

BY OCTOBER, THINGS BEGAN opening up in Kashmir; people were moving out and about. Asad's friends wanted to meet him after the long lockdown. But he would constantly blow them off to talk to Haika. They grew sceptical. Why did the two need to talk all the time? And why was Haika speaking to Asad and not to her own family? Asad didn't pay any heed to haters. The way he saw it—his choices were different, so people made him suffer.

If asked, Asad would say, 'This is why you slip into depression. Your own family doesn't hear you out. If you come out to them, they dismiss you. Everyone just cares about their own fake reputation. They aren't concerned about you, about what is happening within you. You suffer alone. And then you heal alone—if you can.

'The problem is ... people don't believe you. If you are in a relationship with a girl and you appear to be a girl yourself—even if you assert that you are a boy, people won't believe you. They won't believe what your soul feels like. They don't believe in souls. They may believe in it once someone dies and the soul leaves their body. By then, it is too late.'

'*Ye pyaar roohani hai.* This is the love of souls.'

Why 'roohani', one may ask. And Asad says, 'This is a roohani relationship because I don't know if there's going to be a future to it, if we're going to end up together. Everything we are, we are now.

'I told Haika, I don't know how long we will be able to do this. How long I'll be with you. How long you'll be with me. How long we'll be strong. So, let's spend as much time together as we can *now*. Let's not think about tomorrow. Let's think about this second, this minute, this hour. Let's live here and now.'

Subsequently, as the mobile lines opened, Asad and Haika found more ways to stay connected. The internet was restored to 2G speed by early 2020—too slow for video calls, but they made it work. By the time 4G speed were restored, the pandemic hit the world, plunging everyone into another lockdown of a whole different kind. For Kashmiris like Asad and Haika, this was just a continuation of all that they had endured so far.

'But I'm sure you have imagined some future?' his friends ask Asad.

Asad says, 'In Kashmir, you don't know about the next minute. You go to sleep at night and don't know what's going to happen when you wake up—if you're going to be alive, if you will be able to step out of the house, if you will be able to return. What can I tell you about my future?'

Note: Asad and Haika are no longer together. Asad has started his gender affirmation (or transition) journey.

10

DORAEMON

Fifth August 2019 was going to be a very special day for Mahak. There was a wedding in her family, and mind you, it wasn't just any other ceremony. In a family full of daughters, it was the first time in twelve years that a boy had come of age. Mahak's cousin, one of only three other boys in the family, was getting married. The girl was from Delhi. It was a union of love. The bride's entire family had descended in Srinagar for the nuptials and were in the process of getting used to the culture and customs of the region and, of course, to Kashmiri zārè pār, emphatic Kashmiri hospitality sometimes bordering on good-natured smothering.

Mahak was giddily ecstatic about meeting all her cousins who had landed in town just for this. They were all going to be under the same roof after a very long time.

In her early twenties, Mahak was pursuing a BA in English literature in Kashmir and was in her final year. In a few months, she would be graduating. She had lived in downtown Srinagar her whole life; she wasn't sure if she was ready to leave the nest just yet.

Mahak had known a sheltered school life. Though there weren't many restrictions, she could sense the subtle constraints that came with being a girl. She couldn't walk alone to her tuition class or wait for a bus by herself. It was only in college that she truly came into her own. Mahak made friends she knew would anchor her forever. Chief amongst them was Sehrish. Though they had only known each other for three years, theirs was a friendship made in heaven. A bonus was that if she was with Sehrish, she didn't need to be chaperoned anywhere. Mahak finally knew the freedom that she desired with her friend.

On 4 August, on her cousin's mạ̄nzirāth, Sehrish called Mahak. She was missing her terribly. There was news of something ghastly happening in Kashmir, and she wanted some reassurance. Mahak calmed her down, assuring her that she would call her back. She had to take the mehandī for the bride. Sehrish cut the call, feeling dejected.

Mahak wanted to comfort her friend, but she was in a hurry to follow the Kashmiri tradition of taking the mehandī to the bride's house to be applied on her hands and feet. Mahak slipped the phone into her pocket and urged the rest of the mạ̄nzi-kūr—the mehandī girls—to hurry up.

It was dark outside, and the streets were deserted. They had to drive from the house in Bagh-e-Mehtab to where the bride's family was staying in Hyderpora. There were army vehicles stationed everywhere. An eerie silence surrounded them, and Mahak could sense that the air held panic. Her cousin Farah was driving and Mahak was sitting next to her, clutching the basket of henna in her lap. The car with the men from their family had driven up ahead; their vehicle was now out of sight. A pall of terror descended as the girls reached a secluded bridge.

'Let's just go back,' Mahak told Farah. They were a short distance away from Hyderpora, but with the army everywhere, the distance seemed to widen. If anything happened to them, no one would hear for miles. Farah shook her head. Mahak whispered, 'What if we get raped?' Her cousin gave her a sharp look and then glanced behind to look at the younger girls in the car. With resolve, she hit the gas and zoomed out of there. They reached the venue ten minutes later, their hearts thumping in their chests.

They forgot all about the fear that had gripped them when they saw the gorgeous bride. They sang and danced well into the night. As a group of women beat the tumbakhnạr—an ancient Kashmiri percussion instrument—in jubilance, Mahak didn't hear the calls she had been receiving from Sehrish.

The girls got back home well after midnight. Mahak finally checked her phone and saw twenty missed calls. She immediately felt a pang of guilt. Though she was tired after the exhilarating night she'd had, she decided to send wedding pictures to Sehrish as a peace offering for being incommunicado. But the pictures wouldn't go through. There was no Wi-Fi or phone signal. She frowned. This was odd. She tried again and again. She thought something was wrong with her phone, so she turned it off and back on. But the phone network was unresponsive, as was the Wi-Fi.

Exhausted, Mahak put her phone on charge and went to bed. She would talk to Sehrish in the morning, she promised herself.

On the morning of 5 August, she woke up, planning the day in her head. The phone still wasn't working, but she was unfazed. Maybe the Prime Minister was in town. The authorities often cut off mobile internet connections when he visited. He always left by the end of the day, and the phones would start working again.

She got her shaadi clothes out of the cupboard. While typically Mahak wasn't interested in fancy clothes or shopping, for this wedding she had splurged on her outfits and make-up. She wanted to see herself dressed to the nines.

As Mahak got ready, she could hear her relatives stirring awake upstairs and the guests pouring into the house downstairs. She caught snippets of traditional Kashmiri wedding songs with a few Bollywood numbers. Her mother popped in to hand her a stack of clothes to iron. Mahak got to work.

A little later, Mahak came down with the freshly ironed clothes for her mother, when she noticed something unusual. All the men in the family had huddled in one room where the TV was blaring. They were watching the news together. As she handed her mother the ironed clothes, her mother gave her a tray of kahwè-filled cups. She told her to offer it to those watching TV. Mahak went into the room to serve kahwè; she was alarmed by the solemnity all around.

She didn't glance at the TV immediately or listen to what the news anchor was saying; she was much too shocked by the expressions on the men's faces. Offering a cup of kahwè to her father, Mahak asked what was wrong. He gestured towards the TV. Finally, she looked at it and saw what the others were following. Bold letters screamed the truth: Articles 370 and 35A abrogated in Jammu and Kashmir. The Indian home minister was making a speech in the Parliament. Mahak started shivering. The cups in her tray clattered. Hot kahwè spilled all over her new clothes.

'That day I promised myself that I wouldn't wear fancy dresses anymore,' Mahak said.

As her mother helped her clean up, Mahak felt angry tears rolling down her cheeks. She stared at her dead phone. She thought of the twenty missed calls from the night before from Sehrish. What if she never got to talk to her friend? What if she didn't get to reply to her messages? Why had she called twenty times? What if she never found out why?

In a matter of minutes, life shrank for Mahak. Later, she recalled, 'You could have been talking to your friend, or your beloved, or a cousin you loved so much, or somebody who had just given birth ... and it was all stolen from you. Someone may have said, "I'm going to call you after five minutes," and cut the call. Five minutes later, their phone would have been dead. The feeling in itself is devastating.'

As the news became bigger and spread like wildfire, for Mahak what was most heartbreaking was this—that hardly anyone could make it to her brother's wedding. The people who had managed to come, be it from Ganderbal, Tangmarg or Baramulla, were stuck in Srinagar now, with no way of going back. Srinagar was under total lockdown.

A distraught Mahak told her mother, 'I waited for this wedding for twelve years, it was supposed to be the best!' Her mother didn't have the words to comfort her. It was as though something had shattered in all of them.

Mahak changed out of her wedding clothes and refused to dress up. Call it anger, call it hatred, call it angst, but she was adamant. Her mother pleaded with her to get ready at least for her brother's sake. But Mahak couldn't get herself to do it. Her favourite day had been ruined by *them*.

The family had a low-key and sombre wedding. Of the four hundred people invited, only fifty made it. Some relatives who lived a mere ten minutes away couldn't come due to army barricades blocking the roads. The guests and relatives from the bride's side who had flown in from Delhi were in a state of shock. Never had they experienced anything like this, never had their basic human rights been denied to them, never had it occurred to them that for Kashmiris *this* was the norm. While the gracious hosts did everything they could to make the guests comfortable, many were terrified, and a non-Kashmiri friend of the bride ran away on the day of the nikāh; she caught the first flight out she could find.

Mahak felt no sympathy for her. All she could see was her cousin brother's distressed face. This boy—who had fallen in love with a girl and who had been elated when she had agreed to marry him—had been deprived of his big day. It was unfair. What felt even more unfair was to see him being compelled to maintain a brave front. He smiled at his bride in a bid to ease her anxiety, pressed her hand to soothe her after the nikāh-nama had been read, and stayed strong for both of them.

It was peak wedding season in Kashmir. Mahak thought of all the brides and grooms in the Valley facing the same predicament as her cousin and his wife. Had their bārāts even made it to the brides' houses? Who would tell the brides if the bārāts weren't coming? How long would they wait before they gave up hope and took off their lehengas?

Mahak's family made it through the wedding. But they ended up losing a lot of money. The sheep for the wāzèwān meat had already been sacrificed, so the mutton had to be cooked lest it got spoiled. The wāzè had to be paid for all of that. All that wāzèwān, and no one to eat it. Finally, it was Mahak's idea that they should pack and dispatch the food to the poor.

Mahak's hand automatically tried to make a call to Sehrish to lament about the wedding that had nearly unspooled and the despair and the worry. But she couldn't, of course. If hearts could break over and over, hers did for the millionth time that day.

The in-laws from Delhi were scared for their newlywed daughter's safety, and they reluctantly left after the wedding. The new bride was terrified of her surroundings, suddenly stripped of everything she thought was her prerogative. Now she was cut off from her family as well. The honeymoon was cancelled too.

Over the next few days, Mahak's father and uncle took it upon themselves to drop the guests back home safely. One by one, at any hour of the day or night that felt unthreatening, they ensured each person reached home. Mahak would sit with her tạsibī, counting down the minutes on the rosary beads till her family got back.

Farah lived in Lal Bazaar. She had come for the wedding, but her parents hadn't been able to make it. They didn't know of her whereabouts once communication was blocked. After four days of waiting for things to open up, Farah finally left in her car. Her father was a heart patient, and she needed to get back to avoid adding to his stress. Mahak hugged Farah tight, not knowing when she'd see her next.

Mahak would only know of what had happened to Farah once the lockdown lifted. She discovered that Farah hadn't reached home that day. On her way from Bagh-e-Mehtab to Lal Bazaar, she got stopped by the army in Nowshera. They didn't let her move ahead. She tried changing her route, but finally gave up and stopped at a cousin's house in Nowshera. She waited there three days for things to clear up, and after that she went home. Nervous that someone might snatch the gold she was wearing for the wedding, she left it all at Nowshera with her cousin. She would come back to retrieve it a whole year later.

MAHAK WAS ALL ALONE again. She wanted to talk to Sehrish and vent. What would she tell her? Perhaps this. 'We have a phone, we're giving it fuel by recharging it. We know who we want to call, and who we have no desire to talk to. Yet all our communication is being controlled by industrialists and capitalists and those with vested interests who don't want us to express our love. If this isn't exploitation, tell me what is!'

Sehrish lived in Chanpora, close to Bagh-e-Mehtab, but Mahak didn't know her full address. Over the three years they had known each other, they had only ever met in college or outside, never at home. Over the last few months before she graduated, Mahak had plans of having fun with Sehrish and her other friends, of making memories. 'In Kashmir,' she said, 'we look forward to our college years. We don't get that much freedom in school, like they do outside. So, all we hope for in college is at least to have the liberty to bunk classes, hang out with friends and spend those hours building bonds of love, connection and enjoyment. That's what we get in Kashmir. That's all we are given here.' But like so many experiences, commonplace in the lives of others, this, too, was taken away from Mahak.

Weeks passed, with no signs of the lockdown easing. Mahak could feel her inner world collapsing. Sehrish's birthday was in

August, Mahak's in September. Both came and went in silence. Early on during the lockdown, Mahak had come up with a way of giving herself company. She would turn on the front camera of her signal-less phone and talk to her own image. It would seem like a video call. She would press record and pretend that she was talking to Sehrish. She would ask herself questions that Sehrish would typically ask and then answer them. That's how she imagined wishing Sehrish a happy birthday; that's how she wished herself, too.

One day, Mahak had been talking to herself, and her mother overheard her. *'Tum mein djinn ghus gaya hai kya?'* she asked. 'Have you been possessed?'

'Who else do I have to talk to?' Mahak retorted. 'I'm missing Sehrish.'

Her mother, not sure how to respond, let Mahak be.

Besides talking to herself, Mahak started keeping a journal of her memories from that time. It started one day when she had gone to a doctor. She saw an army man swearing at women and children who were, like her, seeking medical care. When she came back home, Mahak had nobody to share this jarring episode with. So, she started keying in what she recalled while hunched over her laptop. She wished to keep the memory alive. To never forget. 'If this were to happen again,' she told herself, 'these memories will help me survive. If I experience an emotional vacuum, these notes will replenish me.'

Mahak wrote her thoughts down: 'When you kill someone, you silence their life. You erase their identity, you wipe them off the face of earth. But here, in Kashmir, our feelings are getting killed. Poets and writers have done so much to capture feeling ... and in the Valley, nobody can feel. However, we are resilient and strong. Regardless of the crimes committed against us, we will continue to love. It's our only secret potion, the remedy.'

THE ONLY ONE KEEPING Mahak sane during the lockdown was her childhood friend Shazia. Mahak and she had reconnected since their houses shared a common wall. Shazia had a boyfriend, Omar. They had been together for three years. Omar lived only an hour away from Bagh-e-Mehtab. Not too far during regular times, but these were not regular times.

One day, an exuberant Shazia came rushing to Mahak's house. When Mahak opened the door, she screamed in glee. 'I saw him!'

'Who?' Mahak asked.

'Omar, of course!' was the reply.

Mahak looked at her friend with sympathy. Isolation sure had a dire effect on people. Poor thing had started hallucinating. Obviously, Omar couldn't *really* make it to Bagh-e-Mehtab through the barricades and high security. Besides, if any of the local residents caught a random guy standing around, they would get suspicious and chase him away. 'You're imagining things. Like a mirage in the desert,' Mahak smiled, patting her back. Shazia rolled her eyes at her cynical friend. 'I swear I saw him!' she almost shouted. Mahak nervously ushered her inside, afraid that her mother would overhear them, but certain that Shazia had seen a ghost.

Mahak and Shazia went up to her room. They lived in downtown Srinagar, which is a congested and conservative area.

People could easily see what was happening in the next house, so it had been drilled into Mahak that it was improper for a young girl to keep her window open. Tentatively, she unlocked her bedroom window. A tiny crack appeared. Both the girls peeped outside. And sure enough, Omar was there, sitting patiently on his scooter in the side lane.

Shazia immediately started screaming and jumping again. Mahak closed the window shut, paranoid. So, he *was* there. Now what were they to do? Shazia couldn't talk to him from her high tower like Rapunzel. Nor could she roam around with this guy outside. Communicating with him seemed not just impractical but entirely impossible. How were they to arrive at a plan that was quiet and discreet?

'Write something,' Mahak suddenly stated. She got out a notebook and a pen and handed it to Shazia. Shazia stared at the blank page, gulped and looked at Mahak. 'I don't know what to write.' Mahak sighed. 'What do you really want to say to him?' Mahak asked.

'I love you.' Shazia said.

'Then write just that.'

Shazia wrote the three words. 'Should I write my name?' They looked at each other and burst into nervous laughter. No way. What if someone else picked it up?

Mahak folded the note deftly into a paper plane and opened the window wide. The hinges, not having been used in years, creaked loudly. Omar looked up, startled by the noise, and his jaw dropped. Shazia waved at him, a stupid grin plastered on her face. His own face broke into a smile. Mahak threw the airplane at him. He plucked it out of the air with a flourish. He read it, blushing slightly. A neighbour passed by downstairs, and the two girls ducked down. This was too stressful.

Mahak told Shazia to send him another note, telling him to go the graveyard behind their houses. It had a direct view from Shazia's window, and no one roamed around there.

After Omar received his second note, Shazia left Mahak's house and bolted off to her own. Out of breath, she opened her bedroom window. Omar had reached the graveyard. From there, they stared at each other for the good part of an hour. Not exchanging notes, not saying anything, just soaking in each other's presence. Amongst the dozens of people laid to their final rest around them, the two lovers came alive.

Later, Shazia would find out that Omar had been coming over for almost a month. This was the first time he had actually managed to see her.

Mahak was happy for Shazia. That night, she recorded a video on her phone, talking to Sehrish, telling her the whole story.

'I wish you were here to see it.'

SEVERAL WEEKS AFTER THE lockdown, Mahak's uncle's landline phone started working. Mahak could finally call Sehrish!

But she didn't have Sehrish's landline number; she wasn't sure if she even had one. She asked her father to get a new phone directory, but all the shops were closed. The old directories didn't have the number she was looking for.

As it happened, a family friend of theirs—Munni—happened to be visiting Mahak's uncle's house. Mahak's ears perked up when she heard a familiar name in their conversation, Hanief Parra. Something clicked, and she sat up straight, her mind racing. She asked Munni who Hanief was. Her boss, she replied. Mahak asked more questions. Where did he live? Chanpora, came the reply. 'Does he have a daughter named Sehrish?' she asked in nervous excitement. Munni nodded. Mahak sprang up. YES!

Munni promised to get their landline and address for Mahak. Many days passed, and finally, Mahak saw her again. Munni handed her a landline number and a basic address without a house number. That was all that she had been able to get hold of. Mahak was thankful. Something was better than nothing.

Mahak dialled the number on her uncle's landline. It didn't go through. She tried again. And again. But it didn't connect. Maybe Sehrish's phone connection was out of order or maybe the number was wrong. Mahak slumped. Dead end.

Finally, her father, seeing her forlorn expression, offered his services. *'Poora Chanpora chaan maar dunga, beta.* I'll scour all of Chanpora for your friend.'

And he did.

Mahak's father went from door to door in Chanpora. Till at last he found Sehrish's house.

Sehrish would later tell Mahak about all that had transpired that day.

Her father was cooking pāchè—lamb trotters—and the whole house carried its aroma. The main gate bell rang, and Sehrish looked out of the window to see a man she had never glimpsed before, but who looked oddly familiar. Familiar—almost like Doraemon. A distant memory came floating back to Sehrish. Of Mahak laughing and telling her that her father resembled the blue robotic cat from the famous Japanese manga series. 'He's short, chubby and fair.'

It was him.

Sehrish ran down and opened the gate. She hugged her friend's dad tight. Mahak's father was taken aback at being greeted with so much affection by someone he had never met before. He patted her head awkwardly. After a moment, Sehrish shyly pulled away and greeted him.

'How did you recognize me?' he asked.

'Dorae ...' Sehrish bit her tongue. She had seen a picture, she said.

Doraemon nodded, amused. He gave her the landline number of Mahak's uncle. Sehrish gave her correct landline number to him. The one they had received had been wrong.

It was October, two months since the best friends had heard one another's voices. The first call saw tears and laughter. Sehrish and Mahak spoke for over two hours, hogging their respective phones. If someone asked for the phone, they would nudge them aside.

This was important.

Sure, people outside Kashmir would take a simple conversation for granted. But not those in the Valley, not Sehrish and Mahak. They would remember this call forever.

'This is what we take with us after everything is done and dusted. Our GPA may get us a good job, but these memories help us survive life. And already we've been robbed of so many of them,' Mahak told Sehrish.

When the internet revived, Mahak's phone got flooded with texts. The first she saw was from a friend in Delhi. It read, 'I hope you're happy, I hope you're alive.'

Mahak wished to tell everyone who messaged her this. 'We can't control death. That is inevitable. But what is within our reach is love—loving the people we can and showing our love to them. When we aren't given the freedom to profess our love, it is the worst kind of cruelty; a crime against a people. Love is humanity, it is everything, existing beyond borders, beyond language. We have seen curfews and lockdowns—and each of them leads to a curfew on love. Love gets caged. A lock is put on it. And yet—here's the miracle—despite the obstacles that do exist, people continue to love, they don't forget each other.'

Many months later, when Mahak, Sehrish and all their other friends met, Mahak was carrying a diary. A diary to note down all their landline numbers.

Just in case the past repeated itself.

II

BLUE SALWAR KAMEEZ

MADEEHA AND FAIZAN HAD grown up in Baramulla. Born a year apart, Faizan was older and Madeeha younger. Their families were hamsāyè or neighbours, and Madeeha and Faizan were chaddi-buddies literally and otherwise.

Madeeha's mother had passed away when she was little. She was the middle child; she had an elder sister, Shazia, and a brother who was seven years younger, Arif.

But the person Madeeha always felt a special affinity with was Faizan. As they were only a year apart in school, Faizan would remember the subjects Madeeha was having problems with and help her out. They went to the same tuition classes and coaching centres near their houses and didn't know a world in which the other didn't exist.

When Madeeha was in the eleventh grade and Faizan was in the twelfth, a girl started messaging him on Facebook. When he investigated her profile, he could tell it was fake, with pictures downloaded from the internet. He ignored the messages, but after a few days, there were more. She said that she had a crush on him and really wanted to talk. Curious, he messaged back. The girl didn't disclose her real name, but she seemed to know a lot about Faizan. She told him that they went to the same tuition centre, and that she had liked him for a long, long time. If he was interested in dating, she would tell him her real name.

Somehow, Faizan was sure this was Madeeha messaging him to gauge his reaction. A tingle went down his spine; his cheeks coloured.

He told the mystery girl that he was interested, but he wanted to put a face to the messages before going any further. She agreed. Faizan told her to wear blue to the tuition class the next day. With excitement and anticipation bubbling up inside him, Faizan went to sleep. He waited anxiously for school to get over, so that he could dart to the tuition centre afterwards.

Faizan scanned the crowds of people in the small, cramped room of the tuition centre. Girls and boys sat at opposite ends of the space, which made it a little easier for him to find the person he was looking for.

Not one of the girls was wearing the colour. This confirmed his suspicion that it was someone from the eleventh grade, as their tuition class started after his ended. And who was in the eleventh grade but Madeeha, of course! So, after his class got over, Faizan loitered at the tea shop outside to see all the eleventh-grade students trickling in.

Still no sign of blue.

Ten minutes later, Madeeha approached from a distance wearing a turquoise blue salwar kameez. Faizan's jaw dropped. She waved at him nonchalantly before walking into the tuition centre, seemingly unaware of the shock that Faizan was feeling right at that moment.

The mystery girl was Madeeha after all. She always wore shades of black and white, with the occasional grey here and there. For her to wear blue—out of the blue that too—was not a coincidence.

As he reeled with the information, Faizan also felt a strange sense of relief. With a visible spring in his step, he went back home.

And that's when he experienced absolute confusion. Faizan opened Facebook and saw a message from the mystery girl saying that she hadn't made it to the tuition class because of a pesky cold. What was this prank, Madeeha? Feeling angry, Faizan didn't reply to her.

The next day, after his tuition class, Faizan was making his way back home, all the happiness from the day before having evaporated. Madeeha passed him by, now in her regular black outfit. He chose to ignore her, but she waved at him just as she had the day before, with a bright smile that made Faizan's stomach do a backflip. He stared at her retreating figure. He was shocked at her audacity and stirred by her presence all at once.

So, in the evening, with the intention of putting the matter to rest, he went to Madeeha's house to meet her. A boy his age would not be allowed to meet her under normal circumstances, but Faizan was an exception. After Madeeha's father asked after the wellbeing of each and every member of his family, Faizan finally got through to Madeeha. She strolled over to him, confused by his sudden appearance. 'I want to talk to you alone,' he pressed. Madeeha was surprised, but she relented.

Once out of everyone's earshot, she asked him what had happened. Faizan plainly stated, 'Stop teasing me. I'm not into your games. So just stop it.' Madeeha stared at him blankly. 'What do you mean?' she asked.

Faizan faltered, looking at her bewildered face. He explained what he meant—Facebook, the mystery girl, the blue salwar kameez, everything. Madeeha's face gave away that this was all news to her, and Faizan felt deep embarrassment. How could he have accused her?

Madeeha swore on her late mother's memory that it wasn't her, that she had nothing to do with this. 'I don't even have my own cell phone, and you know it. I use Aapa's phone to browse the internet.' She fetched her sister's phone and showed it to Faizan. 'Go through it and check if I have an account or anything else incriminating. Go ahead.'

Faizan was mortified now. He pushed the phone away. He had got the proof he needed and was sure it hadn't been Madeeha after all. But there was still something bothering him. She could see it, too, as he hadn't budged from his spot. 'What is it now?' she asked.

Blushing slightly, eyes staring at something inconspicuous on the ground, he replied, 'Whoever it may be doesn't matter. I want it to be you.'

Madeeha's mouth fell open.

She had always felt a deep connection with Faizan and had even started finding him cute in the last couple of years. But she always got the feeling that Faizan only thought of her as a younger cousin, nothing more.

She was wrong.

Given that her father and siblings were barely a small distance away, she said, 'Look at me.'

Faizan's eyes met hers. Madeeha nodded. They both broke into ridiculous smiles.

She ran back into her house, and Faizan walked back to his, his heart full.

And just like that, they were together, easing into a new relationship. In truth, there wasn't much 'easing' that was needed because their bond was already quite strong. Who the mystery girl was didn't matter anymore. But they were thankful that she had messaged Faizan in the first place. If not for her, they wouldn't have spilled the beans and got together.

AS SOON AS MADEEHA and Faizan started dating, Faizan had to go to Srinagar to appear for his twelfth board exams. While he was there, Kashmir was hit with the deadly floods of 2014.

Faizan was living in Bemina, which was one of the worst-hit areas in Srinagar, with flood waters inundating multi-storeyed houses.

Madeeha, back in Baramulla—a district that hadn't been as badly impacted—was a bundle of nerves. Phones weren't working, and she had no way of getting news of Faizan. If she met anyone near her house who knew Faizan, she'd ask after him, no longer worried if her inquisitiveness appeared odd. But nobody had any information. With each passing day, Madeeha prayed that the water would ebb away, and she could talk again to Faizan. At least she would know that he was okay.

One night, a week into the floods, with no sign of the situation getting better, there was a knock at Madeeha's door. Her family cowered, fear writ large on their faces. Who could be visiting at this late hour? It was either an emergency or the army. Neither prospect was pleasant. Madeeha's father went to check. Soon, Madeeha overheard muffled voices through the wall, but the tone seemed relieved rather than troubled. She inched closer to eavesdrop. She gasped slightly. She could discern the voice she had been longing to hear. It was Faizan at the door!

As her father ushered Faizan into the warmth of the house, he asked the boy how he had reached home. At that time, as rural areas weren't as badly affected by the floods, people from there would bring rice, vegetables, relief and aid to those affected in the city. Faizan said that he had met one such group from Baramulla, and he had hitched a ride back home with them. They had dropped him at the main road, and as getting to his own home involved a steep climb—hard to navigate in the dark—he had come here instead. 'I hope you don't mind,' Faizan said quietly.

'You did the right thing. Imagine if you were wandering so late by yourself. It's not safe,' Madeeha's father declared. As the two approached the hamām, Madeeha ran and took her spot, acting as though she were engrossed in a book. Faizan and her father appeared, and she looked up feigning surprise. 'Faizan, thank God, we were all so worried about you!' she said without blinking. He smiled faintly, nodding his head.

As Madeeha's father went to the kitchen to get the dinner organized for them all, she jumped up and stole a quick hug. Faizan hugged her back, whispering 'I missed you' into her freshly washed hair.

Madeeha was literally dying of happiness while serving Faizan food as they all sat around the dastarkhān on the floor. Madeeha's elder sister, Shazia, who knew of their relationship, looked like she would burst into giggles any moment. Faizan, ever so awkward, was avoiding making eye contact with anyone.

Madeeha's father insisted that Faizan stay the night and leave in the morning. A bed was made for him in the hamām. That night, neither Faizan downstairs nor Madeeha upstairs in her room could sleep a wink.

Even though he was back now, Faizan and Madeeha couldn't talk on the phone as networks were still down due to the flood. They could meet in person, but Madeeha wasn't allowed out of the house without a chaperone. With a third person around, it was hard to talk freely. So, they just set up times to see each other every day. By 'see each other', they literally meant that. Faizan would tell Madeeha to come to her main gate at a designated hour, and he would stand on the other side of the road to look at her. They would stare at each other for a few minutes and then move on before anyone noticed their silent exchange. Everyone was home because of the floods, so they had to be extra careful. This went on for weeks, till the phones started working again.

FAIZAN'S TWELFTH BOARDS EXAMS were delayed till March 2015. He appeared for his medical entrance exams soon after and left to pursue an MBBS in Pakistan. By the time he left, Madeeha was in Jammu for her tuition classes, getting ready for her own twelfth board exams.

As soon as he reached Pakistan, Faizan stumbled into the cruel realization that calls to Kashmir could not be made easily from there. Only BSNL numbers in Kashmir were able to receive calls from Pakistan, and Madeeha did not have one. Thankfully for them, WhatsApp voice calls were still an option—though such calls dropped every few minutes due to erratic networks.

Madeeha passed her twelfth board exams in Baramulla towards the end of 2015, and by 2016 she was in Jammu again, applying to colleges. She went back home for Eid in July, hoping to fill the forms in Kashmir University as well. While she was there, Burhan Wani was killed, and the phone lines stopped working yet again. The college forms that Madeeha wanted to fill out also didn't get released due to the hālāth and the hartāl, the circumstances and the strikes.

Again, Madeeha and Faizan were left without any means of communication. This time it was not because of the weather, but because the government didn't want information about the situation on ground disseminating easily. Given how tense the environment was, Madeeha wasn't allowed to go back to Jammu by her father. Every day at home Madeeha wondered if Faizan would come knocking at her door again. But he was in another country now. The chances were slim.

A month and a half later, only trusty BSNL phone lines opened up. By this time, Kashmiri families had learnt to keep at least one BSNL number working. Madeeha's father had procured one. Mobile internet was still cut off, so WhatsApp calls to Faizan weren't possible.

Zarka, who was Madeeha's friend from the PG accommodation in Jammu, was from Kishtwar. She called on Madeeha's father's number to ask about her. Madeeha quickly saw an opportunity. She asked Zarka to call Faizan and ask after him. Always up for a challenge, Zarka quickly agreed.

The next time Zarka called, Madeeha snuck into another room to talk to her. She didn't want her face to give away her feelings for Faizan. Madeeha was in for a surprise. Zarka was innovative, and not only had she spoken to Faizan, but she had also managed to get him on the call. Zarka had borrowed her roommate's phone and had called Faizan from it on WhatsApp, and had then dialled Madeeha from her own phone. She placed the phones on loudspeaker and yelled, 'Enjoy!' Then she left the room. That's how the two lovers spoke after what felt like an eternity. They were so happy to hear each other's voices.

This convoluted mode of speaking went on for a while. Soon, Zarka left Jammu to come home to Kishtwar. Though there was still internet access there—unlike Baramulla where Madeeha was—Zarka didn't have an extra phone to complete the equation. She could only play the messenger now between Madeeha and Faizan.

While phone networks were slowly restored in Kashmir, mobile internet took its time to come back to life. Kashmiris are nothing if not innovative, and they gathered that if they dialled *325# on the phone, they were able to log into Facebook without internet access. Madeeha gave it a go, and it actually worked. She would check her inbox for messages and send replies quickly. She had to be super speedy because the server for the portal tended to collapse at regular intervals.

She would briskly write to Faizan, 'I love you. I miss you. I'm fine. I hope you are okay.' This was what time permitted. This was the extent of their conversation.

After a long time, the internet was restored properly. Jio SIM cards were introduced, and with their promise of free internet everywhere, those in Kashmir went into a frenzy to buy one. The next two years went pretty smoothly for Madeeha and Faizan, but they couldn't meet much as he only came back home once every year.

IN THE BEGINNING OF 2019, Faizan had come back home for a vacation after a gap of nearly one year. As their families were on good terms, Faizan was almost viewed as Madeeha's cousin. It was something that cracked them up and made them uneasy at the same time. Given the perceived nature of their association, Faizan was allowed to visit Madeeha's home. But because Madeeha's sister knew about their relationship, Faizan would always feel shy to come over.

So, this time, while he was home, Faizan tried to make plans for the two of them to meet outside the house. 'I'll come and pick you up in my car, and we'll go for a drive somewhere. I miss being around you,' he said one night on the phone. Madeeha resisted—he knew she wasn't allowed to go out just like that. 'Why are you pushing your luck? You know it's impossible. You'll get me into trouble.' She was miffed, and he was stung.

What followed was a huge fight. A lot of statements like 'whenever I ask for something, you say no' and 'you don't understand what it's like to be a girl in Kashmir' were thrown around. Faizan and Madeeha stopped speaking for some time; they even refused to exchange niceties in the coming days.

Not long after the star-crossed call, there was an encounter in a neighbouring area, and the internet was cut off. When it revived, it only worked alternate weeks. In one of the off weeks, Madeeha found out that Faizan had left for college. He had been called back early and departed for Pakistan without meeting Madeeha or saying goodbye. Classic stubbornness.

Madeeha was livid. Now without any internet connection, she couldn't even call to yell at Faizan. They had wasted his whole vacation fighting over something mundane.

One week later, as the internet hiccupped to life, Madeeha promised herself that she would not call Faizan or forgive him if he did. 'If he can leave without telling me just because he was nettled, I can be offended too.' She was adamant. Madeeha was sure that given how intractable Faizan was, he wouldn't call either.

No wonder she was surprised to see the phone ringing—his name flashing on the screen—the night the internet revived.

'I'm sorry,' he whispered sheepishly. 'I took it too far.' He apologized for their fight, for leaving without telling her, and generally for wasting so much time before saying all of this. Madeeha's staunch vow evaporated into thin air.

MADEEHA JOINED KASHMIR UNIVERSITY'S satellite campus in Sopore in 2019. She was pursuing law. Both she and Faizan were busy with college now and would speak very little whenever exams were around the corner. He had his exams in June, and Madeeha had hers in July. As soon as his ended, hers began. Madeeha's last exam was on 29 July.

Once it was done, they spoke after what seemed like ages. Faizan told her that he was going on a trip with his college friends for a few days and would have patchy signal. Madeeha, who was falling asleep over the call, was fine with it. 'I'll rest for a few days, and then we'll talk at length once you're back.' With the usual 'I love you', they ended the call.

Madeeha was staying at her hostel in Sopore at the time. Everyone around her started to unwind after the long exam season, but the respite was short-lived. On 3 August, the internet stopped working. Sopore was considered a volatile area, which is why it was possibly one of the first parts of Jammu and Kashmir to have its internet obstructed.

Just before Madeeha found out that the internet was about to collapse, she called Faizan. She couldn't connect. She asked her friends and hostel mates to try calling Faizan's friends. They hoped that at least one call would go through, but none of the boys had any network connectivity on their trip. The girls called a total of 110 times between them, before the internet dropped off. Not one call had connected.

Madeeha was used to this. She knew the internet would be back in a few days. All the girls in the hostel had called home to ask if they ought to come back. But their families had urged them to stay put and not venture out anywhere. On 4 August, the cellular network stopped working as well. Still, the girls had hope. They were in this together. Affectionate calls had been made to all their lovers, devoted promises had been made that this storm would be weathered like all the ones that had come before. But what was to happen was unlike all that they had experienced so far. Articles 370 and 35A would be abrogated the next day, and in the process, the entire Valley would be cut off from the world.

Days passed, and the girls got no news from their homes. The cable network on their communal TV had also stopped working. Pen drives were the new currency, as films and TV shows were exchanged to circumvent boredom. A few computers may have succumbed to viruses on account of this. These computers were labelled martyrs.

Madeeha found herself crying when she was alone, and sometimes even when she was not. She would cry during communal movie screenings and over meals. News of the abrogation had reached the hostel through word of mouth. Someone's boyfriend had braved the curfew to come see his beloved. He had given the whole lowdown on what had happened on 5 August. The collective mood of the hostel sank.

Colleges and schools were shut. The reopening dates after the exams were delayed indefinitely for Madeeha's university. Her father came to pick her up from the hostel. It was now mid-August.

Madeeha was back with her family, but only Faizan was on her mind. Months passed this way without any news. Life for everyone was at a standstill. Madeeha could see those around her getting increasingly anxious. Madeeha herself felt she was fading away; each day seemed to blur into the next.

One early October morning, the doorbell rang. Madeeha's heart leapt up. Could it be ...? She ran to the door and opened it. She was out of breath. It wasn't Faizan.

A postman looked back at her quizzically. Madeeha quickly gathered herself and asked what he wanted. He didn't want anything, he had something to give. He handed her a worn-out letter and turned to leave.

Madeeha had never received a letter in her life. Nor was this one addressed to her. It was addressed to the family. She recognized the sender's name and opened it quickly. It was from Sahil bhai, her rakhi brother. Sahil was a Kashmiri Pandit born in Delhi after his parents had left Kashmir in the 1990s. His father was Madeeha's father's best friend as they had grown up together. Even after all this time, they had kept in touch. They had visited Madeeha's home a few years ago, and she had tied a rakhi on Sahil's wrist. An alien concept only seen on TV serials and commercials, Madeeha had rather enjoyed all of it. Especially getting gifts in return.

Madeeha ran through the letter, eager for some communication from the outside world. Sahil had written the letter in August, and it was reaching her family now in October. He wrote that he was worried about all of them. 'I wish I could visit. I can't imagine how you all are.'

Each member of Madeeha's family pored over the simple one-page letter multiple times. Her father wrote back to Sahil saying that they were alive and well and that his letter had brightened their day. The next morning, when Madeeha's father went to the post office to send the letter, Madeeha tagged along. As she stood in the relatively empty but functional post office, it struck her—she could write a letter to Faizan.

Madeeha was immensely thankful that Sahil bhai had written to them because without that occurrence she wouldn't have had this flash of inspiration. That said, writing a letter was easier said than done. Until now, for Madeeha, letter writing had just been a five-mark question in English examinations. This was the first time she was attempting a letter that wouldn't be graded and that was meant to be informal. Madeeha was sceptical—would she manage to draft anything at all? But it all came to her quite naturally. She wrote pages upon pages, and her envelope was plump when stuffed with the letter. She neatly wrote Faizan's name, address and pin code. She added his hostel room number for good measure. She could not have anyone else but him read her most personal thoughts.

Now came the hard part—posting the letter. How was she to go to the post office without a chaperone and with no knowledge of the number of stamps required or the amount of money needed?

No one else in the family had any regular correspondence to take care of. Madeeha realized that she would have to come up with an ingenious solution to this predicament.

Madeeha's cousin Suhail was pursuing his MBBS in the Philippines. His father—her chachu—was in the Indian army. He was posted in Uri, so he was able to talk to his son and relay some information back to his wife (who was Madeeha's neighbour) in Baramulla. Madeeha knew that her chachi was distraught because she couldn't directly speak to her son. Perceiving an opportunity here, Madeeha paid her aunt a visit with her younger brother Arif. Madeeha explained that the post office was working. 'I think we can write Suhail a letter.' Madeeha's aunt's eyes immediately lit up. She said, 'You write the letter from us, and tell him to write back to us as soon as possible.'

Madeeha finally had the excuse she needed to send her letter to Faizan. Of course, she was concerned about Suhail, too, but her missive to Faizan was *extra* special. Once both letters were sealed, she gave them to Arif. By now, Arif had got to learn of Faizan and Madeeha's relationship. 'You know who this one needs to go to, right?' she asked, pointing to the plump envelope. Arif nodded and traipsed off.

Madeeha's siblings weren't the only ones. Most of Madeeha's family by now knew about Faizan's association with her. Madeeha suspected that her Abuji knew, too, but just didn't comment on it.

Suhail got the letter they had sent, and they got a reply from him after a few weeks. His mother read it with tears plopping on the paper; the ink smudged. No letter arrived from Faizan. Madeeha assumed that he hadn't received her note.

Around mid to late October, mobile phones started working again, though only postpaid numbers, and even they came without internet access. Madeeha didn't have a postpaid number. Even if she did, she couldn't call Pakistan without internet access. After the failed letter-writing attempt, Madeeha didn't see the point in trying anything. She eventually bought a new Jio postpaid SIM card since her prepaid card was defunct (prepaid cards had been terminated in Kashmir post abrogation).

A common friend—Rauf from Kishtwar—was studying in Himachal Pradesh. Madeeha called him from her new number, hoping that Faizan had tried contacting him over these months. Rauf didn't take her call, probably assuming it was a spam caller. Madeeha didn't stop calling. After her tenth try, Rauf's irritated voice was heard at the other end. 'Rauf, it's me, Madeeha.' Rauf gasped. After apologizing profusely, he told Madeeha that yes, Faizan had called many, many times, asking about her, wondering if he had heard anything, and if he could organize a call to a landline number in Baramulla. Madeeha's voice broke while talking to Rauf. She told him what he needed to do. Explaining Zarka's complicated strategy over the preceding years, she urged Rauf to set up a similar call.

The entire day before the call, Madeeha was a bundle of nerves. Downstairs, her sister Shazia's wedding date was getting fixed for the next year, but Madeeha's mind was elsewhere.

She expected a call from Rauf at 7 p.m. Instead, at the designated hour, Madeeha got a call from an unknown number. She answered it and heard Faizan clearing his throat. Her legs almost buckled under her. Rauf had found a proxy through which he could route the call directly to Madeeha's number. He had cut out the middleman.

'Hi, my love,' Faizan said.

The first minute of the call saw both crying copiously. After what seemed like forever, Madeeha reminded Faizan that the call could get cut. 'Just say something, anything,' she told him. Faizan whispered, 'I just missed you so, so much.' The tears would not stop. A lot of sentences were repeated for the duration of the call—'I love you'; 'I'm fine'; 'don't worry'—and much was left unsaid. At some point, Madeeha's father walked in and was horrified to see his daughter's red, blotchy face. 'Dear Lord, what has happened?' he asked, preparing for the worst. Madeeha just shook her head. 'Nothing, I'm talking to Zarka di. I missed her so much.' Though not completely convinced, her father stroked her head and left, wishing to give the two 'girls' some privacy. He was never one to pry.

Madeeha and Faizan spoke this way every other day when Rauf was free to connect them through his proxy.

Mobile internet with 2G speeds restarted by January 2020, but access was allowed to only a list of 'whitelisted' websites by the government.[32] Kashmiris weren't allowed to open several social media sites and applications, besides a lot of news and media portals. Madeeha and Faizan found a way around this, too, by relying on a virtual private network (VPN) to bypass these restrictions. APK files of VPNs were being circulated in Kashmir for the same reason. Soon, Madeeha and Faizan were speaking via lagging WhatsApp calls.

AS THE YEAR CREPT forward, broadband and Wi-Fi got restored, and there was freer access to websites, though mobile internet speeds remained at 2G. Faizan was supposed to come home in

March 2020. That's when the pandemic struck. Faizan was stuck in Pakistan. Madeeha couldn't believe their luck.

In the midst of a world health crisis, many people were still going ahead with weddings, albeit austere ones. Madeeha's sister Shazia's wedding had been fixed for mid-June. Given that larger weddings had become Covid-19 hotspots, it was decided that Shazia's wedding would be a small, intimate affair.

It was around this time that Madeeha and Faizan found themselves (again) in the middle of an argument. The bone of contention was his date of return. Madeeha had heard of people flying back from sundry nations, and she couldn't understand why Faizan was unable to. Before he could explain his side of the story, they found themselves deep in the throes of a disagreement. Faizan had ego issues, and Madeeha had anger issues.

Madeeha let the whole argument slide. She was in no mood to pursue it. Shazia's wedding was around the corner, and Madeeha was very, very busy. Without a mother to look into the finer details, she found herself responsible for much of the wedding organization. Worse, due to Covid-19, there were fewer hands than ever to help.

Zarka was staying with Madeeha, helping out. One evening, she stepped into the hamām where Madeeha was organizing the majmè—copper plates heaped with goodies to be sent to the groom's house. She told her that some girl had come to see her. Madeeha frowned and asked who it was. Zarka shrugged and said she didn't recognize the person. Madeeha wasn't in touch with anyone who would show up unannounced in the dark. As she got up to go outside, Zarka's mouth quivered. 'Is that what you'll go out in? Do you want to change?' she asked.

Madeeha looked at herself in the mirror after what seemed like ages. She was wearing pyjamas with a dirty kurta. Her hair was unkempt, and she looked visibly overworked and tense. Just that day her sister had chided her, 'Why aren't you in any of the wedding pictures?' Madeeha had replied, 'I'm in no state.'

She really wasn't in any state at this point either. Ignoring Zarka's slightly shocked expression, she put on the first pair of shoes she could find—her father's bathroom slippers—and went out to meet this mystery girl. She checked her phone to see if there had been any new messages from Faizan. They had spoken last five to six days ago; she had lost count of time ever since the wedding preparations had begun. Faizan had told her that he was going on a trip with his friends. 'Take care. Don't roam around so much during the pandemic,' Madeeha had told him. Faizan had reassured her, 'Don't worry, I'll take care of myself. You concentrate on the wedding. Eat extra tabakh māz on my behalf.' Madeeha had smiled. They hadn't spoken since then.

There were no new messages from him. She felt the glow of the lights on her face. Madeeha looked up at the house sparkling with streams of zūl, those festive wedding lights that looked like sunlit weeping willows. She smiled, taking in the twinkling zūl, savouring these moments of respite from work. Madeeha slipped the phone back into her pocket and opened the front gate.

She stepped out into the dark lane illuminated by a solitary municipality lamp. There was no one around. And then she saw it—a maroon Maruti Swift parked across the road. She could recognize it anywhere. She immediately started screaming with joy. It was Faizan's car. He poked his head out of the window and gave her a wide grin. He gestured to her—shush!— and signalled that she come over. Zarka ran out because of the ruckus Madeeha was creating and covered her mouth. 'You'll get us all caught.'

Zarka was obviously in on Faizan's plan. A gleeful Madeeha nodded to show that she was calm, and Zarka uncovered her mouth. 'How did this happen?' Madeeha managed to ask. Zarka winked and said, 'We have our ways. Now go, I'll cover for you.'

A stark realization hit Madeeha. She looked down. She suddenly wished she were wearing her own slippers or a nicer dupatta. 'Why didn't you tell me to change?' she hissed. Zarka grunted, 'I did!'

Now there was nothing to be done. Zarka smuggled Madeeha into Faizan's car. As soon as she was out of eyeshot, Madeeha started jumping up and down in her seat. She hugged Faizan tightly. 'What about your trip?' she asked. 'I was at the Covid-19 quarantine centre,' he whispered. She looked at him shocked. 'Surprise!' he smiled, starting his car.

They zoomed off. They drove around the neighbourhood for fifteen minutes, but it seemed like forever. Madeeha would break into giggles every thirty seconds. 'You're here. I'm seeing you again!' She kept poking him to check if he was real. After they had travelled through every lane imaginable in the neighbourhood, and just before anyone could get suspicious, Faizan dropped Madeeha back home. With the promise of meeting every single day that Faizan was here, Madeeha got out of the car. As she walked towards the gate, all the thoughts that had been haunting her mind for almost a year came back. They had been through a lot together—all while being so far apart. She had been shaken.

Yet they had survived.

Madeeha's friends would often question Faizan's loyalty. 'How do you know that he doesn't have someone else there? You guys are so far and haven't met for so long.' Faizan was asked similar questions. People would come up to him and say that they'd seen Madeeha with another guy in a restaurant. Neither of them believed these 'fire-starters'. Madeeha would reply, 'I know who he is and what we mean to each other. I know how much he loves me and how much I love him. That's it.'

They had survived.

There had been innumerable gaps in their relationship over the years. The distance, the erratic communication breakdowns, the anxious waiting. It had been difficult. Madeeha's blood pressure would drop inexplicably, and she had been hospitalized a few times due to the stress. She had been depressed. She needed someone. Not just anyone—she needed Faizan. He was her closest friend since childhood, and she longed for him in those dire times.

They had survived.

When Madeeha was certain there would be a war in Kashmir, and everything would be over soon, she wasn't sure if she would see Faizan again. She'd tell those closest to her, 'The terrible state when you don't know where someone is, what is happening to them, how they are ... to constantly live in fear of that ... it is torture.' She would pray every night, 'Even if I am to die, I just want to see Faizan once and talk to him one last time. After that, I will accept my fate. I just don't want to die like this. Please God. Please. Let me see Faizan.'

They had survived.

'Someone from outside Kashmir—if they had to live here for even a little while the way we do, they would go insane,' Madeeha recounted. She didn't even let her younger brother leave the house after the evening azān or bāng. Those times when she didn't know where Faizan was, she had no one but herself to comfort her. That was a fate she didn't wish for anyone at all.

They had survived.

Madeeha reached her gate and turned the handle gingerly. The gate creaked open. She looked around and saw that Faizan's car was still there. He was watching her from his rolled down window.

She smiled.

He smiled.

They had survived.

Note: Madeeha and Faizan are now engaged to be married.

12

FIGHT OR FLIGHT

BATUL WAS A FLIGHT attendant with Saudi Airlines. Her family, originally from Lolab, Kupwara, in North Kashmir, had moved to Srinagar when she was a child. Batul shifted to Riyadh once she started working.

An ardent traveller, Batul's work took her to a number of new places. One day she was in Turkey, another in Paris. Whenever Batul had time off work, she would make it a point to visit Kashmir to spend a few days with her family, before going off on a vacation. She had more reasons to visit now that her elder brother had daughters; she adored them beyond measure.

IT WAS THE END of July 2019. Batul had been back home in Srinagar for fifteen days. Soon, she'd be flying back to Riyadh.

That's when news started coming in of tourists leaving the Valley. There was panic, and Batul didn't want to leave her parents' side. However, her flight to Riyadh connecting through Delhi had already been booked for 4 August. With trepidation, she left her family, promising her mother that she would call as soon as she landed and before her next flight.

For years, Batul had had a ritual of calling her mother before and after every flight. She had never missed it all these years. But this time around, her connecting flight to Riyadh was way past midnight. Not wishing to interrupt her mother's sleep, she didn't call when she boarded the plane in Delhi.

'I'll call her when I land,' she promised herself.

By the time she arrived home in Riyadh, it was 5 August. Batul dialled her mother's number, but the call wouldn't go through. She tried every number that she could think of in Kashmir—family, friends, acquaintances—but all calls dropped.

Batul caught the news, and the reason for the communication breakdown became clear. Article 370 had been abrogated. All phone lines had been suspended in Kashmir; the internet was also dead. All alone in a country far away from home, Batul felt the universe closing in on her. 'Why didn't I call her before I took off?' she chastised herself.

Over the next couple of days, unable to contact her family, Batul's health started deteriorating. She couldn't articulate what she was feeling to the people around her. When a colleague started discussing her own parents at one point, Batul fainted out of sheer stress and exhaustion. She was admitted to a hospital for eight days. When she was discharged, there still seemed no way to reach her family back home.

Batul started seeking out people online in the same position as her—Kashmiris abroad who had been trying to make contact with the Valley. She found a Facebook group named 'Kashmiris in Saudi'. The members there would release information coming in from the Valley, console one another and look out for Kashmiris living abroad. Batul kept posting messages about her parents' locality in the forum, hoping that members would reply to her or perhaps take a message—if they happened to be travelling—to her parents.

One group member was, in fact, travelling. His name was Farhan. Batul called him and gave him her parents' address. He said he had a BSNL VIP satellite number that would work in Kashmir. The plan was that Farhan would go to her family's house and call Batul from there, so that she could speak to her parents. Batul didn't know if trusting a stranger she had met over the internet was advisable, but this was all she had.

By the time Farhan reached Kashmir, it was September. It had been a month since Batul had heard her parents' voices. She waited for Farhan to call her. But he didn't. Her faith turned shaky.

Ten days passed. Farhan was now in Delhi. That's when he called Batul to tell her what had happened. As soon as he had landed in Kashmir, outgoing calls from his satellite phone got barred. Only incoming calls worked. He had gone all the way to Batul's house but had been unable to call her. The whole situation felt cruel and alienating.

Batul had come so close to hearing her parents' voices, yet she remained so far from the possibility of actually hearing them speak. She tried to gather whatever little news she could through this stranger who had met her parents. 'I wish you had taken a picture of them,' she said sadly.

In the days to come. Batul continued to repeatedly dial her parents' numbers, fully aware that the call wouldn't connect. The service provider saying that 'the number is out of coverage area' felt as familiar to her as a caller tune. Batul would imagine that this was, in fact, the caller tune her parents had installed for their numbers rather than it being a service message; that at any moment they would answer and greet her with affection. They'd tell her that it was all a big fat joke.

Little did she know that this would become her most vivid memory of that agonizing period.

BATUL CONTINUED HER SEARCH for good Samaritans. Along the way, she found the number of a policeman in Srinagar who had a satellite phone. She called him repeatedly until he finally answered her call. He lived near her parents' house and agreed to visit them at a designated date and time.

However, on the scheduled day, due to a sudden work commitment, he couldn't travel and sent his PSOs (personal security officers) instead to her family's house with a phone. His guards encountered the same problem that Farhan had. The policeman's personal satellite phone had outgoing call facility but not the official satellite phone he had given to his PSOs. An oversight on his behalf. Batul waited and waited, but no call came through.

Some landline phones slowly started working in Kashmir, but Batul's family didn't have a connection.

Seventh September was Batul's birthday. With no hope of making contact with her family, she decided she needed to do something to clear her head. She decided to go to Dubai all alone to spend her birthday there.

Batul was on the subway in Dubai when her phone started ringing. It was an unknown number, so Batul didn't bother answering the call. The caller persisted, and finally, Batul answered. She heard a Kashmiri accent. Her heart leapt. Then the call fell through. She tried calling back, but the line was busy. Holding her breath, she decided to wait for the person to call her back. But no call came through. She shook her head in disbelief.

After half an hour, when she got off the subway, the phone rang again. Batul answered at once.

'Batul, *myōn zuv*?' It was her mother's voice. 'My life, my love?'

Batul got goosebumps immediately. Her mother was calling to wish her happy birthday. She broke down.

In Kashmir, after the abrogation, phone booths had been set up at different places—police stations, hospitals, schools. People would line up each day to talk to their loved ones outside the Valley. They would wait for five or six hours and get sixty seconds to convey their message. How were they supposed to enunciate all that they had been thinking and feeling in sixty seconds? How were they to articulate episodes from the past after standing in the heat and knowing absolute exhaustion? What if their call didn't go through? Would they be given special treatment the next day? Or would they go back to standing at the end of a long queue?

If they were fortunate, and the call did happen, it would end before it began.

Batul's mother was calling from one such phone booth centre in Lal Chowk—the busy marketplace in the heart of Srinagar; home to the famous Ghanta Ghar or clock tower, from which the Indian flag would be hoisted without fail each Indian Independence Day, the army guarding it from all sides.

For several days now, Batul's mother had been going to this centre to speak to her daughter, but she had failed to get hold of the phone. The centre would shut before she could reach the front of the line. Today of all days, on her daughter's birthday, her chance had finally come! After waiting for eight hours, she got one minute to wish her daughter. She told Batul that everything was okay and that there was no cause for worry. Before Batul could ask her for any neighbour's landline number that could be working, the line got cut. Sixty seconds done.

Sixty seconds, which can seem excruciating if you want them to come to an end, had gone by in a blink of an eye for Batul who was hanging on to every second.

Batul continued pressing the phone to her ear after the call ended, listening for delayed traces of her mother's voice. Nothing came through.

Her mother had wished her on her birthday. There was something so poetic about it. Perhaps it was poetic justice—though nothing about the whole situation felt 'just'.

There, in a country that was not her own, Batul sat down and wept.

BACK IN KASHMIR, BATUL'S mother was as innovative as her daughter. She sought out a doctor who lived near their house. He would get internet access in his government hospital from time to time. The Wi-Fi connection in hospitals had been kept functional for medical emergencies but was slower than a dial-up broadband connection from the 1990s. Even though she barely knew him, Batul's mother went to the doctor's house and recorded a voice message for her daughter on his phone. He promised her that when he got access to the internet, he would send the message across to Batul.

A few days later, the stars aligned, and he was able to send the recording over WhatsApp to Batul. Batul was on a flight and only heard it once she landed. He had also asked her to send him a voice message in return that he could relay to her mother. She did.

By the time Batul sent her recording, the doctor was back home from hospital duty. As a result, the message remained undelivered. Batul waited for the single tick to turn into a double tick, for the double tick to turn blue. But for days, it didn't.

The doctor's number disappeared off WhatsApp altogether. There were rumours that people who had been relaying messages or using the hospital internet for reasons other than medical emergencies were getting caught. Batul was never able to contact the doctor again nor did she receive any more voice messages from him.

The message he had sent—Batul would listen to it on loop as though it were a song she loved. She hung on to her mother's sweet voice telling her not to worry, that her father was well, that her little nieces were getting bored at home. She laughed and cried at the same time, something she didn't think was possible.

Meanwhile, Batul's father wasn't far behind in his own innovation. During the lockdown following 5 August, since no one had anything to do or anywhere to go, Kashmiri men would pass time and try keeping human connection alive by taking on mundane tasks—purchasing bread from the kāndur, buying milk, going to the mosque or getting the occasional haircut, whether or not it was required. Batul's father was no different. One day, at the mosque, he heard that a neighbour's son would be travelling to Bangalore soon. He gave him Batul's number. By end September, the son contacted Batul. He told her that her father's message was simple—do not worry. He added that her father was concerned for her wellbeing and that everyone was fine.

'We are all fine'. 'Don't worry'. The simplest of words, and her parents kept reiterating them to *her* as they went through the most difficult of times themselves. She wanted to comfort them, but it seemed like they were the ones comforting her all the time. Maybe they felt that since they were all in it together, at least they had each other for reassurance. She was all alone in Saudi Arabia.

A few months after the abrogation, Batul's father called her. Someone's home landline happened to be working, and he had found out. It was a bit far from where they lived, but he made the journey on foot. When he reached, he discovered that while the landline was working, it didn't have international calling facility.

As they say, necessity is the mother of invention. Across Kashmir—and Batul's father was aware of this—people had adopted a special way of calling those abroad if their phones didn't have international calling facility or ISD. A local call would be made to someone in India who had an ISD facility. That person would then call the international number and initiate a conference call. The mediator would have to give up the use of his/her phone for the duration of the call.

This was how Batul heard her father's voice after whole months. She could tell from his voice that he was conscious about talking to her from a stranger's house. He was very aware of his surroundings and the people listening, so he didn't reveal very much about the family and stuck to niceties. He had always been shy—which Batul found very endearing—and now, doubly so. He kept the call brief. Besides, there were others in queue after him, waiting to call their loved ones. It would be wrong to prolong the conversation. He ended the call by telling Batul not to spend too much time on social media, that it would only mess with her head and heart. She chuckled to herself. Some things would never change. After telling him to get her nieces along next time, so she could hear from them, she cut the call.

Weeks went by. She didn't get another call from that number.

DURING THIS TIME OF estrangement, Batul came to learn of the kindness of strangers.

One day, through the Facebook group Batul frequented, a Kashmiri man named Aamir from Delhi contacted her. His cousin Sarib was going to Kashmir, and he had a BSNL satellite phone. Aamir himself was trying to get in touch with his wife and son, and Sarib was helping him out. Sarib agreed to go to Batul's house too and arrange a call.

It felt like the past was repeating itself. Batul didn't expect much of the visit. She did tell Sarib though to make sure that outgoing call facility was activated on his phone number.

A few days later, Batul was completing her nẹmāz in the evening. She had just offered her duā when the phone rang. She picked it up, and it was her seven-year-old niece. '*Hello puphi, kaisi ho?* How are you?'

Batul started crying. This time around, there were no restrictions because there was no one else waiting in queue. Batul was speaking to her brother, his wife and her nieces after months. When she asked about her parents, her brother told her that they had gone to their ancestral home in Lolab. Batul missed speaking to them. But after hearing the chatter of her nieces, her heart was full.

Batul managed to remain in touch with her family off and on. But the constant fear that they'd get taken away from her again used to haunt her. 'What if the landlines get cut? What if the satellite phones are disconnected? What if, what if, what ...' These thoughts ran through her head.

Though she didn't communicate her fears during her calls with her family, her panic coloured her waking life. Batul wasn't keeping well physically and mentally. Her blood pressure kept dipping. Though the airlines' doctor said she didn't have any major ailment, she wasn't 'fit to fly' with a distracted mind and waning energy. He told Batul that if this became a recurrent occurrence, she would be barred from flying till she got better.

Batul's colleagues, aware of her deteriorating condition, kept constant tabs on her. There was an Egyptian flight attendant Batul was friends with on Facebook, but they had never really met. After reading Batul's anxious posts online, she reached out to her. She wanted to give Batul something personally. Batul was sceptical as she had never met this flight attendant before; in any case, she was wary of discussing things to do with Kashmir with those she didn't know. Under normal circumstances, Batul may have refused the flight attendant's request. But times were not normal, and Batul was lonely and miserable. She let her visit.

Since the Egyptian was adept at making Buddhist mandalas, Batul assumed that the wrapped package she was given contained just that. Instead, she discovered that it held a painted portrait of Batul in her flight attendant's uniform. It carried the words 'stay strong'. The very thing Batul needed to carry out her work duties at the moment.

It was a remarkable act of generosity by a stranger from a faraway country. It touched Batul all the more because colleagues closer from home, from mainland India, hadn't checked on her even once. There could be many reasons for this, Batul deduced—that they felt guilty, or that they believed that what was happening in Kashmir was just, or that they simply felt uncomfortable discussing politics with a Kashmiri. Whatever it was, after the radio silence from these people she considered her friends, the startling warmth of an Egyptian she barely knew overwhelmed her.

Another kindly stranger came in the form of a cab driver. In Riyadh, flight attendants with Saudi Airlines got personal cars from the company to take them to and from the airport. Somehow, most of the drivers were Pakistani. One such Pakistani driver was driving Batul to the airport, when he asked where she was from. When she said Kashmir, he looked at her intently in the rear-view mirror. He paused, then said, '*Sab theek ho jayega*. Everything will be okay.' Batul was startled that he was following the news so closely. The driver asked Batul how many family members she had. Batul hesitated—she didn't want to reveal very much—but finally told him the truth. His response once again startled her. He told her that he was a Pathan from Peshawar, and that he had a big house there. 'You should get your whole family there, there's enough room for everybody!' Batul thought the sentiment was sweet. But she said, '*Ghar ghar hota hai. Ghar chodna gaddari hoti hai.*' Our home is our forever home, and leaving it is an act of betrayal—she stood by these words.

A few days later, the driver got home-cooked food for Batul—a token of comfort for someone far from home.

Adding to these small bits of goodwill—once, on one of her flights, the man who managed the catering came up to her to talk. He was Sri Lankan and knew that she was Kashmiri.

Before this, the only interaction they had had was when he handed her the catering papers. Now, he asked if everything was okay at home. He knew a little bit of Hindi and conversed with her in the language. Much like the Pakistani driver, he, too, told her that he had a big house in Sri Lanka where her family could come stay if things got bad.

Batul wondered what all these men were doing in alien countries, so far from home, while their big houses stayed desolate. Maybe they weren't sure when they would return, so they offered their homes to others.

Batul remembered that she wasn't unlike the people she met. She was away from home, too. 'Houses shouldn't be empty; families should be together.' The thought stayed with her.

BATUL WOULD LOOK OUT of the window at night and watch the moon for hours, knowing that her mother could see the same moon in Kashmir. Something so massive—a white orb in the sky—made her feel insignificant yet deeply connected with another person. It also made Batul's problems seem less complicated. She would wait for the full moon more fervently than ever before.

A few years' prior, her parents had come to Saudi Arabia to complete their umrah. To meet them, she had to submit their identification verification slips to her airline company. She still had their passport-sized pictures from those documents. Now, she would keep those pictures in a transparent pouch in her wallet at all times—her personal guardian angels. Batul developed a habit of looking at them during her flights when all the passengers were snoozing.

Batul used to journal a lot as a kid, but those diaries had been lost in the floods that engulfed Kashmir in 2014. After the abrogation, she took to journaling again. This time around, Batul started writing to a particular person each day—to her parents, her brother, her nieces or a close friend who lived in Kupwara.

Batul's father was adept at Urdu. She started honing her Urdu skills to compensate for his absence. She practised the language by watching YouTube videos of Pakistani women. She googled new words to add to her vocabulary. She found Urdu websites like Rekhta so she could sharpen her language skills.

All of this, so she could write a letter to her father to impress him. He had always wanted her to practice her Urdu grammar, and now she wanted to show him that she cared about what he cared for.

Batul finished writing the letter and posted it. But it was returned to her due to some internal issues. Batul promised herself that whenever she'd meet her father next, she would hand it over to him in person.

By October, more people in Kashmir had reactivated their landlines. Landlines had been forgotten for years because of the advent of mobile phones, but now they were popular and relevant once again. Batul got a call around this time from the landline of a deputy superintendent of police (DSP) who lived in her neighbourhood. The familiar 0194 area code flashed on her phone screen and Batul knew it was a call from home! Finally, there was a connection a few minutes away by foot from her family's home. Her parents and nieces and their parents could come there to talk to her. At long last, Batul felt like she was home with all of them around her.

When Batul was hesitant to overstep, the DSP uncle was warm. 'Think of this as your own home, beta. Call whenever you want.' From that day, Batul was able to communicate routinely with her family. The DSP's house became the heart of all conversations. Sometimes, she would leave messages for her family, and the DSP's kin would send it across.

Batul's health started improving. She didn't make it to the dreaded 'not fit to fly' list after all. The doctor was happy with her progress.

The communication restrictions started lifting in Kashmir slowly. Batul was able to go home to see her family. The weight that had been constricting her chest for months lifted. She could *see* her parents, her brother, her nieces—they were real people. She could touch them, hold them, be held by them.

Batul was finally at peace.

She went and thanked the DSP's family—she had never met them before—for all that they had done for her. She could give faces to the voices that had been speaking to her for weeks. The families, in turn, had become close thanks to the landline. So much so, if fish was being prepared in one house, it *had* to be sent to the other. This was especially true if a delicacy like họkhè gāḍè or họ-gāḍ was being prepared. The sheer effort of drying the fish made sharing the joy a necessity.

If there's one thing Batul learnt from those excruciating months, it's this—connections can be formed in the strangest of places. No amount of darkness can truly kill the will to reach out to another person.

Now, only one matter remains. Batul is yet to give the Urdu letter to her father. She doesn't think it's quite ready.

It may never be ready, Batul admits. 'There is so much more I wish to say.'

13

FORTY-FOUR DAYS

'IT'S BEEN REALLY HARD for all the people who love each other. Not just the couples. Parents and children, too. Anyone who has ever loved anyone. Only the ones who go through it realize it. For the rest of the world—it's something that just *happened*.'

Saniya got engaged on 21 June 2019. An orthodontist from Srinagar, her fiancé Mehraan was from Bangalore and worked in the IT sector. The rishta had come through close family friends in Bangalore. It was an arranged marriage, and Saniya had met Mehraan only once briefly before the engagement.

In traditional Kashmiri culture, since the bride and groom couldn't visit each other's houses before marriage, engagements often happened either in the bride's house with the groom's family (but without the groom present) or in an event hall or hotel with both the bride and groom present. Mehraan's family chose the former option. They had come down to Srinagar for the ceremony without him. The engagement happened remotely. The bride- and groom-to-be remained in separate states, one in the north, the other in the south.

Saniya and Mehraan only started speaking properly on the phone from the time of their engagement. If they were to count the time they had for uninterrupted talking up to the moment the phone lines got cut on 4 August, it would amount to forty-four days. Forty-four days of courtship. Enough to form a connection, but not enough to weather the mental storm that was to come.

All day on 4 August, Saniya had been hearing rumours that something big was around the corner in Kashmir. She called Mehraan to tell him, but he didn't answer. She left him a message to call her back. She alerted him at night again, 'The phones and internet here are going to get disconnected soon.' The message went through. But before Mehraan could call her, Saniya's phone lost signal. It was 11.30 p.m. and one by one, the network dropped across all her family members' phones. Saniya hadn't been able to tell her fiancé of forty-four days not to worry, that she would be in touch soon. Hopefully.

Bangalore, where Mehraan lived, was miles away from Kashmir, but the distance wasn't what bothered Saniya. What concerned her was that Mehraan probably had never closely known anyone from Kashmir before, and now he was engaged to a Kashmiri. He hadn't experienced lockdowns and curfews—experiences that were common in Saniya's world. She started imagining the way he perceived the situation he was in—engaged to someone and then suddenly confronting a void; knowing nothing about their whereabouts or their wellbeing.

Saniya's brother, Sabeel, lived in Bangalore, too. Like many Kashmiris away from home, he had no way of contacting his family. He assumed that in a few days, things would ease up, and the phones and internet would start working again. When Mehraan called him to ask after Saniya, Sabeel could see that what he perceived as normal was most disconcerting for Mehraan. Sensing the growing panic in Mehraan's voice, he told him, 'Wait for a few days, it will be fine. It always is.'

A few days passed and nothing changed. Mehraan tried contacting Saniya day and night, but the calls wouldn't go through.

Saniya, on her part, sensed pangs of withdrawal. She felt disconnected from Mehraan and from the world at large. She was constantly restless, tired and uneasy. She could hear the helicopters flying over the house at night and army jeeps zipping through the roads during the day. That agonized her even more.

Bạḍ Īd came, but the family didn't go out of the house to meet anyone. After all, there was a curfew. Saniya couldn't even meet her sister, Baseera, who lived at a walking distance from her. There was a BSF camp where Baseera lived, so they had cordoned that whole area off for non-resident civilians. This would remain the story for at least two more months. Saniya's father had locked their own front gate. Usually anyone from the neighbourhood could come in for a salām or a cup of nun-chai. Not anymore.

EIGHTEEN TO TWENTY DAYS after the abrogation was announced, there was no sign of the lockdown easing up. This, despite the fact that Saniya and her family lived in the Nishat area of Srinagar, which was relatively peaceful.

Saniya's cousins teased her, 'Mehraan must be cursing his luck. His bride has disappeared into thin air.' Saniya didn't find any of this funny. In fact, their comments stirred something deep within her. They were right. Mehraan must think she had disappeared for good. Saniya had no idea how long this would go on for. Was it fair to make him wait? She wasn't even sure what he knew of the politics of Kashmir, what his own politics were. They hadn't discussed such matters yet. Saniya felt weighed down by the unknown.

After almost three weeks of no contact, Saniya decided to take matters into her own hands. She had heard that there was a working phone in the Nishat police station. She was going to make a phone call to Mehraan.

Now, visiting a police station was not the norm in Kashmir. In a place where locals didn't trust the Indian paramilitary forces, the Jammu and Kashmir Police was often seen as being complicit. So, inhabitants of the Valley would hesitate before venturing in. In the current political climate, they'd be even more cautious; who knew what kind of surveillance would be in place?

For Saniya, these concerns receded due to her need to communicate. She was taking a big step, and she knew it. She wasn't allowed out of her house alone, so her cousin Abid accompanied her. They started on foot to the police station. There were barricades and concertina wire fences guarding the police station that was all the way up on a hill. The guard patrolling down below at the entrance didn't allow them up. He gave no particular reason. It seemed like much depended on his mood. Not wanting to argue, Saniya returned home. But she was not going to give up so easily.

She made another trip to the police station with her cousin after a few days. This time, the guard let them through. Saniya and Abid hiked up the hill and reached the station. They were panting, but the hardest part was yet to come—convincing the policemen that they wished to make a phone call. Saniya was almost sure the policemen wouldn't help her. If they let *her* make a phone call, a line of other civilians would follow. Had she been married to Mehraan, they may still have made an exception for her. A wife could have something urgent to communicate to her husband. But a fiancée? What did she have to say that was so earth-shattering after all?

Saniya couldn't get herself to lie about her relationship with Mehraan and call him her spouse.

Along with Abid, she was sent to the station house officer (SHO). There, the two placed a request for a phone call. The SHO asked Saniya the dreaded question, 'Who do you want to talk to?' Terrified of rejection yet cornered, she stuttered, 'My fiancé.'

During the abrogation, the Jammu and Kashmir Police had been ordered by the higher authorities to deposit all their weapons; they had no access to them any longer.[33] Downgraded to being sidekicks of the army, policemen were now no longer trusted by the Centre, nor were they fully trusted by the locals.

Saniya knew that, given the situation, they had no reason to be especially nice to her. She couldn't tell what the policeman thought of her confession.

Much to her surprise, he let her make the phone call. 'It's not allowed really. But for one minute, I will let you.' He gave Saniya his satellite phone.

Saniya felt knots in her stomach immediately. She had put in so much thought into the eventuality of this not happening that suddenly, when it did happen, she was at a loss for words. She had sixty seconds to talk to Mehraan. Sixty seconds to communicate whatever she could. Sixty seconds to speak of all the uncertainty she had been feeling. And all under the watchful gaze of the SHO, and with her cousin within earshot. None of this was ideal for the calming of her nerves.

Saniya squinted at her hand where she had written Mehraan's number. It had almost smudged off due to her nervous sweating and the hike up the hill. She had been writing it on her hand every day, not sure when she would be able to go to the station.

Saniya dialled the number on the basic white Nokia phone, and the line beeped slowly. With each beep, she grew more anxious. Would it connect or not? Beep ... beep ... beep. Would he pick up? Beep ... beep ... beep. Would he recognize her voice? Beep ...

And it started ringing. Saniya felt a shiver down her spine. Two rings, and a familiar voice answered, 'Hello?' Maybe she was imagining it, but Saniya could hear the longing in Mehraan's voice, hoping it was her at the other end.

Mehraan said hello again, and it finally kicked in that Saniya only had one minute to talk. Suddenly, she felt the need to introduce herself all over again. Maybe he had forgotten her. In a very formal tone she said, '*As-Salām-Alaikum*. This is Saniya Qadri speaking.'

A beat of silence in which she heard a sharp intake of breath. Then—'Saniya, thank God. How are you? Where are you calling from?'

Saniya cradled the phone close to whisper. In the middle of the police station with the SHO, hawaldars, her cousin watching, she felt exposed. She couldn't talk about the two of them with an audience around. So, she chose a more generic route.

'I am fine, I am fine. I just ... I don't know what's going to happen here. If the situation is going to change ...'

'I'm going to fly down there. I have been looking for flights, but they keep getting cancelled,' Mehraan interrupted.

Saniya gasped, 'No, please don't do that. There are no phones, no modes of transport, nothing. You are not used to this. Just stay in touch with my brother. My father will call him somehow with updates. I don't know how things are going to be here. If they get worse, I don't want you to get stuck.'

Mehraan asked quietly, 'And it's okay for you to be there?'

Saniya choked. The SHO tapped his watch. She had twenty seconds to go.

Something came over her, and all the ambivalence of the past few weeks asserted itself. She said, 'I think, Mehraan, you should consider moving on. From us.'

Abid gasped in shock. 'What are you doing?' he nudged her.

Saniya ignored him and continued. 'There's too much uncertainty here. You didn't sign up for this. You don't need to be part of this!' The words left Saniya's mouth without her having a chance to mull over them.

There was silence at the other end. And then—'I am coming there.'

Saniya said, 'No, no, don't! Don't think of coming here, unless ... God forbid, something bad happens. You just take care of yourself. Okay, take care, bye.'

She cut the call. The screen displayed fifty-two seconds. She still had eight seconds to go. Why did she cut the call early? She looked up to see Abid's stunned face. Even the SHO was astonished. 'You called to break up with him? Kind of harsh.'

Saniya walked back, feeling a mixture of fretfulness and an odd kind of peace. She was at ease because she'd heard Mehraan's voice but unsettled because of what she had said. Then again, if she had felt the need to reintroduce herself to the person she was going to spend the rest of her life with, wasn't that something to look into?

Abid, walking by her side, was losing his mind. 'Everyone's going to blame me ... how did I let this happen! How could you say that? I should have snatched the phone away from you. *Ya Allah!*'

'It's not about you, bhai.'

But he wasn't listening.

Saniya had just started talking to Mehraan a few weeks ago, getting to know him as a person. They were beginning to understand each other as individuals, discovering their likes and dislikes. And now suddenly—nothing.

Saniya had articulated what she felt would be the healthiest path for both of them. She didn't want the engagement to end—she was sure of this. But she also knew that sometimes the heart clouded the mind, and one didn't know how wrong one's choices were till it was too late. She was trusting her mind right now. She had no idea if that was the way to go.

Saniya's father soon caught wind of what had transpired at the station. Rather than getting angry, he understood. Saniya explained what she had been feeling. Mehraan and she had only been engaged for two months or so. They had spoken on the phone for a few weeks. Nothing major had transpired between the families. Even the wedding date had not been fixed.

'After the abrogation, maybe his family won't want to go ahead with this. Why would they want to get their son married in Kashmir? Is it fair to bind Mehraan to someone from such a volatile place?' she asked her father. He was at a loss for words.

'We don't know about our own tomorrow, Baba. Why would Mehraan wish to build a new relationship here?' Saniya added.

She didn't want to make someone commit to her out of a sense of obligation.

Saniya's father—while he saw her point of view—tried to talk her out of the decision. Saniya remained immovable. She didn't want to ruin anyone's life. Everyone in the house started bearing the collective burden of this decision. *Lukh kyā wanan*—what will people say—was usually doled out aplenty in such situations. But in Saniya's household, they didn't care about what other people would think about breaking off the engagement; they were worried for Saniya's mental health. That she was choosing someone else's happiness over her own future could have a less than desirable result. She was their priority.

Since the family couldn't reason with Saniya, they let her be. Mehraan's father contacted Saniya's father—this wasn't an easy feat to achieve—to ask about the police station phone call. Saniya's father told him to wait it out. 'I know my daughter. She puts a lot of pressure on herself. She will come around.'

SANIYA WAS KNOWN TO pen down her thoughts. For the first eighteen days she hadn't spoken to Mehraan, she had handwritten everything on paper—whatever she wanted to tell him, whatever she was feeling, date-wise, time-wise. She continued to do this even after the police station phone call. While writing, Saniya realized that it wasn't 'over' for her, but she didn't want to tell anyone. She had wanted to give Mehraan a choice, and she was firm about that.

A few weeks post 'the call', Sabeel came down from Bangalore to check on the family and to talk to Saniya. He was empathetic and told her that he would stand by her no matter the decision she took. 'But even this will get over one day, Saanu, consider that. And that day when the phone lines open, who do you want to call first?'

'Mehraan,' she replied without a thought.

Her brother smiled.

Saniya nodded slowly. There was hope yet. She got up and gathered the letters that she had written to Mehraan and gave them to her brother. 'Hand these over to him. If he still wants to go ahead, it's a yes from me, too.'

Sabeel carried the letters with him to Bangalore and gave them all to Mehraan. He was relieved when Mehraan said he would read them. It wasn't over for him either.

Mehraan absorbed everything Saniya had written across those pages. He knew where she was coming from. He knew her chief concern remained him. *Them.* Saniya didn't want either of them to resent the other in the long run. Mehraan knew now more than ever that Saniya was the one for him. Reading those letters—each of them held her deepest thoughts, anxieties and vulnerabilities—confirmed this.

Slowly, the landlines started working. Saniya made her first call to Mehraan. Nothing needed to be said or re-affirmed.

They were okay.

After that, to get on a call with Mehraan wasn't always possible. Even if Saniya managed to wrangle the landline from whoever was hogging it, there was zero privacy when she spoke.

Left on her own, Saniya would feel very restless again. She didn't know what was happening in Mehraan's life. There was barely anything happening in hers. On the calls, there was never any time to ask what Mehraan had felt when he read the letters and whether he wanted to respond to anything, now that he had the chance.

FOUR MONTHS PASSED AFTER the abrogation, and all Kashmiris under lockdown started getting removed from WhatsApp groups they were a part of. After all, the application followed the policy that accounts that remained inactive for 120 days would automatically expire. The world outside Kashmir noticed this, while the people in the Valley remained oblivious.

In November 2019, Saniya decided to fly to Bangalore. She would be meeting Mehraan for the second time in her life. She was scared and exhilarated.

The two met at a restaurant. Over a steaming cup of tea, Saniya and Mehraan finally got the closure they needed.

'I choose you, and I hope you choose me, Saniya,' Mehraan said. 'Everything else is just background noise.'

Saniya nodded. 'I choose you, too. I just worry. In Kashmir, everyone has a bullet carrying their name. I just don't want such a fate for you.' Saniya articulated her worst fears.

Mehraan held her hand. 'I read all your letters, and I felt what you were going through. All your predicaments, all your fears. I'm not much of a writer, so I didn't know what to say. But ... there is no *me* without *you*.'

A weight lifted off Saniya. She smiled widely for the first time in ages.

She went back to Kashmir feeling buoyant about her relationship with Mehraan. Her parents had been waiting to hear what she had to say. She just nodded a 'yes' when she saw her father. The poor man—worried for such a long time—was relieved. He immediately called Mehraan's father. 'Haanji, let's set the date, bhaisaab.'

By then, mobile phones had started working in Kashmir. Saniya was elated—only to discover that her own phone was still without a signal. Saniya had a Karnataka circle number (as she had once studied there), and for some reason, although the communication lockdown seemed to be lifting, her own SIM card refused to kickstart to life. To add to her woes, the customer care executives in Kashmir told her to go to the Jammu office to figure it out. By the time Saniya got her number working again, it was December. And until then, she had to rely on her family members' phones to talk to Mehraan.

Just as their relationship started feeling somewhat 'normal', the pandemic struck. Saniya and Mehraan had to remain away from each other again. They missed the date set for the wedding.

Yet suddenly, this seemed like a minor impasse. They could talk to each other at least. See each other on video calls. They were grateful for small mercies.

IN NOVEMBER 2020, MEHRAAN and his family flew down to Kashmir. Saniya and he had an intimate wedding at home. There were barely ten people present for the nikāh ceremony. But Saniya and Mehraan couldn't have been happier. As soon as they were married, Saniya teased Mehraan mercilessly, 'Now not only are you wedded to a Kashmiri, but you can also buy land here. Happy?' They laughed bitterly at the painfully absurd reality of this. They still have this inside joke.

Post the nikāh, Saniya flew with her husband to Bangalore. The moment she landed in the city and reached his house, she looked for her letters in Mehraan's room—the one that was now also hers. She went through them again. A wave of nostalgia swept over her.

It was as though Saniya had experienced losing a lover and getting him back, all in the same breath.

Saniya tried to make light of the moment. She turned to Mehraan and said, 'God forbid I lose my memory ... these letters will help you revive it.' He laughed.

Saniya knew that she would tell her children about those letters.

As for her and Mehraan—'We will talk about that abrogation for the rest of our lives. We will ask each other—do you remember how difficult it was? Do you remember how we made it?

'We survived. We lived. We loved.'

14

LILLY

SHIRIN GREW UP IN Mumbai. Her mother was Kashmiri, and her father was Maharashtrian. When she was a baby, she would routinely visit her grandparents in Kashmir. As she grew up, these visits were reserved for school vacations.

Shirin made many friends in Kashmir, but there was no one she could keep in touch with while she was away—for she wasn't allowed internet access as yet.

When she reached the fourth grade, Shirin was finally permitted to have a Facebook account. She posted a picture of herself with her father to begin with. The account was open to the public, and within a few days, a boy commented on her picture. The comment read, 'Do you remember me?'

Shirin was curious. She went to the boy's profile. His face wasn't familiar, but his name 'Moin' did ring a bell. His Facebook bio revealed that he was from Kashmir and six months younger than her.

When Shirin asked her mother if they knew a Moin from Kashmir, she learnt that there was one near her grandparents' house in Srinagar. He was a neighbour's son; Shirin had played with him as an infant. Could this be the same Moin? Before she could ask, she received a message in her Facebook inbox from Moin, explaining who he was. He was the same boy.

The two of them got talking over Facebook and very soon, developed a steady friendship. Shirin would look forward to her allotted hour at the computer every day so that she could chat with Moin. Even though they didn't have a whole lot in common, they would share pieces of their own worlds with each other—worlds that were sometimes similar, sometimes different, but always carried something of Kashmir.

Shirin now waited for her Kashmir vacation more fervently than ever before. Besides her grandparents, she was excited about spending time with Moin. It may not have been apparent to them just yet, but the start of puppy love had them both enraptured.

After reminding her parents for the millionth time, her tickets to Kashmir got booked. Shirin immediately told Moin the dates she would be visiting. Instead of being jubilant, he sounded miserable. Moin's family would holiday every year in Delhi where his uncle stayed. He was going to be away during Shirin's visit. Her enthusiasm got punctured like a tyre.

As both of them were very young, neither Shirin nor Moin could dictate the schedule for their vacations. They kept missing each other for several years, their timetables never aligning.

Yet, their association remained steady, and Shirin's puppy love grew into stronger feelings. Facebook messaging blossomed into texting, which, in turn, led to long phone calls. Moin had lovingly started calling Shirin 'Lilly'. 'I don't like lotuses too much, water lilies are the best,' he explained to her.

The summer she turned sixteen, Shirin asked her parents for a vacation in Kashmir. She felt more in command of her schedule and asked for specific travel dates as well. She knew that Moin would be there this time. Shirin assumed that her parents would cross-question her, and she had prepared a whole list of reasons to travel, with rebuttals for any and every argument that could be thrown her way. Curiously, her parents readily agreed. She didn't have to persuade them. The three of them would go to Kashmir exactly when Shirin proposed.

Shirin was elated. She was finally going to meet Moin after seven years of trying desperately to. There were butterflies in her tummy at the thought of him calling her Lilly in person. She had even chosen the outfit she was going to wear when she met Moin for the first time.

Three days before the trip to Kashmir, Shirin's father had an urgent work commitment come up. Her parents were compelled to cancel the trip, even as Shirin pleaded with her mother that only the two of them go. 'We'll go next year for a longer period of time,' they said.

Shirin was inconsolable.

In faraway Kashmir, Moin was distressed as well. His family only ever went to Delhi and never to Mumbai where Shirin was. 'It's too humid,' they'd reply if he suggested visiting India's business capital. When he said he wanted to see the ocean, they told him, 'Why would you want to see the ocean when we have Dal Lake right here?'

The longer trip promised to Shirin the following year never came. Shirin was an only child to strict parents who valued academics above all else. There were the tenth board exams to contend with, then the twelfth board exams, then the entrance examinations. Shirin realized that she wasn't going on vacation any time soon.

Once, when Shirin was in the eleventh grade, she had to travel with her parents to Kashmir for a week as her grandfather was unwell. By now, Shirin had resorted to teasing Moin about visiting Kashmir. It helped defuse the tension between the two of them. When Shirin told Moin that she would be visiting, he thought she was crying wolf again. He had a trek planned to Himachal, and he left just as she reached.

Shirin arrived and called him, but Moin's phone was out of coverage area. Shirin didn't know he was trekking; she thought he was still around in Srinagar and his phone wasn't working. She tried tracking him down, looking for his house in the neighbourhood—only to find out that his family had moved further away. Shirin knew that asking persistently about a boy wasn't looked upon kindly in Kashmir. Nor did she want to start an expedition to a new address on her own. She was left with no option but to fly back to Mumbai with her parents. When Moin finally returned from his trek and saw her messages, he was mad with himself. It seemed that they were just not destined to meet.

Shirin turned seventeen, then eighteen, then nineteen and twenty. They were yet to meet each other. Video calls made communication easier; they could even see each other now. Still, they yearned for something more tangible.

BY THE YEAR 2019, Shirin and Moin had been friends for a whole decade. Both had romantic feelings for one another and were aware of it, but they refrained from putting a label to their long-distance association.

On 1 August of that year, they decided to change that. Shirin was going to visit Kashmir in October, and this time Moin was going to be there for certain. While they had been talking for ten whole years, they felt the need to ease themselves into a deeper relationship. 'If we start talking like boyfriend–girlfriend now, we can get over the initial awkwardness over the phone. So, by the time we meet in person, we'll be fine!' This was Shirin's master plan.

Just as they made it official, things started turning sour in Kashmir. As everyone around him started stocking up on essentials—as if a long, harsh winter was around the corner—Moin told Shirin that something terrible was going to happen in the Valley. Shirin wasn't perturbed. She felt that Moin was trying his own version of 'crying wolf' on her.

On 4 August, Shirin's grandfather called to inform the family that in all probability he would not be in communication with them for a bit. Shirin stopped taking Moin's fears lightly. The gravity of the situation was finally affecting her. Shirin's mother burst into tears while talking to her father. He was eighty years old. Shirin was very attached to him as well and couldn't bear to imagine anything happening to him and not finding out in time. To add to her woes, she realized that she would also be estranged from Moin.

'I will find a way to contact you. Don't worry,' Moin tried telling her when Shirin bawled over their call.

At midnight on 4 August, the phone lines died; the internet collapsed. Shirin had experienced this many times before with Moin—but at those points they hadn't declared their love for one another. Now, everything felt more ominous and unpredictable. Besides, the cruelty of fate pressed down on Shirin; they had finally said the magic words and *now* they were being made to separate. 'Did we jinx it all by opening our hearts?' Shirin wondered.

The next day, 5 August, saw the abrogation being announced. Shirin's mother, who had grown up in Kashmir and had spent most of her life there, couldn't bear to hear the news. Her blood pressure shot up and she had to be hospitalized. In the hours that Shirin waited for her mother to regain consciousness, thoughts of her family in Kashmir and Moin preoccupied her. 'Will they survive?' she asked herself.

Shirin was in college in Pune at that time. She went back after her mother was discharged. She was sure Moin would find a way to call her like he had promised. She ensured that her phone was always with her and never on silent mode. Once or twice, her phone rang loudly in class, much to the chagrin of her college professors. But the calls weren't from Moin.

Days turned into weeks. A month passed without any news from Moin. Shirin was panicking. She had heard that people were getting hold of satellite phones and certain landlines in Kashmir. Facebook support groups had sprouted up like mushrooms that kept offering updates with phone numbers. Her mother religiously scoured those pages each morning to find a working number in her father's area in Kashmir. After Shirin realized that Moin wasn't calling, she joined her mother in the search. Whatever number they could find, it would help them check on both Shirin's grandfather and Moin.

Shirin tried calling all sorts of phone numbers—PCOs, post offices, police stations, anything that would ring. For the most part, no one picked up. The few times they did, they would get annoyed by her requests to send messages to Fatehkadal, which was far from where they were stationed. She called her grandfather and Moin's landlines as well, but only got multiple mind-numbing beeps that tapered off like a broken cassette.

Not knowing what else to do, Shirin started writing letters to Moin. She wrote to him every other day and posted them all. She didn't know if these missives would even reach Kashmir, but she sent almost thirty of them. 'Even if one reaches, I will be happy,' she told herself.

When Shirin got a haircut, she realized she couldn't send Moin a picture asking him how she looked. So, she decided to courier him a big box of goodies. With printed pictures of her fresh haircut, she packed wind chimes, some toys for his little cousins, a perfume bottle for him and a scarf. 'I want you to know how I'm looking now,' she wrote.

The courier company, though uncertain about whether anything would reach Kashmir at that time, finally yielded to Shirin's requests. She paid them extra and pleaded with them to try their best. If Moin replied, she would know that she had succeeded. But there was no reply.

Shirin was at her PG in college during this whole time. There were entire days when she could not get out of bed as she was depressed. She would often charge her phone out in the hall as the power socket in her room had stopped working. She had instructed her roommates to inform her at once if her phone rang when she was asleep or away from it.

After months of waiting, Shirin got a call from an unknown number. She was in her room, and the phone began ringing outside in the hall while charging. Her roommate screamed that the call was from Jammu and Kashmir. Shirin bolted out and almost yanked the socket off the wall in her attempt to answer immediately. Sure enough, it was the familiar 0194 area code flashing.

'Hello?' she panted, fingers crossed.

'Lilly?' the voice said.

And just like that, Shirin became a puddle of tears. She sank to the floor. After so much time that she had lost count, she was hearing Moin's voice.

'Lilly, I don't have much time. I just have two minutes, and there are five hundred people behind me waiting to call. I have been standing for two hours just to call you. I'm fine and your nanu is fine too. I saw him on his walk.'

Shirin didn't utter a single word. She just cried.

'Are you going to say anything?' Moin asked.

'I just wanted to know you are okay,' she sniffed.

Moin went on to say that he didn't know when he'd be able to call her again.

'That's okay,' she said. 'I heard your voice, that's all I wanted.'

Before Moin could say anything else, the call dropped. Barely two minutes after months of silence. Shirin held the phone close.

THE NEWS COMING OUT of Kashmir was sparse. The media outlets there were allowed an internet speed that made dial-up connections seem lightning fast. Local channels and newspapers struggled to release the news as well. Shirin found it hard to believe the little that emerged on national news from or about Kashmir.

All she got was that the Uttar Pradesh chief minister was calling for lunch with Kashmiri students to discuss the advantages of the abrogation of Article 370.[34] And that the national security advisor was breaking bread with a few Kashmiri men somewhere in South Kashmir; over biryani, he was saying that the recent decision in Jammu and Kashmir was for the development and prosperity of the locals.[35] How was one supposed to know if the said locals would actually know prosperity? Much of the news felt like an obvious photo op—an attempt to show that everything was 'normal' in Kashmir post-abrogation.

Rumours of houses getting torched down started spreading. Tear gas, pellet guns, pepper spray—common jargon in Kashmir—kept resurfacing in conversations; all of it was affecting Shirin. There were times when she would read stories and articles late into the night and weep. She hadn't seen the unrest affect her family up close. But here she was, lamenting all lives in Kashmir like they were to her kith and kin. She garnered a deeper understanding of the conflict and how bad it could get.

A PCO number that Shirin had been trying for a while finally picked up her call after weeks. The PCO was in Fatehkadal where Moin and her grandfather both stayed. She gave the shopkeeper Moin's name and address and told him to give him a message. 'Tell him that Shirin had called.' The shopkeeper had probably heard many such requests by now. He agreed grudgingly. He found the house after asking around. Moin's aunt looked at him quizzically when he said that 'Shirin had called'. His aunt knew nothing of Shirin and was about to shoo the shopkeeper away, when Moin's mother overheard the conversation. She knew about Shirin and Moin's relationship and took the message for him. Her sister-in-law looked perplexed by this exchange.

Moin got the message and went to the same PCO to call. He was impressed by Shirin's inventiveness. 'You've become quite the smarty-pants,' he laughed.

'The things we do for love,' she replied, glad that her mission had succeeded.

Shirin and Moin spoke about mundane things, nothing too serious—that Moin had again seen her grandfather on a morning walk, and that his younger cousins were getting study assignments and notes on pen drives from their school.

Shirin grasped that when everything around one felt uncertain, one held on to simple things for comfort.

Shirin's travel date in October, when she was supposed to go to Kashmir, came and went by. Her parents forbade her from taking the risky journey. She complied once again.

Shirin and Moin spoke through the PCO she had identified for a few months till mobile phones started working again in October or November. Shirin was glad when mobile networks revived—not least because the shopkeeper at the PCO had got sick of her calling and often snapped when she phoned. 'Don't you have any other work, missy?'

First, texting was restored. Shirin and Moin went back to sending messages without the internet. About twenty days later, mobile phones were able to receive and make calls. Moin had a postpaid number that started working immediately.

While talking on the phone, Shirin and Moin were both careful. They had heard rumours that phones were getting tapped since the restoration. They were cautious about not using certain words while speaking. If the conversation turned political in any way, they would immediately change the subject.

IN DECEMBER, PROTESTS AGAINST the Citizenship Amendment Act (CAA) and the National Register of Citizens (NRC) erupted across the country. If Shirin remained idle, she would start worrying about Kashmir. So, she joined the protests as well. She organized the rallies and petitions, and along with seeking equal treatment of all citizens in India, she pushed for the rights of Kashmiris as well. She talked to anyone and everyone she met during those protests and educated them about what was happening in the Valley at that moment.

If Shirin received any information at all from Moin, she passed it on. She spoke of how communication channels were being denied to the people there; that although phones had revived, the internet was still not working. She raised the fact that students who wished to fill out college application forms had to travel long distances to get internet access. She mentioned that freedom of speech was being curbed, and with it, basic human rights.

Moin had received some of Shirin's letters and the big box of goodies. He had posted her a letter instantly, but Shirin was yet to receive it.

One day, in December, Shirin opened the door to see the postman. She was surprised because she never received letters from anyone but was quick to get excited because she could guess who this missive was from. Her excitement, however, faded when she saw the state of the letter. It had been tampered with. It was smudged and dirty, and the writing on it was barely legible. Shirin got mad and yelled at the postman, before realizing that it wasn't his fault after all. The letter had arrived this way; it had probably been opened by someone in the Valley to see if it held anything incriminatory or if it carried stories that the popular news networks hadn't relayed. She calmed down and apologized to the postman before closing the door.

A letter written in October, received in December, that too in tatters. When she tried deciphering the letter, she could vaguely tell that Moin had thanked her for all the gifts she had sent him. Shirin preserved the letter (or what was left of it).

She hoped that the internet would be restored in Kashmir soon, so she could see Moin's face on video call again. December flew by, and at the end of the year, Shirin found herself weeping. She had been praying for a new beginning for Kashmir with the new year, but 2020 was around the corner, and it seemed to offer little respite to Kashmiris.

One day, towards the end of January, at around 6 p.m., Shirin got a news notification that 2G internet had come back to life in Kashmir. She immediately tried video calling Moin. It didn't connect. She tried again and yet again, her fingers growing tired of tapping icons. Maybe he still needed to buy an internet pack, and the crowds at the shop were overwhelming. Shirin dozed off. Finally, around 8:30 p.m., when she was waking up from her nap, she saw Moin's name flashing on a WhatsApp video call. She asked her roommate if it was real. 'I think I am still dreaming,' she whispered, 'Pick it up or it'll get cut!' her roommate yelled.

Shirin took a deep breath and picked up the call. Moin's anxious face filled the screen. The first thing she did was take a screenshot. Shirin wasn't sure when the call would get cut, and she wanted to remember what he looked like now. His hair had grown scraggly, but he still had a mischievous glint in his eye. 'Lilly ...' he said as though he hadn't seen spring in years.

They were both in tears, unable to form words, let alone string a sentence together. The sadness didn't last long as Moin's young cousins hijacked the call. They yelled their hellos and thanked Shirin for all the toys. Shirin's heart was full. Since the internet was slow and patchy, their faces got pixelated and the audio lagged. But Shirin didn't care. She was in love with every moment she got. 'I miss you, Lilly,' Moin tried to say over the excited children. 'I miss you, too, my love,' Shirin smiled.

Shirin and her mother spoke to her grandfather on video call as well. He was awfully cheery for someone who had been cooped up for so long. 'We didn't have phones when we grew up, so this is all very familiar to me,' he laughed.

On the eve of the Indian Republic Day, the internet stopped again in Kashmir. A familiar panic engulfed Shirin. But thankfully, it was restored by the evening, and she had Moin back.

Shirin and Moin had gone through the unrest of 2010 and 2016 together, as well as the floods of 2014. Somehow, back then it didn't bother them as much as it did in 2019. Post the abrogation, they went through more emotional ups and downs than most full-fledged romantic relationships did.

'I have a love-hate relationship with those days,' Shirin told Moin later. 'Now when you call too much, I get so annoyed. Back then, I yearned for it all the time.'

After all they have gone through, Shirin and Moin have yet to meet. They hope to—very, very soon.

15

NEWSPAPER

ON THE NIGHT OF 4 August 2019, Maryam and Daniyal were talking on the phone. Maryam was keeping her voice low so no one outside her room could tell that she was speaking so late.

Daniyal was stressed out; he had been this way for many weeks now. 'Two months! It's been two months. The results were supposed to be out by now. Why aren't they out? Why?' he fretted.

Maryam yawned and said, 'They'll come out soon. I can feel it. Don't worry.'

'Where can you feel it?' scoffed Daniyal.

'In my bones. All 206 of them,' came the reply.

'Okay, doctor sahiba!' Daniyal rolled his eyes.

Daniyal had appeared for his Kashmir administrative services exams recently and had gone through the interview round two months ago. The final results were still pending and should have been out a few weeks prior. He was all nerves and nakhras now. 'Do you think it's because of what they're saying will happen tomorrow? That the Article will be removed? Is that why the results aren't being declared?' Daniyal's thoughts were spiralling in all directions.

Maryam was used to his antics by now. A medical student herself, pursing her MBBS internship at that juncture, she knew what it felt like to wait for exam results. The days leading up to it were always slow and painful. In a few months' time, Maryam would be appearing for her NEET PG exams, and then she'd be in the same boat as Daniyal, and probably turn even more insufferable. Right now though she was the epitome of Zen. She coaxed Daniyal, 'Just go to sleep, baby. Inshallah, the rumours you mention are all a hoax. Let's talk in the morning. I ... am ... so ... sleepy.' Maryam's breathing got heavier with each word. Daniyal sighed, 'Good night, baby.'

MARYAM AND DANIYAL HAD been dating since the time they were in school. These late-night calls were a norm by now. Both were adept at training their voices low and keeping an ear out for movements outside their respective bedrooms. They had come close to being caught way too many times and were experts at feigning sleep. They'd rub their eyes while opening the door to suspicious parents and say, 'Whatttt ... I was having such a good dream.' Cue: yawn.

Daniyal had been waiting for his results, but so was Maryam. Both of them had decided soon enough in their relationship that this was forever. They were going to get married, they were certain. There were a few hurdles though. Maryam came from a family of doctors and was training to be one herself. The expectation was that she'd marry a doctor from a family of doctors as well. 'He will understand you and your erratic schedule in the long run. If you pursue a stream like gynaecology and have night duty, only in-laws who are doctors will sympathize!' This had been drilled into Maryam from a young age.

Maryam knew this wasn't an unshakeable rule. But coming from a traditional Kashmiri joint family, she was aware that even if the man she married wasn't a doctor, he needed to have a good job and be well-settled. Daniyal was acquainted with this and was doing his best to enter the administrative services. Not only was he genuinely interested in this vocational stream, he also knew it was a sure shot way to send Maryam a rishtè.

Maryam woke up on 5 August to zero network and no Wi-Fi. Bleary eyed, she trudged downstairs. Both her parents were in the hamām, having tea. When she asked if their phones were working, they shook their head. Maryam needed to get to the hospital in an hour for her internship duty. 'Don't go. Stay home today,' her father told her. 'Anyway, the army won't let you pass in your own car.' He wasn't going to his hospital either.

That's when Maryam knew something serious was going on. The TV was turned on in the room, and as she sat down to pour herself some tea, the headlines read that an important announcement was due in the Lok Sabha soon. Daniyal's words about the Article rang in her ears. In a few hours' time, his prophecy would turn true.

Post the abrogation, the day passed in a daze. Everyone in the house seemed to be carrying an aura of sadness. Maryam went to see her cousins who lived next door, and even they were talking in monosyllables. Worse, the desire to check their phones for messages or calls was driving everyone crazy. Their hands went to their mobiles involuntarily and suddenly they were reminded of the impossibility of communicating. 'They're just cameras and calculators now,' her younger cousin Arshiya complained. Maryam hugged her close, already fearing the night when she wouldn't be able to talk to Daniyal.

In all the years they'd been together, Maryam and Daniyal had seldom missed a good night call, except when they had been fighting. On those nights, a message sufficed. But there was always *something*. Until today.

Dinner was had with the TV news blaring. Huge panel discussions about the repercussions of the abrogation flashed across news channels. A lone Kashmiri was on each discussion panel, face downcast and talking through his/her dejection, carrying the weight of the millions of people in the Valley who had no voice right now. The family ate in silence and retired to bed early.

The first night was the hardest. Not only was Maryam in despair because of what was happening around her, but she was also terrified of the future. The state had been bifurcated. What if the Kashmir Administrative Service (KAS) didn't exist after the abrogation? What if they introduced a new exam? What if Daniyal got to know that the exams he had appeared for were rendered null and void? What if only the Indian Administrative Service became the standard henceforth, and Daniyal would have to prepare all over again? What would happen to Maryam and Daniyal then? Would Maryam have to marry someone else ... someone her parents chose for her?

Maryam had thought of this possibility thousands of times—of not getting to marry Daniyal. She loved him very much, but she also knew she didn't want to turn her back on her parents for him. She didn't have it in her to elope. With a heavy heart, she had made this clear to Daniyal a long time ago. So, Maryam's hopes, her entire future, were linked to Daniyal getting into the KAS and then breaking the news to her parents. She would fight tooth and nail for her love at that point and get engaged. Without Daniyal having a job though, she knew the fight didn't stand a chance.

Now, on the night of 5 August, Maryam wasn't sure if their life together would ever be a reality. She took out her defunct phone and typed a message in Daniyal's chat window. 'I love you, Daniyal. I miss you,' she wrote. She pressed 'send'. The message displayed a tiny clock next to it. Undelivered. Maryam said a prayer; she wished to see Daniyal the next day. They lived close, a kilometre away. She hoped he would find a way to come see her.

The next day, Maryam opened the curtains to the main French windows in the house that overlooked the whole neighbourhood. Her prayers seemed to have been answered way too fast because a few hundred metres away, outside Maryam's other cousins' house, was Daniyal's car. She could see Daniyal from a distance talking to her cousin, Owais. Maryam rubbed her eyes in shock and stared again. Daniyal was still there.

Maryam ran to her room and glanced into the mirror to check if she looked okay. She looked half-asleep, her hair unkempt. 'Whatever ... he's seen worse,' she thought. She flew down the stairs and out of the main gate. By the time she reached her cousins' house, Daniyal was gone. His car had turned a corner and left. Owais bhai, a few years older than Maryam, frowned at her. 'Why are you running?'

Maryam caught her breath as her mind raced. No one knew about her and Daniyal's relationship in the family yet. She would have to play it cool. 'Nothing, I just thought I'd go jogging.'

Owais stared at Maryam's slippers and back at her. He laughed.

Maryam quickly tried to change the subject. 'What were you doing out here? I saw you talking to someone from the window.'

'Inquisitive much?' Owais raised an eyebrow.

His younger sister Sehreen came out of the house to call Owais for breakfast. Owais continued, 'It was Daniyal. He went to school with you two, right?' Sehreen nodded and Maryam feigned ignorance. Sehreen frowned—Maryam was clearly overacting. She didn't know about the two either, but Maryam was sure that she suspected.

'What did he want?' Sehreen asked Owais.

Owais told them that Daniyal had been around to ask whether he'd heard about the KAS results yet. Owais had appeared for the exams as well.

'Have you heard anything?' Maryam managed to ask.

Owais shook his head. 'Abbu has gone to Jammu. Maybe he'll hear something.'

Maryam nodded, stress lines on her face.

Sehreen was watching her closely throughout this exchange with narrowed eyes.

Later that evening, Sehreen landed up at Maryam's house. She barged into the bedroom and closed the door. Maryam was sprawled on the bed reading a book, sipping water through a bottle lazily. 'Daniyal and you are an item. Accept it,' Sehreen stated matter of factly. Maryam choked on the water that she was sipping. Sehreen patted her back till Maryam settled. Maryam looked at Sehreen like a cat caught peeing on a rug. She nodded. 'Yes.'

'Why didn't you tell me!' Sehreen yelled at her, hitting her with a pillow. Sehreen, Maryam and Daniyal had been in the same batch in school. Sehreen had known Daniyal for years. Maryam explained everything to her, how it started, when it started, why she was afraid of anyone knowing ... all of it. Sehreen, though still a bit miffed, nodded. Maryam felt the invisible weight that she had been carrying on her shoulders lighten. Sehreen was supportive about the whole thing. 'Don't worry, I'll help you when the time comes to talk about Daniyal with the family.' Maryam hugged her cousin tightly.

Sehreen told Maryam to come to her house the next day to hang out in case Daniyal showed up again. He had told Owais that he would keep coming over to check—just in case his father had news to share. 'Abbu is coming tomorrow. Daniyal might show up to see if he has updates. You can quickly meet him then.' Maryam was thrilled with the plan. That night, Maryam prayed harder than she ever had for Daniyal to get selected in the KAS.

The next day, Maryam dressed up after days and made her way to Sehreen's house with their younger cousin, Arshiya. The three girls sat with Owais in the hamām, laughing, joking, gossiping. All along, Maryam's eyes kept flitting to the gate, hoping that Daniyal would magically appear. She sat for several hours, but Daniyal didn't show up. Finally, she gave up, aware that her parents would be waiting for her for lunch. She rose and asked Arshiya to follow—they lived next to each other.

Right then, the front gate creaked open. Maryam rushed to the window. It was Sehreen's father walking in through the gate. He was holding a small briefcase in one hand and a folded newspaper in the other. Maryam felt a knot in her stomach. A few moments later, her uncle walked into the room looking grim and stared at Owais. 'Your name isn't on the list.'

In all her lifetime, Maryam had never seen her uncle joke. But at this moment she, along with everyone in the room, thought he was joking. Sehreen smiled. 'Abbu, don't lie. He got through, didn't he?' But her father's face remained morose. Owais didn't move a muscle as the news slowly sank in. Sehreen's face withered as well. Maryam was aware of the kind of perseverance it took to study for these exams; she had seen Daniyal toil away for years preparing. She was disappointed for her brother. Yet she was also dying with curiosity—what did the newspaper say about Daniyal?

Maryam sat there staring at the newspaper, unable to touch it. So close to the truth. Arshiya held her hand. 'You're shivering, baaji!' she said. Maryam gulped. She turned to Sehreen and whispered, 'I'm going upstairs to pray. Check the newspaper for Daniyal's name and send Arshiya up to tell me.' Sehreen nodded.

Maryam went to Sehreen's room and offered nẹmāz. She prayed while her sisters studied the newspaper downstairs. Maryam rocked back and forth, knowing she couldn't change what was printed in the newspaper, but at the same time willing it to be what she and Daniyal had hoped for. 'Please don't disappoint me, dear God. Please.'

Knock. Knock. Knock. Maryam's eyes flew open. She got up gingerly and opened the door. Arshiya's excited little face filled the door frame. 'He got it, baaji!' Maryam let out a breath that she didn't know she was holding on to tightly. She hugged Arshiya, and the two of them jumped around the room in celebration, making sure not to make too much noise, as the house was still reeling with the news of Owais's results.

Maryam ran down and snatched the paper from an amused Sehreen. With one finger, Maryam made her way down the list. Stop. There it was. At number fifty. She took out her phone and clicked a picture for posterity. She was happy. So very happy.

Grinning from ear to ear, Maryam walked back home. Finally, all her prayers had been answered. And the most bizarre part of all of this was that Daniyal didn't know that he had cleared the KAS yet. She couldn't believe that she knew before he did.

Maryam sent Arshiya in the evening to check if Daniyal had come to Sehreen's. She came back shaking her head. Now a new kind of stress engulfed Maryam. 'He said he would come. Why isn't he coming?'

The next morning, Arshiya came to her bedroom panting. 'He. Is. Here.' She collapsed, holding a stitch in her side. Maryam jumped over her and ran to Sehreen's house. From the distance she saw Daniyal standing with Sehreen and Owais. He was holding the newspaper and reading it.

Maryam ran up to them, and Daniyal looked at her. Always awkward around other people, he didn't say anything at all. He went back to staring at the newspaper, while Maryam scowled. Sehreen interjected, 'You got in! Show some emotion at least.' Daniyal just smiled and nodded. 'Thank you.' He took a picture of the paper and muttered, 'Need to show Abbu.'

Maryam rolled her eyes at Sehreen. 'What's the meaning of his reaction?' Sehreen whispered. Maryam shrugged but wasn't really surprised. Daniyal wasn't an overtly expressive person. He had always been shy ever since Maryam had known him. She was the only person before whom he let go and displayed his goofy side.

Later Maryam would learn that Daniyal hadn't celebrated right there because he was thinking about Owais and what he was going through. Most others had not extended this courtesy to Owais. How many KAS applicants had visited Owais's house after learning that he had the newspaper with the results. They would come to check. If they had made it, they'd jump around in joy. If they hadn't, they'd start crying then and there. Owais had to witness it all. Daniyal was one of the few empathetic souls around. When Maryam gathered this back story, she loved him even more—if it was possible.

'Congratulations,' Maryam said before Daniyal left that day. 'Are you happy?' she asked.

Daniyal looked at her, unable to keep a straight face. 'Very.'

Sehreen cleared her throat to dissipate the tension. Owais was clueless.

Daniyal mumbled something more about needing to inform his family and left.

Sehreen nudged Maryam after Daniyal's car rounded the corner. 'What a Pappu!'

Maryam giggled. 'My Pappu!'

FOR THE NEXT TEN days or so, Maryam didn't see Daniyal. She would later find out that he used to drive up to her house or the vicinity each day to catch a glimpse of her. But she had no way of knowing, nor could Daniyal ask anyone to call Maryam outside.

It was so peculiar to Maryam. This moment that Daniyal and she had been waiting for, for so very long, was finally here. It was a reality. They had a newspaper with his name as part of the list of selected KAS candidates. After all those nights spent speaking about this moment, fretting over it—minds and bodies churning with anxiety—the moment had unfurled exactly as they had hoped.

Only for the abrogation to steal their thunder.

'We can't even talk to each other about it, let alone celebrate it,' Maryam texted Daniyal at night. All the messages from the preceding days were still undelivered. Maryam wondered how long texts remained on WhatsApp servers. What if phone services didn't open for so long that her messages never made their way to Daniyal? It was a possibility. A depressing one at that.

Maryam imagined conversations in her head with Daniyal when she was alone. In these conversations, they talked and laughed and celebrated his win. Daniyal had got what he had worked for years to achieve. And both of them were one step closer to being married. The thought made Maryam tingly.

But the old worry about the veracity of these results also resurfaced. Jammu and Kashmir as a state didn't exist. It was a union territory now. What if that meant that the KAS exams would be quashed and replaced with something else? If statehood and the articles governing the region for decades could be snatched away, just about anything else could happen in Kashmir. The apprehensions clouded Maryam's mind. 'Why can't I feel happy about this in peace?' she wondered.

MARYAM HADN'T GONE TO her hospital in ages. Neither she nor her fellow interns had been summoned. Her father had started travelling to his hospital. An ambulance would pick and drop him and other doctors and staff from the area. Ambulances were given precedence over private vehicles on the roads, the latter getting stopped at various checkpoints and often not being allowed to go ahead by the army and police.

As the phone and internet services remained blocked, Maryam had more things to worry about. Her NEET PG exams were due in a few months' time. She had started studying for it but found her preparation lacking. It was an online, computer-based exam, a format that was new to her. Besides, most of the study and prep needed an internet connection. Just before the abrogation, Maryam had bought a subscription to a medical study app that would give her notes, videos, books and exam simulations. Doing these online practice tests on a regular basis, along with studying, was a key part of preparing for the NEET PG exams, where time was the biggest challenge to completing all the questions. The subscription held little value now as Maryam couldn't access any of the material. Unnerved, she resorted to studying from textbooks again; this was like attempting to dig a hole with a fork. The tools were all wrong. As the days blurred into each other, Maryam couldn't concentrate on her exam prep like she would have liked to.

IN THE MEANTIME, MARYAM was getting increasingly restless about meeting Daniyal. She'd land up at Sehreen's house at different times of the day, trying to catch him. And he did come. But he would just meet Owais and leave. On most of these days, even Sehreen wouldn't know he had visited till after he had left. And as a result, she couldn't keep Maryam posted on time. Their timings never seemed to coincide.

Bạḍ Īd passed without the phone lines reviving. Indian Independence Day, too, went by. There was no change in the situation, Maryam was a bag of nerves. 'I have to meet Daniyal. Do something,' she pleaded with Sehreen. On seeing her sister in distress, Sehreen said that if they had to do something, it would have to be done together. The family wouldn't allow them out of the house in the current hālāth, unless they worked as a team.

Sehreen got her car out one afternoon after pleading with her parents to let her go. 'I won't be alone. Maryam is with me,' she said. Maryam and Sehreen went for a drive around the neighbourhood. Once they were around Daniyal's house, they started circling the area. Maryam knew that Daniyal went to the gym at 4 p.m., so they waited. The roads only had a few cars running and some people walking. They'd give Maryam and Sehreen an odd look when they passed by. The girls didn't see Daniyal that day, and went back home. Down but not out.

Maryam and Sehreen tried again after a few days. This time they got out Maryam's car and waited closer to Daniyal's house. Finally, a car emerged from Daniyal's lane. It was his father's car. Maryam recognized it at once and honked. She honked several times to grab Daniyal's attention. At some point, she was tempted to get out and wave at him. But this was a known neighbourhood; word would get around, her parents would find out, and not only would Maryam get into trouble, but her relationship with Daniyal would also be in jeopardy. Not to mention Sehreen—she would be in hot water as well.

Luckily, Daniyal noticed the mindless honking and recognized Maryam's car. He got out and started running towards it. Maryam saw him getting closer in the rear-view mirror and smiled. But suddenly, he stopped. Daniyal turned around and walked back calmly. He got into his car and drove off. Sehreen stared at Maryam. She was at a loss for words. 'What was that?' she asked.

Maryam refused to give up hope. 'He must have seen a relative and stopped. I think I know what he's going to do.' Maryam started the car. She drove it into a narrow lane where Daniyal and she would often meet. It was their private spot to park and talk. She was almost certain that he'd come there. They waited for some time, and sure enough, after fifteen minutes, Daniyal's car turned into the lane.

Daniyal drove up to Maryam's car. Both their windows slid down. 'I'll take her from here,' he told Sehreen. Maryam gave her car keys to Sehreen. 'I'll be back in fifteen minutes,' she said. Maryam jumped out of her car and into his. Daniyal drove off.

They drove around the neighbouring lanes, keeping away from the main roads. This was the first time they were getting some privacy after weeks. Maryam caught her reflection in the mirror. She was wearing her night clothes and looking unkempt. She looked at Daniyal. He was as shabby as her. 'A good-looking pair we make,' she said. They burst out laughing.

It was now that Maryam finally got to see Daniyal excited about his result. He was so, so happy. He held Maryam's hand throughout the drive, shifting the gear with it. For the first time, Maryam wasn't the one blabbering. Daniyal was. He was unstoppable. The one time Maryam interrupted him, he said, 'Shut up. I need to tell you a lot of things. I will forget them. So just let me talk.' So, she let him. Maryam watched in amazement and with love as Daniyal turned into the most animated version of himself that she had ever seen. He was gesticulating, his face a canvas of expressions.

Daniyal told her in chronological order—how he felt when he saw the result; how his parents reacted to the news; how he missed talking to her about it immediately; how he used to drive by her house every day to catch a glimpse of her.

Maryam was finally content.

Back in the lane where Sehreen was waiting, Daniyal stopped the car. They hugged each other tightly and made a pact that they would try to meet like this every alternate day at 4 p.m. If Maryam couldn't make it or didn't have the car that day, Daniyal would drive around her house and honk three times. If she heard, she would come to the window to see him. If possible, go for a drive from there if no one was watching the road.

Of course, these plans didn't always work out. Without phones or any other means of communication, coordination was close to impossible. More than that, because of the lockdown, everyone was for the most part at home. It was impossible to slip out of the house unnoticed. And then there was the fact that expecting Sehreen to play Maryam's chaperone-cum-alibi every other day felt like a big ask.

Still, Sehreen was helpful. 'We are bored at home and sick of sitting indoors,' she would say when Maryam needed to slip out. The family would relent, knowing that staying at home was unnerving for them all, but especially hard for younger people. Before seeing them off, the family would always offer words of caution. 'Come back before dark. Don't talk to anyone. Don't go too far. You'll get caught in a kani-jang or stopped at a checkpoint.' After hearing this for the millionth time, Sehreen and Maryam would get into the car and zoom off, sometimes taking Arshiya along. Maryam was thankful she had sisters—not only because they helped her meet Daniyal, but also because when times are fraught, one relies on personal connections. Not everyone was blessed with a supportive family, she knew.

If Maryam couldn't make it to Daniyal's neighbourhood, sometimes, Daniyal would throw notes and snacks into Arshiya's garden. Her house was right next to Maryam's, the garden didn't have any lights, and, therefore, love-tokens could be tossed over inconspicuously in the evenings. Sometimes the notes read: 'Let's go for a drive.' And Maryam, on receiving them from Arshiya, would go to her window and gesture a yes or a no. If snacks (such as Maryam's favourite chips) landed in the garden, Arshiya and Maryam would feast on them later. 'I approve of him,' Arshiya would say while munching.

For a few weeks, Maryam and Daniyal caught some moments of stolen time over these covert drives. By September, Maryam was summoned back to college for hospital duty (though not daily). She was desperate to find out more about her NEET PG exams and how her friends were faring. Denied any connection to the outside world, she didn't even know when the exam forms would be released. Then there was the challenge of filling the forms online. How was she going to do that? After all, internet access was still out of reach.

Returning to college came with an additional advantage for Maryam. The selected KAS candidates needed to compulsorily undergo medical check-ups. Daniyal was assigned SMHS hospital, which GMC, Maryam's medical college, was a part of. Maryam bunked her classes the day Daniyal was there. The two of them reached the hospital early. After Daniyal's check-ups were done, they sat in the car in the parking lot and chatted the whole day. Restaurants weren't open yet, so they couldn't visit one. But the car proved to be the perfect place—if not the only place—to talk in privacy.

By end September, Maryam started going to college more regularly. Daniyal would have work around the area as well. GMC was always their meeting point. While Maryam was in classes or on hospital duty, Daniyal left notes on her car's windshield about his whereabouts, mostly on receipts or tissue paper. *I'm here. I'll get free by this time. Don't go home. Wait for me* ... and so on.

In all of this, Maryam realized she hadn't been able to meet her friends and fellow students at GMC. As none of them had working phones, coordination was impossible. Besides, she was trying to spend the little time she had free with Daniyal. One day, quite by chance, Maryam saw her friends huddled around her car in the parking lot. They had cheeky grins on their faces. When they saw Maryam, one of them started pulling her leg. 'Hmm ... we can see why you don't have any time for us.' Confused, Maryam looked past them and saw a note on her car's windshield. She blushed. 'Romance is in the air, we see,' another friend chuckled. Maryam plucked the note and read it. *'Wait for me. I am around. I will get free by 3.30.'* Maryam looked at her watch and then at her friends. 'Let's have tea? I have an hour to kill.' All of them burst out laughing.

After this incident, Maryam would leave her car window open just a crack, enough for a piece of paper to pass through. Daniyal would pass her the notes through the window, so that Maryam's friends couldn't tease her again. Maryam would see the notes resting on her car seat whenever she got back. Then she'd wait for him.

One day, when Maryam had gone to Lal Ded Hospital for her ob-gyn internship, she saw a note from Daniyal in her car. *'I'm here. Just keep looking for me. I will be around.'* In the big maternity hospital, without a phone, it was hard to find anybody. Nonetheless Maryam started looking for him. She roamed around in the halls for almost an hour, walking as fast as she could to cover more ground. One senior doctor frowned when she saw her. 'I thought you were done for the day. Do you want more work?' Maryam smiled and shook her head, getting away so that the doctor didn't actually give her more tasks to complete.

Then, out of nowhere, Maryam saw Daniyal up ahead. He caught sight of her from a distance, and he smiled. They started walking towards each other. As it happens in Bollywood films, the world slowed down and an imaginary path cleared in front of them. Almost in slow motion, they met in the middle. Shy, coy, reserved.

'Hi.'

'Hi.'

'Hello? Move.' They both jumped in shock. A disgruntled nurse was wheeling in a patient, and the two lovers were blocking her way. They moved aside and she zipped across, grumbling under her breath. Maryam and Daniyal giggled. 'Let's get out of here before my senior sees me,' Maryam said.

Only a few restaurants had opened by now, so they made do with whatever was—in this case, RK Sarovar, a hotel in Srinagar which was also serving as the media centre for the press during this turbulent period.[36] With no internet access anywhere else in Kashmir, journalists had to make a beeline for RK Sarovar, which had a few computers and extremely slow internet speeds. The journalists would wait in long queues that would test their patience, file their stories and painstakingly upload their reportage. All they wanted was to get the ground reality out into the world, but the entire process was a nerve-racking ordeal. It was breaking away at their perseverence, one kbps at a time.

Maryam and Daniyal were having lunch in RK Sarovar's lounge garden. There were many cameras on the ground floor as a lot of reporters filmed there. Maryam was immediately worried. 'What if they film us in the background?' Daniyal looked around and waved off the concern. 'We're safe, don't worry.' They finished lunch, and Daniyal drove Maryam back to her car parked closer to home. She drove back home the rest of the way.

Maryam walked into the hamām where her parents were watching the evening news. She glanced at the screen, and her heart flipped. The news correspondent was speaking from RK Sarovar. It was a pre-recorded clip from the time that Maryam and Daniyal had been there, a few hours ago. Maryam sat on the carpet next to her mother, her heart pounding. She could see Daniyal's blue Hyundai i20 in the parking lot behind the correspondent. Of course, no one knew that was Daniyal's car except her. But as she watched the screen, panicking, all she could think of was one possibility—that if the camera panned even a little bit, she would be seen eating in the restaurant with Daniyal. Then her parents would know where she had been that day and with whom.

Maryam tried to distract her parents so they would look away from the TV screen. But they were glued to it; this was the only bit of fresh news they got every day about what was happening in Kashmir. Maryam hyperventilated. Any moment now she would be exposed.

Thankfully, the camera did not pan. The correspondent finished what he was saying, and the visuals went back to the news anchor in the studio in New Delhi. Maryam collapsed into a cushion. Her mother stared at her in confusion. 'Did you not eat today?' she asked. Maryam sighed heavily. 'I think I've had enough.'

Soon, Maryam and Daniyal's landlines started working. While Daniyal had a cordless phone that he could keep in his room at night, Maryam didn't. Each night, she had to wait for everyone in the family to fall sleep, while she pretended to sleep in her room. Then, at midnight, she would sneak down the stairs silently and call Daniyal from the hamām's phone. To her family—when they realized she wasn't asleep—she claimed that she liked watching movies in the hamām late into the night. 'We're living life on the edge, aren't we?' she'd whisper into the phone's receiver. With the RK Sarovar near-miss and now the covert phone calls, things sure were getting exciting.

By October, Daniyal had to go to Jammu for some KAS training. Maryam could no longer call him on the landline. She'd have to wait for him to call from somewhere. It was a frustrating and painful wait every day.

'I heard the phones are opening this week,' Daniyal told Maryam in mid-October. It was almost midnight, and Maryam yawned. 'Sure, sure,' she said. 'I hear that every day.'

'Call me first when your phone starts,' Daniyal continued.

Maryam agreed, though she was sure that nothing was going to happen. These false promises had been made for months to Kashmiris.

A few days later, Maryam was in the hospital when she felt a vibration in her bag. Thinking she had left a rogue alarm on, she rummaged only to find her phone buzzing. 'Daniyal calling,' it read. She had been so long without a working phone that she hadn't recognized the buzzing of her own. All around her, people's phones started pinging in unison. Everyone stopped listening to what the senior doctor had been saying, who herself was busy checking her phone.

Maryam picked up her phone call excitedly. 'I was supposed to call you first!'

'Well, I beat you to it, doctor sahiba.'

'Noted, KAS sahab.'

Both of them giggled at their lame joke. It felt like the first time they had spoken when they were teenagers—the giddiness, the excitement, the awkwardness of it all; the need to keep voices low so that no one would hear.

WHILE PHONES WERE NOW working in Kashmir, the internet still was not functional. And by the looks of it, it wasn't going to start working any time soon.

Maryam's exam prep had taken a severe hit. She was used to studying with online mock tests and videos, so the textbooks were not cutting it. As the rest of the country prepared for the NEET PG exams with all resources a click away, Maryam, her friends and fellow students were at a disadvantage. By end November, Maryam learnt that exam forms were out. They had been out for a while now, but word travelled slowly and sporadically to Kashmir. Maryam scrambled to find a place where she could fill her online form. One of her mother's relatives worked in the income tax department. The office had slow internet access for work purposes. Maryam landed up there and, despite the frustrating internet speed, managed to fill her form. She returned every alternate day for a couple of hours to gather whatever study material the internet allowed. She downloaded practice tests, took screenshots, screen-recorded study videos on her phone to watch later, all in the midst of the hustle, bustle and noise in the office. She often got distracted, and could memorize very little, but was determined to go on.

Now it was time for Daniyal to calm Maryam down as she fretted over her exams. Maryam said, 'I'm still not as annoying as you were!' Daniyal smiled. He comforted her and pushed her on.

As the exam date got closer, Maryam thought there would be no more surprises in store. Wrong. News was spreading that the students appearing for the NEET PG exams from Kashmir had been allotted exam centres in Jammu. Maryam reeled on hearing this information. Already her nerves were frayed; would she also have to travel to Jammu?

Maryam had given her email address and password to a friend in Mumbai, asking her to keep a lookout for mails from the National Board of Education (NBE) and specifically one that offered an 'admit card'. That would solve the Jammu mystery once and for all. But while the rest of the country got their admit cards, Maryam's didn't even show up on the website. Maryam's friend sent several emails to the NBE but received no response. With no admit card and no other intimation, Maryam—and all the others in Kashmir wishing to appear for the NEET PG exams —didn't know whether to go to Jammu or stay put.

The NEET PG exams were in the first week of January in 2020; this coincided with the height of chilạy kalān, the harshest period of winter in Kashmir spanning forty days. Maryam was just about making peace with the fact that she would have to travel to Jammu, when the weather forecast for the exam week showed heavy snowfall in the region. The students were anxious. What if they travelled to Jammu by road and got stuck somewhere on the highway in the snow? What if flights didn't take off because of the weather? What if they didn't reach the exam centre on time?

Barely a week before the exam, luckily or unluckily for the students, they got emails from the NBE telling them that they had the option of changing their exam centres to Kashmir on account of extreme weather conditions. These were emails no one knew they had received since there was no internet access. It was Maryam's friend in Mumbai who called to tell her the news. Maryam told her to respond at once saying that she wanted to shift her centre to Srinagar. Her friend did that, but the mail bounced back. Again and again. Finally, at the umpteenth attempt, it went through.

The last week before the exam seemed to crawl. There had been no reply from the NBE yet. As the exam day started inching close, Maryam and her friends again didn't know whether to stay in Kashmir or travel to Jammu. This was an absolutely soul-crushing, mind-numbing exercise. What had they done to deserve such disregard?

Three days before the exam, Maryam woke up to a blanket of snow outside. It had snowed heavily like the weather department had predicted. Flights to Jammu were getting cancelled. Maryam and the others were stuck in Kashmir for good now.

Two days before the exam, Maryam's friend called her from Mumbai. There was an email from the NBE saying that the exam centre had been shifted for her. Maryam sighed in relief, only momentarily, the stress of not knowing whether she could appear for the exam quickly getting replaced by the stress of actually appearing for it.

Finally, the day arrived. It's safe to say that Maryam was not terribly confident about faring well in the NEET PG. With limited practice prior for a computer-based exam, it took her a while to understand the commands and buttons on the keyboard, and she lost precious time. She had to leave out some questions to avoid negative marking, and by the end of it all, Maryam was underwhelmed by her performance. She knew that she wasn't going to get the score that she wanted.

Daniyal did everything he could to cheer Maryam up, but she felt dejected. Mentally, she had already told herself that she would appear for the exam again. Internet access couldn't be barred forever. Or could it?

As she had anticipated, Maryam's results weren't as good as she had wanted them to be. They weren't bad either, because after the counselling sessions, Maryam found out that she was eligible for some medical branches. They were just not the branches she had wanted.

Maryam mulled over the possibilities before her. She didn't want to take a decision and regret it her whole life, especially while knowing that she was capable of cracking the exam if she had the tools she desired—if she had internet access. She had it in her to fare superbly. Daniyal knew this, too, who told her not to settle for anything less than what she wanted. Maryam decided to drop the year and give the NEET PG exams another go.

Maryam appeared for the exams after almost a year-and-a-half; they had been severely delayed this time due to the Covid-19 pandemic. However, with internet access now available, and practice tests within reach, she got a good score. And she secured her preferred branch—gynaecology. Unlike Daniyal's KAS result, Maryam's results could be properly celebrated. 'It'll be lots of night duty, mind you. Don't miss me too much when I'm away,' Maryam teased. Daniyal chuckled, 'I have spent enough nights for a lifetime talking to you already. I will be fine.'

Maryam was posted in Lal Ded Hospital, the big maternity centre where Daniyal and she had found each other in the midst of the communication blockade. That cheesy moment still brought a smile to her face whenever she passed that corridor. So much time had gone past since then, yet it felt like just a heartbeat away.

Now both Maryam and Daniyal were where they wanted to be, doing the work that they wanted for themselves and for each other. From covert chats in cars and almost getting caught at RK Sarovar, they would finally be able to disclose their association. It didn't have to be hush-hush any longer. Not much longer indeed.

Note: Maryam and Daniyal are now married and have a son.

16

AGLI HARTĀL

NADIYA AND SHAHID WERE from two different schools in Srinagar. In 2009, they were both in the eighth grade. Neither knew that the other existed.

Eighth grade is also when most kids in Kashmir start attending tuition classes. Nadiya's father was extremely strict and particular about her academic pursuits. He always had the final word in the household, and because of him, Nadiya wasn't allowed to go to tuition classes just yet. She was highly studious anyway, so tuition classes didn't matter. Her life revolved around going to school, getting good grades, homework and then studying some more.

Mobile phones and social networking sites were on the rise. Nadiya's friends constantly gossiped about the boys they saw at the tuition centres they attended, but Nadiya couldn't be bothered. Her schedule had been set in stone for so many years now that nothing could get in the way, however cute 'it' may be. Dating was not even on the horizon.

For all of the eighth grade, Nadiya kept hearing about a 'Shahid' who attended her friends' tuition class. He was from another school and apparently a total dreamboat. Her friends just needed an excuse to speak about him. The conversations ranged from what he had said in class that day to how his school muffler was styled to how he'd passed them a textbook. Nadiya's friends had a huge crush on Shahid, but when Nadiya suggested this to them, they denied it in a peel of giggles. Nadiya hadn't seen him yet, but sure was curious about this mystery boy who had taken up a huge chunk of her daily conversations.

Towards the end of 2009, Nadiya appeared for her eighth grade Jammu and Kashmir board exams and passed with distinction. Ninth grade would soon commence, and she decided that it was time to join tuition classes. Her first choice was to go to the one her friends went to. But before deciding anything, she needed permission from her parents. They discussed the matter between themselves and agreed to send her. Nadiya who had already readied a pros-and-cons list was pleasantly surprised to see that her folks had relented so easily. She had learnt over time that her father was unyielding when it came to letting Nadiya leave the house for something other than 'studies'. To her luck, tuition classes fell under the general umbrella of 'studies', and she was enrolled into her friends' tuition classes the very next day.

Nadiya hadn't confided in her friends yet, but she had always been curious about Shahid. From the first time they had mentioned Shahid, she had wanted to see him, know him, talk to him. She had not even seen a picture of Shahid, yet she felt a strange connection to him. Maybe at a subconscious level, that's why she wanted to attend the tuition class as well.

The first day of the tuition class, Nadiya told her friends casually, 'Point *that boy* out to me when he arrives. I also want to see what you guys keep harping on about.' Her straight face didn't give anything away. As the class filled with more students and the chatter grew louder, one of Nadiya's friends nudged her, and with the slightest tilt of her chin, pointed to Shahid. Nadiya turned and stared.

Shahid had just walked in with a group of his friends. By his demeanour he looked shy and reserved. All the boys sat together at the far end of the room. Nadiya saw him for the first time, and well ... she did not like him at all.

Nadiya was disappointed. Having built him up in her mind for so long, she was devastated that reality didn't match up. She couldn't put a finger on what had irked her. She turned back to her friends, who were still staring at Shahid with googly eyes. 'Are you crazy? You've been speaking about *this* guy for a whole year? What's so special about him?' They withered under her critical stare. The class started, and they didn't bring up Shahid for the rest of the session.

Days passed at the tuition class, and Nadiya didn't speak to Shahid—not even to ask for an extra pen when her ink ran out, or to close the door to stop the heat from escaping in the winters. Nothing. The fact that they didn't converse didn't bother her. Till it did. She discerned that he was ignoring her back. She noticed it one day when Shahid came to class late. The only empty seat was next to Nadiya, but he sat down on the carpet. Nadiya was offended. That's when she started noticing more of this behaviour. If all the seats were empty and only Nadiya was sitting in the room, Shahid would still find the seat farthest away from her.

Stung, Nadiya tried to talk to him. But all her efforts were in vain. If she asked Shahid for the time, he wouldn't reply or pretend not to hear. It was tit for tat, Nadiya decided. 'I don't even know him,' she fumed, 'and he doesn't know me. What's his damn problem?' All the feelings that Nadiya had been suppressing until now came bubbling to the surface.

Unwittingly, Shahid had become someone she looked forward to seeing every day. Unable to grapple with her muddled feelings as she had always been a 'good, studious girl', she resorted to ignoring him. In any case, he was ignoring her—but now she wondered if he had developed feelings for her as well.

Over the next few days, Nadiya took extra note of Shahid. He was inherently a shy person—her first impression was correct—but he *did* talk to the other girls in class, just not her. Once, as a ploy to initiate conversation, Nadiya held on to Shahid's guidebook that was being shared by a few of them. He would *have* to ask for it back. But instead, Shahid left without taking his book back from her. Nadiya handed it to his friends later, frowning at his antics.

The mystery unravelled quickly one day when Nadiya was exiting the bathroom. She overheard Shahid's friends talking in whispers near a corridor. 'Shahid likes Nadiya. That's why he's always in a funk around her ... because she keeps ignoring him.' The boys sniggered amongst themselves. 'How the hell do you know?' one of them enquired. Nadiya crept closer to listen, staying deathly quiet. 'He told me himself, duh. He's such a lovelorn puppy. When I gave back his guidebook that she returned, he looked at it like it was gold.'

Nadiya had finally heard what she had wanted to. She was elated. To put an end to the strange cold war between Shahid and her, she decided to take matters into her own hands. She didn't have a mobile phone to speak to him, so didn't try to get his number. The only way to talk to him was in the tuition classes, so she devised ways in which Shahid would be compelled to respond to her.

The next day in class, when the tuition teacher announced that she would be taking a surprise mock test, Nadiya's hand shot up. 'Ma'am, I'd like to ask the questions please?'

The teacher gave her a quizzical look. But since Nadiya was a class topper and least in need of the test, she agreed. Taking the clipboard with the questions from the teacher, Nadiya stood in front of her peers, all of whom looked bewildered at the turn of events.

Nadiya went through the questions and nonchalantly glanced around the class, choosing her prey. 'Yes, Shahid?' she asked. Shahid, who had been purposefully staring out the window, turned to look at her. Unlike all the other times, his eyes didn't flit to the floor. Nadiya realized that this was the first time she had said his name aloud, to him and to herself. With her friends, she spoke about boys, even Shahid, using pronouns, never imparting any degree of importance to them.

As Shahid stared at her, Nadiya quickly recomposed herself. 'Give one difference between mitosis and meiosis.' The whole class went silent, waiting for Shahid to open his mouth. Several seconds passed. Shahid and Nadiya didn't break eye contact.

The impatient teacher was about to chastise him when Shahid spoke. 'Mitosis results in two daughter cells that are identical to the parent cell. Meiosis, on the other hand, results in four non-identical daughter cells, each having half the number of chromosomes of the parent cell.' Everyone sighed in relief. Nadiya smiled at Shahid.

A beat.

A breath.

Shahid smiled back.

From that day onwards, they started talking. Every day after the tuition class got over, Shahid waited outside for Nadiya to emerge. The tuition classes were after school, so they would come directly in their school uniforms. Across two hours or longer, the teachers would cover six subjects. It was basically like going to school all over again. The boys got done sooner than the girls, and Shahid would have to wait almost an hour for Nadiya to get free. It was really a tactic used by the tuition classes to stop the boys and girls from mingling after they dispersed.

On getting free, Nadiya would start off in the direction of her home. Shahid would walk on the other side of the road. As soon as she was out the eyeshot of her friends, Shahid would cross over and join her. Her home was a twenty-minute walk away. Shahid accompanied her to a point close to her residence, just a few steps shy of it, to avoid the gawking of hamsāyè—neighbours or known people—and the possibility of them ratting Nadiya and Shahid out to their parents. If Nadiya's father got to know, it would be goodbye to tuition classes for her. Shahid was aware of this, and never tried dropping Nadiya to her gate.

Nadiya and Shahid would separate, and he'd walk back to his own house, which wasn't too far from hers. She lived in Bagh-e-Mehtab and he lived in Chanpora.

As they were in different schools, neither knew the other's teachers, class clowns or had any inside jokes. Thus, the walks would be filled with long explanations, so the context of every story and joke was clear. They still hadn't said out loud that they liked or loved each other, but these walks were perceived as dates. They were dating.

In 2010, they faced their first major hartāl during their relationship. In April that year, the Indian army claimed to have foiled an infiltration bid from across the line of control.[37] They killed three armed militants from Pakistan in an encounter in Machil, Kupwara. However, it was found out that the encounter had been staged and that the three alleged militants were, in fact, civilians who had been lured into the army camp with the promise of jobs and then shot in cold blood. The civilian men had been handed over to the army by their sources in exchange for a cash reward. Kashmir rose in protest.

During one of the protests following the killings, Tufail Ahmad Mattoo, a seventeen-year-old student who had been heading out from his tuition class, was hit on the head by a tear gas shell.[38] He bled to death on the spot. A regular student a day before, just like Nadiya and Shahid, he was laid to rest at the Martyr's Graveyard in Srinagar. What followed were months of curfew and hartāls.

Nadiya and Shahid didn't go to school for a really long time due to the shutdowns. Tuition classes were still open and at a walking distance from home, so they got to meet each other—but there was a degree of uncertainty that dictated all comings and goings. They were still young kids, so the concept of longing for someone hadn't formed yet. Nadiya and Shahid's conversations primarily consisted of teasing each other and cracking jokes. As the months of unrest continued, Nadiya and Shahid had each other as constants in a fast-shifting world.

As the unrest settled, they moved from the ninth to the tenth grade. The walks home from tuition classes continued as usual. Nadiya had a hunch that her friends still had a crush on Shahid. She hadn't confided in them about her relationship, so she never asked. Both Shahid and Nadiya had done pretty well to hide their relationship even from their friends, and no one was suspicious. Yet.

At some point though, her friends realized that Nadiya and Shahid seemed to be leaving together every day. Out of envy, they tattled to the tuition teacher.

The next day, the teacher summoned Nadiya to her office. Once the door was closed behind her, she slapped Nadiya tightly across the face. Nadiya was petrified. As she came back to her senses, she heard the teacher berating her. 'What's going on between you and Shahid? Do you come here to study or roam around with boys?' she spat out.

Nadiya mumbled that they were just friends. Unconvinced, the teacher carried on, 'I've seen many such "friends" who bunk class and go for shikạ̄ra rides. Do you want me to call your parents and tell them?' Nadiya shook her head furiously. Pleased with the effect her scolding had had, the teacher calmed down. 'If I see you near him again, your parents will hear about it. Do you understand?' Nadiya nodded, staring at the floor, angry tears gathering in her eyes. The teacher settled back into her chair and slurped her tea loudly. 'Get lost now.'

Nadiya scurried out of there in a hurry. She didn't speak to her friends who she was sure were behind this. Even they were shaken when they saw her face, a deep shade of red, in class. When they tried to talk to her once the teacher left, she took her stuff and ran out. Nadiya changed her route, bypassing the one where she knew Shahid would be waiting at, and caught an auto-rickshaw to go back home.

The impact of the slap on Nadiya was huge. She felt hurt and betrayed by her friends and perturbed by her teacher's moral policing—moral policing that was only reserved for the girls. The boys could do no wrong or were let off easy. Nadiya was also aware that the teacher wanted some favours from Shahid as his family had affluent connections; she was sure this was partly why he had not been scolded at all.

Hurt that, besides all else, Shahid had not got a raw deal like her, Nadiya stopped speaking to him altogether and said nothing about the incident. She also didn't want him to argue with the teacher—which would only invite more attention on herself—so Nadiya kept him at bay.

Shahid knew nothing of the slap and was baffled and bruised by Nadiya's cold behaviour. He tried to talk to her in class and continued to wait for her afterwards, but Nadiya had changed her route and wasn't about to take the old one.

After many days, Shahid finally caught Nadiya while she was walking down the alternate route. He looked so vulnerable and confused that Nadiya spilled the beans. Shahid's face turned sombre. 'How dare she hit you and not say a word to me! I'm an equal part of this. I'm going there right now.' Shahid turned to leave, but Nadiya stopped him.

'Please don't create a scene. I don't want more attention!' Nadiya could see that none of this was Shahid's fault; he had simply become the target of her anger and hurt. At that moment, as she stood with Shahid, she decided to stop punishing him. She dug into her bag and brought out a pen and notebook. She scribbled something on a page and tore it off. She handed it to Shahid. 'Now write yours,' Nadiya said and gave him her notebook. Shahid saw that the piece of paper held a ten-digit mobile number. 'It's my father's mobile number, so you can't call,' Nadiya said. 'I will take it from him in the evening for some time and call you.' Shahid nodded as he scrawled his own number in her notebook.

Both decided to hang out less in public and have all their conversations via phone, so that no one found out about them.

At 7 p.m. every day, Nadiya would call Shahid. They'd speak for half an hour, and at 7.30 p.m. sharp, they'd cut the call. Nadiya would delete the call logs and give the phone back to her unsuspecting father. Shahid never called the number even by mistake.

Neither knew how to 'act' in a romantic relationship or what to talk about. What they cared about was daily gossip and academics, and these were the two topics that dominated all their conversations. Even if they fought with each other, the calls never stopped. If they were angry, they didn't speak for the whole duration of the call, but they made sure not to skip calling. The fights didn't last long anyway.

The only time Nadiya got extremely pissed off with Shahid was during the last days of their tenth grade. A girl at the tuition class had given Nadiya a piece of paper. She had told Nadiya that a junior girl in her school bus had asked to pass it on to her. Nadiya opened the note to find a phone number. 'She asked you to call her.' Nadiya knew that the girl passing on the note was from Shahid's school. But she didn't know anyone else from there who would want to talk to her. Better safe than sorry, Nadiya thought, and threw the paper away. When she told Shahid about this, even he was bewildered. 'Who could it be?' he asked. Then he added, 'I'll look into it.'

A few days later at the tuition class, the girl who had scribbled the note, landed up herself. She confronted Nadiya. 'I had sent my number to you. I wanted to speak to you. Why didn't you call me?'

Nadiya was taken aback. 'I don't call strangers. How do you know me?' she asked.

The girl told Nadiya that she had been dating Shahid before her. That Nadiya had come in between them.

This landed like a tonne of bricks on Nadiya. She hadn't known anything of Shahid's past and had always assumed that they were each other's 'firsts'. Shahid hadn't ever mentioned an ex-girlfriend or the fact that he had left someone high and dry for her. Stung but stoic, Nadiya told the girl that if she had come in between them, she would step back. 'If he wants to be with you, he can,' she said. With that, she walked away, tears stinging her eyes.

Nadiya didn't call Shahid that night. She was distraught. Shahid knew better than to call her father's number—so he didn't either. The next day he tracked Nadiya down at the tuition class. 'Why are you ignoring me?' he asked woefully. Nadiya hissed, 'Because there was something brewing between you and that girl who sent me the note—back when she was in the seventh grade and you were in the eighth. Then in the ninth grade you left her for me.' Shahid blinked, confused, as though this were news to him. Nadiya continued, 'You can go back to her if you like. I won't stand in the way.'

Shahid calmed Nadiya down. He told her that he had never dated the girl. 'She liked me at one point, but it was one-sided, and it never amounted to anything.' Shahid added that when he figured out that the note was from her, he had even told her to stay away from Nadiya and him. 'I'm sorry I didn't tell you about her or any of this. That's all in the past. You are the only person I have ever dated, and I don't want to be with her or anyone else.'

Nadiya was irked for some days, but she eventually moved on. That was the first big fight they had had.

In a few months, their tenth board exams passed them by. Nadiya was a school topper and had secured a ranking in the Valley as well.

She shifted schools for the eleventh and twelfth grades—she enrolled herself in a government school—as her previous educational institution only offered classes till the tenth. Shahid's school was bigger, and he didn't need to switch.

Now, Nadiya entered a world of fewer boundaries. Government schools weren't as strict as private ones. They didn't have their own buses and were extremely lax about attendance. For roll call, someone else could say 'yes, ma'am' on one's behalf, and the teacher wouldn't even look up from the register.

Nadiya was no longer tethered. Whereas in her previous school, her routine was fixed—school, tuition, home and repeat—now, she could improvise. Since she was technically always 'present' in class, the school had no reason to call her parents. In other words, Shahid and she could meet as often as they wanted.

The two finally started going out on dates around Srinagar. Nadiya would leave for school each day, and on most days she attended classes. But when the mood struck, she'd take the day off from school along with Shahid. He would pick her up in the morning from outside her school gates and they would go for shikāra rides (realizing with amusement that the tuition teacher had been right after all) or walk along the Jhelum river bund after having ice cream at Zero Inn. Or they'd have tuj at Makai Point or traipse through the Mughal gardens in Srinagar.

They'd usually travel by local buses or Sumo cars, receiving a few inquisitive glares as they'd be in school uniform in the middle of the day. But the two learnt to stare back till all judgemental onlookers were forced to look away. This is how Nadiya and Shahid would spend their dates together—free of incessant phone calls and tension.

Nadiya had opted for PCBM (Physics, Chemistry, Biology and Maths), and Shahid had chosen commerce as his stream of choice. He didn't have tuition classes to attend, but she had long ones. When Shahid and Nadiya weren't on dates, Shahid would pick her up from school and drop her to her tuition classes, then pick her up again and drop her home. It would be dark by the time Nadiya finished, so she was thankful that Shahid was around to take her home.

By now, Shahid had given her a small button-pad Nokia phone. These were called 'illegal phones' in Kashmir, as one's parents didn't know about them. Nadiya was always on tenterhooks, convinced that someone at home would find the phone in its hiding spot or hear it because the ringer would be left on loud accidentally. Thankfully, none of this transpired. Shahid and Nadiya talked through the night, no longer dependent on Nadiya's father's phone. Nadiya whispered under her bedcovers, while remaining deeply aware of the night sounds around her—a creaking floorboard or the distant rumble of toilets flushing.

The anxiety of keeping the Nokia phone a secret ended in the twelfth grade when Nadiya was deemed old enough to be given a cell phone by her parents.

This is when Nadiya discovered social media and texting (something the good old Nokia didn't accommodate)—a world that had always been alluded to by people, but that she had never experienced on her own. She could text with Shahid for hours without having to talk in whispers and could even do this in front of her parents without them getting suspicious—of course, she'd have to maintain a deadpan face.

While her father had bought the phone for her, Nadiya knew that this gesture didn't mean that his views had changed. He was still the strict patriarch who hated the term 'love marriage'. If he got even a whiff of her relationship, Nadiya would be banned from leaving the house till she was married off to someone of his choice. 'For marriage, your views don't matter. The family selects the boy!' From the time she was a little girl, this statement had been dinned into Nadiya. She was fully aware of the dangerous step she had taken.

That she wanted to be with Shahid she was absolutely sure of. How they were going to get to a place of permanence was a matter she couldn't make sense of. Thrilled as she was with her newfound freedom in the eleventh and twelfth grades, Nadiya decided to keep all thoughts about the future at bay.

NADIYA AND SHAHID GOT into different colleges after the twelfth board exams.

Nadiya decided to pursue a BSc in biology, and Shahid opted for a business administration degree. He had his driver's license by now and a car as well. Gone were the days of fighting for an empty seat in the local buses. Nadiya and Shahid travelled in his car everywhere. Furthermore, this meant that no one would recognize them in public transport and try snitching.

By now, Shahid's family knew about Nadiya and were very happy. Nadiya had even spoken to Shahid's mother on the phone. 'You just tell us when, beta, and we will send the rishtè,' she had said. But since Nadiya's family could potentially oppose the match, the two had to tread carefully till the time to talk marriage arrived.

Nadiya and Shahid viewed family opposition as just one more hiccup in what had been a long courtship in turbulent times. The real impact of hartāls hit them in 2016 when Burhan Wani was killed. Nadiya and Shahid were in college and had been in a relationship for several years now. Nadiya's final year of her BSc degree had just begun. Phone networks stopped working. Only landlines and BSNL SIM cards were functional, both of which Nadiya didn't have. There was no Wi-Fi at home either. Maybe if she could meet Shahid outside under the guise of attending tuition classes, he could have given her a BSNL SIM card, but Nadiya's family didn't let her venture out. The lockdown continued for a few months, and the two of them didn't talk for the entirety of it.

The day colleges reopened, Nadiya was awake at 5 a.m. to get ready. The excitement of finally being able to see Shahid had kept her up all night. She literally ran out the gate and went through the entire day at college in a state of total distraction. At the end of it, she came out of her college and scanned the crowds for Shahid's car. Sure enough, he was standing next to it, waving at her.

Nadiya entered the car, and Shahid got into the driver's seat. In the privacy of the vehicle, they hugged each other tightly. After all the sweet nothings had been exchanged, Shahid stared into Nadiya's moist eyes, his own the same, and said, '*Agli hartāl se pehle main tujhe le jaaonga.*' He assured her that he would marry her before the next hartāl. 'I can't take it anymore,' he added.

ONCE BOTH SHAHID AND Nadiya had graduated, Shahid decided to pursue business and Nadiya appeared for the entrance exams for her bachelor of education degree. She got through and joined Kashmir University. It was a long way from her house, and a daily commute to and fro would be extremely difficult for her. So it was decided that she would go stay at her maasi's house in Nowhatta for the duration of her course, which was three years.

At first, the idea of a move was met with resistance from Nadiya's father. Nadiya's mother convinced him. 'How will she travel for so long every day? Will you drop her and pick her up? No, right? She will be exhausted. When will she study? She will burn out in no time.' Her father accepted the reasoning.

Shahid supported Nadiya's decision. They were both also relaxed because Nadiya's aunt knew about their relationship; in fact, she was the first person in her family Nadiya had confided in. Before moving to her house, Nadiya had called her. 'There's a boy, and I like him. I want to marry him,' she had said. Nadiya knew it was time to start warming her family up to the idea, so that eventually she'd have help to convince her father. Her maasi understood. They had always been close.

Nadiya had been yearning to tell someone in her family. She had a brother and sister, both younger than her. As the eldest child, she didn't want to place the weight of her disclosure on either of them. So, she had chosen her maasi. What she didn't know was that her maasi had passed on the news to Nadiya's mother; after all, Nadiya's mother was her elder sister, and she didn't want to back the relationship without her consent. Nadiya's mother approached her daughter when she found out, and to Nadiya's surprise, she was fine with it. 'But on one condition,' she told Nadiya. 'I want to speak to Shahid's mother first to get to know their family, their intentions and if they are serious about marriage.'

Nadiya and Shahid's mothers spoke on the phone. The lovers remained nervous the whole time as they tried to eavesdrop on the conversation. Finally, Nadiya's mother's door opened. Seeing her daughter's panic-stricken face, she smiled. She hugged her warmly and said, 'It's all good.' Nadiya collapsed into her mother's arms, relieved that her love would not go in vain. Both mother and maasi accepted the relationship.

Nadiya and Shahid remained awake the whole night, excitedly talking on the phone about what was to come. 'I told you I'll come get you before the next hartāl.' Of course, this being Kashmir, they knew there would be a next hartāl. When or where it would emerge from were the variables. They pushed the thought away for now and revelled in the joy of the knowledge that they had. Added to that was the fact that in Nowhatta, Nadiya would have fewer restrictions than in her own home; the two would be able to talk at ease and meet more freely.

Nadiya packed her bags and moved to her maasi's house. While living there, Shahid and she got closer. For the most part this was because Nadiya didn't have to lie to meet him anymore. All she had to tell her aunt was, 'I'm going to meet Shahid.' That was it. She didn't have to invent convoluted stories about where she was going, which 'friend' she was seeing and why she was going to be late. Back home, the number of female friends she had thrown under the bus in a bid to explain her whereabouts was insane. 'You owe me one,' her friends would tell her via text with a winking emoji each time Nadiya's mother called them to ask about her daughter.

Nadiya would go home for Eid and other special occasions. Shahid would drop her off to a certain point and then her brother Amaan would pick her up from there. On one of these occasions, Amaan saw Nadiya getting out of Shahid's car. After a lot of reflection, he confronted her about it. By then, as her mother knew about the whole thing, Nadiya was not too worried. Plus, Amaan was her younger brother, so she did have some authority in the matter. 'I like him, and I'm going to marry him,' was her straight reply. She watched her younger brother's face express shock and embarrassment. He didn't talk to Nadiya for a while as he struggled with the thought of his elder sister being in a relationship. It was unthinkable in the context of their household. It took some time for him to come around. In due course, Shahid and Amaan became good friends.

Shahid had ventured into the pharmaceutical business. He started building a pharmacy that he'd be running in the future. By 2019, when Nadiya was in the last semester of her degree, his work was 90 per cent done.

ON 4 AUGUST, SHAHID had come to pick Nadiya up—as he did every day from university. As they drove to Nowhatta, Nadiya noticed long lines at the gas station. 'Are the petrol prices going up tomorrow?' she asked. Shahid shrugged; he didn't know.

Once home at her maasi's, Nadiya noticed extra groceries piled up on the kitchen table. 'What's all this?' she asked. Her maasi, who was washing a gigantic wad of hākh—collard greens—told her that there were rumours of a hartāl the next day. 'Phone, internet, everything will be shut.' Nadiya poured herself some nun-chai and proceeded to help her aunt in cleaning the hākh.

'Even if they shut them all down, they will revive soon,' she replied.

The phones were still working that night, so Nadiya felt that there had been a hue and cry over nothing. That was until her phone buzzed with Shahid's name. She picked it up. 'I'm coming there. Meet me outside. I need to talk to you,' Shahid said.

Nadiya looked outside the window. It was pitch dark with a solitary streetlamp illuminating the dead street. 'It's dark outside ... maasi won't let me go.'

He insisted. 'Everything will be shut from tomorrow. How will we meet in the future?'

Nadiya smiled. 'You're overreacting. This is an everyday thing, and even you know it. One day there's a hartāl, the next day it's not there. We'll meet the day after tomorrow.'

But Shahid wouldn't listen to her. He was adamant that things were going to get especially terrible, and it was imperative that they meet. 'Make an excuse and come. Please.'

Thinking on her feet, Nadiya told her maasi that Shahid had got her some important medicines that would be hard to find during the hartāl. 'He's coming right now. I'll go get them and come back.'

Her maasi looked sceptical. It was 9 p.m., and they lived in Nowhatta, which was in downtown Srinagar. Things could get heated here fast. But she saw merit in what Nadiya was saying. 'Go fast and get it.' Maasi kept a lookout so that her husband wouldn't know that Nadiya was going to the gate. He didn't know anything about Shahid.

Nadiya gingerly opened the latch of the metal gate so that it didn't make any sound in the quiet of the night. She walked extra fast to the point where Shahid always parked his car, so that he wouldn't be noticed. He was waiting there already with his headlights off. Nadiya got into the car. Shahid enveloped her into a tight hug. 'They're saying it'll go on for a long time.'

Nadiya patted his head softly. 'If not this week, we will meet the next. Don't worry.'

He moved away. 'You're taking this too lightly, Nadiya. It's going to get bad. They are removing the Article.'

Nadiya scoffed, 'And how many times have we heard that? We'll be fine.'

Shahid sighed at her stubbornness and hugged her again. Nadiya took the medicines from him that she'd asked him to buy on the way, so she'd have proof for her aunt. She jumped out of the car and scurried back home. Shahid waited till he heard the sound of the metal gate closing and then started the car.

Nadiya and Shahid began speaking on the phone once he got home. Dinner was done, and the families were asleep. It was 11 p.m. Nadiya was amused. 'See, the phones are still working.' And as if she jinxed it, the call dropped. Nadiya tried to call Shahid back, but the phone didn't have any network access. The Wi-Fi was down too. Nadiya had a sinking feeling in her tummy; she wondered if Shahid had been right all long about a long hartāl. Now all she could hope was that the rest of stuff he had told her wouldn't come true as well.

She turned her lights off and got into her bed. In the warmth of her covers, she said to herself, 'They'll open phone lines by 2 p.m. tomorrow. Like they do every Indian Independence Day.'

The next morning when Nadiya woke up, there still wasn't any network access on her phone. She checked the phones belonging to everyone else—her cousins, aunt, uncle. No one had signal. They turned on the TV to watch the news. Sure enough, the news confirmed their fears. Article 370 was gone. Shahid had been right again. Nadiya's heart sank. She couldn't even go home to Bagh-e-Mehtab because of the lockdown outside. She was stuck.

With nowhere to go and no place to be at, Nadiya went to the garden every five minutes. A familiar imaginary car horn would toot, and she'd rush outside, only to realize that Shahid wasn't there. The hustle from the roads that usually crossed the boundary walls and crept in through the gate was all gone. It was replaced by the sounds of mayhem. Nadiya heard men of all ages protesting, shouting slogans against the abrogation. There were stones being thrown and tear gas shells being used in retaliation. Nadiya's maasi yelled from the kitchen window. 'Are you crazy? Come back inside at once.' Nadiya rushed back in. But she kept going back to the lawn when no one was looking, haunted by that familiar car horn.

But Shahid never came.

As tear gas shells kept getting lobbed, the gas seeped in through the cracks in the doors and windows of the house—this, even if the doors and windows were tightly shut and the thick curtains were drawn. Everyone in the neighbourhood had watery eyes and kept coughing for hours. In those hours of distress and confusion, Nadiya imagined Shahid once more, braving the tear gas outside and appearing at the house's gate. In her half-delirious state, she would run to the gate and peep outside, only to find the road empty, strewn with remainders of all that had transpired.

There was a window on the top floor of the house from which one could see the whole neighbourhood. Nadiya often went there to check for Shahid's car. Opening the windows was not allowed. The army personnel standing guard downstairs forbade residents from peeking as the protests happened right underneath. So Nadiya had to be especially careful, looking out furtively without anyone's knowledge.

No Shahid still.

As the hartāl went on, there was little else to do but watch the news. The family checked the headlines, first at 9 a.m., then at 11 a.m., then at 3 p.m., then at 4 p.m., 6 p.m., 9 p.m., scanning the news tickers for any indication that phone and internet services will be restored soon—in twenty-four hours, three days, a week, anything. They just wanted to know that this ordeal had an end. But again, nothing came.

Their mobile phones were referred to as 'dabbas' now. They were of no use. After a few days of diligent charging, with dreams of phone service restoration, by the fourth day they stopped doing that as well.

Days slowly crept on. Weeks crawled. Nadiya started losing track of time. One day, when she spotted a calendar, she was surprised to see that two weeks had passed. As slow as time seemed for her, it flew by whenever it wanted to. This was the longest that Shahid and she hadn't spoken in the recent past.

Before the abrogation, the semester exams had preoccupied Nadiya. The dates had been announced. With the abrogation, were they still going to be the same? Homes weren't getting newspapers, so she had no idea if an update about the exams had been printed. Sure that the exams would still happen at some point, if not now then later, Nadiya continued studying. Studying helped create a sense of normalcy and schedule in her life.

By the third week, Nadiya's maasi's household had formed a new daily time-table. All of them woke up and finished the house chores first, before they got lazy. The food was cooked, the floors were cleaned, furniture was dusted and the clothes were put to wash and dry. Everyone had their chores assigned to them. After that, all of them sat in front of the TV for the rest of the day.

The market was closed, but the grocer next door opened his shop for some time in the evening. They bought vegetables and pulses from him, a day's worth, and never so much that another family wouldn't get its share. Mutton and chicken were the stuff of dreams now. Nadiya and her family didn't dare venture to the main road to buy some. Going to the grocer next door was adventure enough. They learnt to be happy with their vegetables, rice and dal.

One day, there was a knock on the front gate. Nadiya's uncle went to investigate. It turned out to be Amaan. He had come to take Nadiya home. 'Papa asked me to come get you,' he said. Nadiya couldn't believe how much she had missed her brother till she saw him, nor did she realize how intensely she missed her parents. She quickly packed some clothes and a few of her textbooks. She was happy that she was going home. And if she were in Bagh-e-Mehtab, at least she would be close to Shahid's house. Maybe they'd be able to see each other from the window.

Taking her maasi's leave, Nadiya set out with her brother. As he took her bag to carry, she looked around the street. It was evening, and a lot of army guys were roaming around. Gossipy neighbourhood uncles were sitting and chatting by a shuttered shop. Their eyes followed Nadiya, who turned to her brother in confusion. 'How did you come here? Are we going by bike?'

Nadiya's brother smiled and didn't reply. They walked some more, and Nadiya recognized the path they were taking. It led to where Shahid used to park his car.

And sure enough, from a distance, she saw him waiting outside his vehicle. He was pacing up and down nervously, and he hadn't seen Nadiya yet.

Nadiya stopped in her tracks and stared at her brother in awe. He winked. Shahid and Amaan had been co-conspirators.

As though he felt Nadiya's presence, Shahid looked up. His face broke into a smile. Nadiya's pace quickened, tears already making their way down her cheeks. When they were face to face, Nadiya and Shahid just stared at each other. They couldn't hug because of the audience. Shahid opened the door for her, and Nadiya sat inside. As Amaan kept the baggage at the back, Nadiya stole a quick hug with Shahid. 'I can't believe it's you,' she said. 'Me too,' he whispered as he inhaled the fragrance she carried.

During the drive, Nadiya pieced together all that had been happening. The two boys spoke non-stop, talking over each other. Immediately after the abrogation, nobody had been allowed to venture out. But a few days in, a ḍhīl of an hour got introduced, during which time people could buy groceries. Shahid saw an opportunity here and started coming to Nowhatta. He'd ride his bike through narrow lanes and shortcuts to avoid the high security. But always, he'd get stopped at a checkpoint at the Khanyar police station. Beyond the police station, the authorities didn't let anyone move ahead. Shahid would plead with the police, they'd remain firm, and finally, he'd have to give up and go home. Shahid would repeat the ritual every day, hoping that at some point, the police would take pity on him. Eventually, the policemen started recognizing Shahid; they were even bemused by his tenacity. But they never let him get past the concertina fencing.

When Shahid couldn't take the separation from Nadiya any longer, he tracked Amaan down. 'We will go get Nadiya back,' he said. Shahid knew that even if he got past the Khanyar police station and reached Nadiya's maasi's house, he wouldn't be able to step inside. If he walked in, he'd jeopardize whatever future they had together. So Shahid waited till such time that the duration of the ḍhīl increased and the security cover became lighter. The two of them set off. At the Khanyar check post, Amaan pleaded with the policemen, saying that he urgently needed to get his sister back home. Shahid hid his face from the cops this time. Finally, the two were let through. Amaan landed up at the doorstep of his maasi's home claiming that Nadiya had been summoned—which was a lie in itself since Nadiya's parents had no idea she was coming. For once, the communication blockade felt like a blessing; no one could call to cross-check.

Nadiya listened to the whole story amazed. 'All this so that we could be close to each other?' she asked. Shahid nodded, looking at her like one would at the first snowfall of winter.

Shahid dropped Nadiya and Amaan home.

Nadiya whispered to him, 'Come see me every day. I'll stand at the window.'

Shahid smiled. 'That was the plan, baby.'

Nadiya's parents were ecstatic to see Nadiya but also concerned about the journey. 'Don't tell me you came alone?' her mother scolded her. They had no idea that Amaan was behind this; they assumed he had been playing cricket in a park nearby. So Nadiya came up with a cock-and-bull story about her uncle having some work in the area. 'I wanted to spend time with you all, so I requested him to drop me. I told him to come inside, but he was in a hurry.' Amaan's eyebrows shot up, marvelling at his sister's improvisation skills. 'I met Amaan outside, and he helped me get my bags.' Amaan nodded fervently. Again, there was no way to corroborate the story about the uncle.

Now that she was home, Nadiya could see Shahid, but only from a distance. They caught each other's gaze from the window, but this felt inadequate.

Since Nadiya wasn't allowed outside the gate—whereas Amaan could roam freely—Shahid started sending Nadiya letters through Amaan. The first offered detailed instructions on the letter exchange cycle. Letters had to be traded twice a day—once in the morning and once in the evening. In other words, Nadiya and Shahid had to write two letters each per day. Amaan would carry the post back and forth, meeting Shahid in the park where he played cricket.

The letters, besides declarations of love and longing, also carried details of the news floating around and the errands that Nadiya needed Shahid to run as she couldn't leave the house. Whether it was getting a doctor's appointment or checking on the new landline connections, Shahid had to keep pace with the requests being made. More than once, Nadiya and Shahid spoke of Amaan and how grateful they were to him. 'If he hadn't found out about us, we would have remained cooped up in our rooms without contact!' Shahid said.

In one of his letters, Shahid told Nadiya that the work on his pharmacy had been halted because of the hartāl. But given that all medical shops in Kashmir remained open even during hartāls, Shahid could see that his was a viable business choice. 'See, I took a good decision!' he bragged.

The one assertion that remained a constant in the letters was this—'I promise, before the next hartāl happens, I *will* take you with me. I said it in 2016, and now I'm writing it in

2019. You have written proof. We'll be married. Then we'll show our children all that we used to write to each other during this time!'

Twenty-fifth August was Nadiya's birthday. Shahid sent her chocolates through Amaan, with a letter saying—'It's the first time we have been apart on this day. I won't let it happen again.'

THE NEXT MONTH AND a half saw a flurry of letters being exchanged.

Nadiya had finished studying from the textbooks she had carried with her. She knew there would be exams, even if they were delayed. She needed to go back to Nowhatta to study from the books that were still at her maasi's house and revise more efficiently.

There was one more reason prompting the decision. She was getting frustrated sitting at home, reading Shahid's letters, and trying to catch his distant gaze from her window. She wanted more. She wanted to be near him. And this was possible only in Nowhatta—not near her own home where her father closed the gate at 5 p.m. even for Amaan.

Nadiya now had to convince two people. She started with her father, who remained strongly of the view that 'girls should not step out of the house unless it's for studying'. Using this stance to her advantage *again*, Nadiya told her father that she needed to go back to Nowhatta to study and complete her syllabus before the exams. The argument worked *again*.

Her next big challenge was to convince Shahid. Nadiya knew that he would be angry that she was going away. She was right, because she got an extra-long letter from him, lamenting her decision. He was scared that she would be far away and wouldn't come back for a long time. Nadiya promised him that she knew what she was doing, and it was in their best interest. 'We can't even meet here ... what's the point?' she said.

So it was, one Wednesday, Nadiya packed up to leave again. She sent a letter to Shahid asking him to meet her the next day at 5 p.m. It was a ḍhīl day. Her father dropped her off at her maasi's house. They were happy to welcome her back.

The next day, Nadiya was ready at 4.45 p.m. and told her maasi that she was meeting Shahid. 'I'll be back by 6.30 p.m.,' she reassured her. Nadiya's maasi accompanied her to the car. Shahid was waiting and got a slight shock when he saw Nadiya's maasi—for the first time at that. She just smiled on witnessing his startled expression and said, 'Get her back on time. She is my responsibility. And for this amount of time, yours.' Shahid gulped and nodded. Maasi walked back. Nadiya burst out laughing. 'See, I told you my plan would work.' Instead of laughing with her, Shahid started crying. 'What happened?' Nadiya asked.

Shahid said, 'I ... I can't take it anymore. I swear I'll take you with me before the next hartāl!'

Nadiya, who had always found the statement slightly funny, didn't see any humour in it this time. She looked at Shahid. 'I believe you,' she said.

They drove around the neighbourhood for some time, and then Shahid dropped her back home.

'Same time, next week. Thursday, 5 p.m.,' Nadiya said.

This was their meeting ritual. No communication till then. They drove around the city during these meetings for as long as time and hālāth permitted. To Lal Chowk or Boulevard and back.

BY OCTOBER, PHONE NETWORKS were restored sans internet. Nadiya and Shahid finally felt a semblance of normalcy returning. At least they didn't need to wait a whole week before hearing each other's voices.

Nadiya's university opened in December. Shahid's pharmacy's construction restarted as well. Nadiya's exam date sheet got released, as she knew it would. It was just as well she had been studying. In December, she appeared for her final exams, and her course was officially over and done. She had to pack up the life she had built in her maasi's house for three years and move back home.

Nadiya knew the natural course of things in her household. Now that she wasn't studying anymore, her father would start thinking of marriage. Even though her mother knew about Shahid, Nadiya wasn't sure how well she could fight her battle given that Shahid's pharmacy hadn't started yet. She didn't have an answer to the question that was bound to crop up—'What does he do for a living?'

As Nadiya had anticipated, a few days after she came back home, the marriage conversation started. 'Just keep delaying. I'll be ready soon,' Shahid told Nadiya. 'If any rishtas come, keep saying no.'

This was the final stretch. Nadiya agreed to wait, but there was a hitch. It would take at least a year for the pharmacy to become profitable. Even if she rejected the rishtas left, right and centre, Nadiya needed a back-up excuse justifying her spate of refusals.

So, Nadiya told her parents that she wanted to study further. She wanted to appear for the master of education entrance exam. Her father was not impressed. 'Enough studying. Shaadi first.'

So, without telling anyone at home, Nadiya filled out the entrance forms and started preparing for the exam.

Meanwhile, she kept rejecting the marriage offers that she was getting. Her father, who thought that a girl shouldn't have a choice in marriage, was getting fed up with Nadiya's antics. Her mother came to her rescue, 'She needs to spend her life with this person. Do you want her to be miserable? Just trust her instincts.' He backed off momentarily.

Nadiya appeared for the entrance exams and got selected. There was an uproar at home when she told her father. 'So what if you got selected? You are not getting admission!' Nadiya pleaded with her dad. 'Let me do four semesters at least. Then I'll leave,' she begged.

By now the pandemic had overturned the world, and since classes were online and Nadiya didn't have to travel to Kashmir University, her father reluctantly agreed. Nadiya secured admission. So, with some quick thinking and her mother's help, Nadiya was able to fend off rishtas for a year.

Over that year, Shahid's pharmacy business took off and became profitable. He certainly was 'marriage material' now. His mother reached out to Nadiya's mother again. 'If you are ready, we are coming with the rishtè ourselves,' she said. Nadiya's mother asked her for some time; she would have to coax her husband.

She told Nadiya, 'If they come out of the blue, your father will get suspicious. I'll handle everything. You be quiet. A peep out of you, and your father will kill us both. We have to pretend that Shahid and you don't know each other and that the rishtè has come organically. Turn this love marriage into an arranged marriage. Understand?' Nadiya nodded, unable to hide her excitement.

Nadiya's mother then approached her husband with Shahid's rishtè, explaining that she and Shahid's mother had been childhood friends from school. 'She has a son who is Nadiya's age. She wants Nadiya to become her daughter-in-law. I think it will be a good match. I told her that I'll talk to you first and respond.'

Nadiya's father was slightly suspicious. He asked her a barrage of questions, 'Why have I not heard of this friend? Has her son seen Nadiya? Has Nadiya seen her son? Where has *she* seen Nadiya?'

'No one has seen anyone,' Nadiya's mother said. 'The girl and boy don't know anything. We have just spoken amongst friends.'

When Nadiya's father was suitably convinced, they decided to go ahead with the nazar din', which essentially meant doing a background check on Shahid and his family. It involved talking to people who knew them, inquiring with neighbours and relatives, before making a decision. If all went well, they'd accept the rishtè.

Nadiya's father and uncle went to do this recce. They saw Shahid's house, looked into his business and asked about the family. That whole day, Nadiya was a bundle of nerves. *This was it.* Today when her father returned, he would make the decision, whichever way it went. Even the thought of it going awry made her anxious.

Nadiya and Shahid had promised each other a long time ago that in case the rishtè didn't work out, neither would marry another. They would remain single forever. Nadiya didn't have the heart to rebel and elope, so this seemed like the only alternative. That day, as she waited, Nadiya hoped and prayed that her future had Shahid in it.

Nadiya's father returned in the afternoon. Her mother set out the afternoon snacks and gestured that Nadiya keep calm. Her father sat down and slurped his tea, his face not giving anything away. Nadiya's mother placed a plate of tsọchiwōr in front of him and asked as though she were wondering about the current price of mutton, 'So what did you think of them?'

Nadiya stiffened as her father dipped a buttered tsọchiwōr in the tea and ate the soaking bread. He mumbled with a full mouth, 'Good. Let's accept it.'

Nadiya had been listening out of eyeshot. She shot up the stairs on hearing this and locked herself in her bedroom. Then she started jumping up and down with joy. She called Shahid to tell him the good news. 'It's happening, it's happening,' she shrieked. Shahid yelled in triumph. This was 2021. They had been together for eleven years now. 'This is the happiest day of my life.'

Unfortunately, the happiness was short-lived. Someone told Nadiya's father that she had known Shahid from childhood, and that they used to go to the same tuition class. Nadiya didn't know who this person was; all she knew was that the hope that had been lit in her life seemed to be steadily getting extinguished. Her father confronted her mother about this, who vehemently denied all allegations. 'Believe me, for God's sake, it's my friend's son. This person must be misinformed.' But Nadiya's father wasn't convinced. He yelled, 'This is what she does in university? This is why she does degree after degree? So that she can go gallivanting with boys?'

Nadiya's father stopped talking to her. He wouldn't even look at her. If Nadiya entered a room, he would get up and leave. Convinced that the dreaded 'love marriage' was taking place under his own roof, he now believed that Nadiya had betrayed him. The silent treatment went on for a while. Nadiya was a wreck, sure now that her father wouldn't let the rishtè happen. Her mother took Nadiya into her arms and consoled her. 'He doesn't have any proof. All this is hearsay. Just give it some time,' she said.

Shahid remained stoic. 'Don't break down now. If you do, it's over. We've been together eleven years ... what's one more hurdle? He'll come around, don't worry.'

Nadiya had always been dismayed by the way her culture and her family functioned. She was dismayed that a girl was never given the right to choose; that she wasn't viewed as being significant enough to have a voice. She was dismayed that a girl couldn't question her parents' choices, that she had to remain coy and demure and never air an opinion about her own marriage.

It made no sense. All her life, she had been told to stay away from strangers. Then why was she expected to marry one?

This is why, Nadiya believed, love marriages made sense. A girl wasn't spending a lifetime with a stranger but committing to a person she shared love and comfort with.

That Nadiya's father would ever see this side of the argument was unlikely.

On 26 July 2021, Nadiya got a call from her university. She had been nominated for a gold medal for topping her previous course. The Indian President was coming to Sher-i-Kashmir International Conference Centre (SKICC) the next day to present the medals.

All these days, Nadiya had been a shadow of herself. Now, suddenly, she felt invigorated. She ran into the room where everyone, including her father, was watching TV and yelled, 'I've been nominated for a gold medal!' The family was jubilant.

Even her father couldn't hide his pride. He said, 'I'll drop you to SKICC tomorrow.'

Later that night, Nadiya's mother, before going to bed, whispered to her husband, 'See, she wasn't gallivanting. She's a university topper. Gold medallist.'

Something turned in the man.

He dropped Nadiya the next day. The drive was quiet, but it was without any kind of tension. Nadiya came back home wearing the gold medal. Her father was on top of the world, having already called the entire extended family. 'My daughter is a gold medallist. I will send you a picture of it!' he told them.

It was a first in the family, after all.

That's how the cold war ended. Nadiya's father forgot all about the mystery person and their gossip about Nadiya and Shahid. It didn't matter anymore.

In a few days, Nadiya's mother told Shahid's mother, 'Send the rishtè.'

The following Sunday, Shahid's folks came over to Nadiya's house. The families met. Nadiya's father accepted the rishtè.

On 8 August, they had their thaph—they formally accepted the marriage proposal. Shahid's mother told Nadiya's, 'In exactly a year, we will come to take her home.'

After the thaph, Nadiya met Shahid for the first time as a couple at the threshold of marriage. Both of them were exuberant about the turn of events. They sat in Shahid's car and spoke about all that it had taken them to get here—the ups and downs, the hardship and separation, and the love, all the love. Most of all, they spoke of the freedom they could now savour.

Freedom—the word especially excited Nadiya, who until then hadn't been allowed to explore the world around her because she was a girl. She wanted to travel, have picnics, stay in hotels, go out with Shahid wherever and whenever she felt like, and do all the 'couple things' that people did. She wanted to know an existence without boundaries and inhibitions, without a looming authority figure saying no.

Nadiya sought that freedom through marriage. It was a kind of freedom that was finally within reach.

Shahid held her hand and said, 'See, I'm keeping my promise.'

Nadiya laughed. 'This is Kashmir, baby. Anything can happen before the wedding!'

Shahid shushed her. *'Wo sab ka nahi pata. Magar agli hartāl se pehle tujhe le jaa raha hoon main.'*

Once more, he promised—he'd whisk her off before the next hartāl in Kashmir.

And he did.

Note: Nadiya and Shahid got married in September 2022. Before the next hartāl.

ACKNOWLEDGEMENTS

Lōal Kashmir FIRST TOOK form in my mind at the end of 2020, and as I interviewed over seventy people for it, their stories took over my heart.

Shepherding these beautiful stories has been a great privilege and responsibility, and I am glad that I found people who saw my vision and helped me transform it into a book. I would like to thank and extend my utmost gratitude to the following people who have been a part of this spectacular four-year long journey—from inception to publication.

To the contributors of these sixteen accounts, named and unnamed. You have made this book possible and I hope I've done justice to your life stories.

To the contributors whose stories did not make it to the final manuscript. This book would not exist without my conversations with each and every one of you. For in each interaction, I was reminded of why *Lōal Kashmir* needed to be out in the world.

To my mentor at South Asia Speaks, Rahul Bhatia, who encouraged me from the get-go and told me this book would be special. He has matched my excitement at every step of this incredible ride. A huge thank you to Sonia Faleiro for setting up South Asia Speaks, and creating a platform for writers to find their voices.

To Rahul Soni from HarperCollins India, for championing *Lōal Kashmir* from the very beginning. To Dharini Bhaskar, for being a wonderful collaborator and shaping the book with sensitivity and care. To both of them for seeing the book through till the end. An extended thank you to the team at HarperCollins India for bringing this book to life.

To my agents at A Suitable Agency, Ranjana Sengupta, Hemali Sodhi and their team—for believing in *Lōal Kashmir* and finding it a home.

All my love and appreciation for my sister, Aashna, who has always been my biggest cheerleader. For never letting me take the easy road. For helping me out whenever I felt stuck—no question was silly or unimportant.

To my parents, Surabhi and Parvez, for not constraining my sister and me to a mould. Some extra love to my mother for being one of the most beloved English teachers in Srinagar. I may not be able to point out all the ways in which she has inspired me, but I want to let her know that she has.

To my grandmother, Dr Wijaya Altekar, to whom this book is dedicated. She is ninety-three years old as this book comes out, having lived an incredible life—with a PhD in biochemistry, and having worked at Bhabha Atomic Research Centre and NASA. She is better travelled than me and remembers to mention it when she can.

A big hug to Arbeena Riyaz, for helping me with the Kashmiri phonetics in the book.

To Basita Shah, for visualizing the cover illustrations of *Lōal Kashmir*, taking from what I gave you, and making it your own.

To Mona Bhan and Deepti Misri, for pointing me in the right direction when I was missing crucial pieces to complete *Lōal Kashmir*. To Fatimah, thank you for answering my queries with patience and warmth.

To Shanker Raman, for being the first person who heard about *Lōal Kashmir*, when it was the seed of an idea. Thank you for urging me to take the plunge when I was uncertain.

To Kanishka, Antareep and Nicholas for reading excerpts from the book and reaffirming my faith that *Lōal Kashmir* could touch people, even if they're not from Kashmir. Love and longing are indeed universal.

And lastly, infinite kisses and head scratches for my cat, Ellie, my favourite writing and editing companion. Thank you for not walking over my keyboard and deleting my manuscript.

GLOSSARY OF KASHMIRI AND URDU WORDS

Ahan haz	Respectful way of saying 'yes'.
Azaadi	Freedom.
Bādāmwạr	Almond orchard.
Chilạy kalān	The harshest and coldest part of winter in the Kashmir Valley, lasting forty days, starting from 21 December to 31 January.
Dāwath	A feast.
Dāl-e-battè	Literally meaning 'lentil Pandit', this term is used as a slur for Kashmiri Pandits. It is a pun on the term 'Dāl-e-batè' that means lentils and rice.
Dastarkhān	A traditional spread or tablecloth that is laid out on the floor on which food items are served for a meal.
Dejhoor	A traditional and culturally significant ear ornament worn by married Kashmiri Pandit women.

Ḍhīl	A temporary and short relaxation in curfew in order to run daily chores.
Duā	The act of supplication during prayer.
Gọshtabè	A Kashmiri dish consisting of meatballs in a yoghurt-based curry. Typically served as the last dish of the wāzèwān.
Hākh	Local Kashmiri collard greens.
Hālāth	Circumstances or conditions.
Hạlụwè	A sweet dish made with semolina and dry fruits.
Hamām	A Kashmiri heating system consisting of a room with a subfloor that holds a wood-fired furnace. It is used in winter to provide warmth.
Hamsāyè	Neighbour.
Hạrisè	A rich, slow-cooked meat dish prepared specifically in the winter months in Kashmir, often eaten as breakfast.
Hartāl	A strike or protest often accompanied with the shutdown of public institutions.
Hạ̄zīrī	Attendance or reporting for duty. The context here is of a surrendered militant reporting to the authorities at timely intervals to prove that he hasn't left the state.
Họkhè gāḍè or họ-gāḍ	Dried fish.
Ikhwạ̄n'	A group of pro-Indian government militia or 'renegades' consisting of surrendered Kashmiri militants who defected from various insurgent groups.

Kahwè	A Kashmiri hot beverage traditionally made with cardamom, cinnamon, almonds and saffron.
Kāndur	Baker of local Kashmiri breads.
Kāngèr	A traditional heating device used in the Kashmir region, particularly during winter. It consists of an earthenware pot filled with hot coal embers and encased in a wicker basket.
Kani-jang	Stone pelting.
Kaum-kabila	A community, tribe or group of people sharing religious, cultural, geographical or ethnic similarities.
Khabri gatshun or khabar	A post-wedding ritual in Kashmir, in which the bride's relatives pay a visit to the newly married couple and also gift them gold and money.
Khọftan phạkīr	Literally meaning 'vagabonds of the night'. These men were members of the 'Peace Brigade' instituted in Kashmir by the local government for surveillance after Indian independence. The name was given as the men raided families—sometimes on suspicion of dissent—at khọftan (Isha nẹmāz or night prayers).
Lōal	Love, affection.
Mātāmāl	Maternal grandparents' home.
Mạnzi-kūr	Young girls and women from the groom's side who take henna for the bride to her house on mạnzirāth.

Mạnzirāth	One of the events in a multi-day Kashmiri wedding, centred around mehandī or henna application, music and revelry.
Mahrāz	Groom.
Mahrin'	Bride.
Majmè	Copper plates or baskets heaped with goodies to be given as gifts.
Mạnzimyōr (singular), mạnzimyạ̄yr (plural)	Marriage matchmakers.
Mukhbir	Informant for the army.
Myōn zuv	My life.
Nadụr' mọnji	Lotus stem fritters.
Nazar din'	Literally meaning 'going to check on someone'. The context here is an informal background check done on suitable matches by families before accepting a marriage proposal.
Nun-chai	A salted tea prepared in Kashmir, known for its distinct pink hue.
Pāchè	A dish prepared with lamb trotters.
Paithai bānè	The eldest born in a family.
Pakh	Let's go.
Phẹran	A traditional Kashmiri garment worn by both men and women. It is a loose, long-sleeved gown that reaches down to the knees or ankles, typically made from wool, and is designed to provide warmth during the winters.

Phirsāl	A post-wedding ritual in Kashmir when the newly married couple visit the bride's parents' house for a meal. The groom's family is invited as well.
Pujj	A butcher.
Rishtè (Kashmiri), Rishta (Urdu)	A marriage proposal.
Rooh	Soul.
Rọkhsạtī	The part of a Kashmiri wedding when the bride leaves her parents' home to go to her husband's house.
Shikạ̄ra	A wooden boat found in the Kashmir region.
Tabakh māz	A Kashmiri wāzèwān dish made with lamb ribs.
Tạhrīk	The political, social and armed movements advocating for the rights and self-determination of the people of the Kashmir region.
Tạsibī	Prayer or rosary beads.
Tāziyat	Condolences given after a death.
Thaph	The formal acceptance of a marriage proposal between two families.
Tsoṭ	A Kashmiri flat-bread baked in a clay oven.
Tsọchiwōr	A bagel-shaped Kashmiri bread baked in a clay oven, known for its soft top with sesame seeds and a harder bottom.
Tuj	A barbeque dish made with different meats in Kashmir.

Tumbakhnạ̄r	An ancient Kashmiri percussion instrument used for singing and revelry in weddings and celebrations.
Wāzè	The cooks who prepare the wāzèwān.
Wāzèwān	A traditional multi-course meal in Kashmiri cuisine, known for its elaborate preparation and rich flavours. It is often served at weddings, celebrations and over other special occasions.
Wạlīma	A wedding feast held after the marriage ceremony, common in many South Asian cultures. In Kashmir, it is thrown by the groom's family a day after the bride is brought to his home after the rọkhsạtī.
Wanè wun	A style of Kashmiri folk singing characterized by its melancholic and soulful tone. It is commonly sung by women at weddings.
Watan	Nation or country.
Zārè pār	Emphatic Kashmiri hospitality as a gesture of goodwill, sometimes bordering on good-natured smothering. The term can also be used to describe the act of convincing someone in an incessant manner.
Zūl	Lights used to decorate houses and venues at weddings.

NOTES

Scan this QR code to access the detailed notes.

ABOUT THE AUTHOR

MEHAK JAMAL is a filmmaker and writer. She was born and raised in Srinagar, Kashmir, and has always wanted to tell stories from her homeland.

Mehak is a 2022 South Asia Speaks Fellow, awarded to outstanding emerging writers from the region. Her film *Bad Egg* premiered at the 19th Indian Film Festival Stuttgart and won the Audience Award. It went on to screen at multiple film festivals all over the world.

Mehak is a film alumna of Srishti Institute of Art, Design and Technology, Bengaluru. She lives in Mumbai with her cat, Ellie. *Lōal Kashmir* is her first book.